STEVE JONES

WITH BEN THOMPSON

LONELY BOY

TALES FROM A SEX PISTOL

FOREWORD BY CHRISSIE HYNDE

DA CAPO PRESS

First Da Capo Press edition 2017
Reprinted by arrangement with Penguin Random House UK

Cataloging-in-Publication data for this book is available from the Library of Congress.
ISBN: 978-0-306-82481-4 (hardcover)
ISBN: 978-0-306-82482-1 (e-book)
Library of Congress Control Number: 2016952378

Published by Da Capo Press, an imprint of Perseus Books, LLC,
a subsidiary of Hachette Book Group, Inc.
www.dacapopress.com

Da Capo Press books are available at special discounts for bulk purchases in the U.S. by cor-
porations, institutions, and other organizations. For more information, please contact the
Special Markets Department at Perseus Books, 2300 Chestnut Street, Suite 200, Philadelphia,
PA 19103, or call (800) 810-4145, ext. 5000, or e-mail special.markets@perseusbooks.com.

10 9 8 7 6 5 4 3 2 1

I'm all alone,
I ain't got no home

'Lonely Boy', Sex Pistols

CONTENTS

PART III – AFTER

FOREWORD

He was a teenager when I met him. I didn't notice him carrying a sack full of dreams around, but he was. Like all of us, he wanted to play guitar in a rock 'n' roll band. But none of the bands out there fit.

We hung around Malcolm and Viv, and with them, the prog rock and *Top of the Pops* candy floss of the day seemed irrelevant. When he appeared onstage one night in a nihilistic little outfit, the Sex Pistols, only the girly decals on his Les Paul betrayed the pose.

Here was an Elvis fan. A dandy.

The girls had a soft spot for this shy West London thug and he took full advantage. (The crack of dawn wasn't safe around him.) When it all fell apart with the band, he pulled a Lemmy and absconded to LA. Got a truck and a dog.

No one could have predicted that he'd become host to the best radio show in the state. But then, no one could have predicted Jonesy.

Chrissie Hynde, July 2016

PART I: BEFORE

1. THE ARTFUL DODGER

One of the main things I remember about growing up in West London in the 1960s was the corrugated iron, that and the odd Ford Anglia driving about. There were building sites and debris everywhere – it was like the whole place was falling down around us. And the corrugated iron was a real nause (i.e. a fucking pain in the arse) to climb over. It was eight feet high and sharp enough to cut into your hands as you pulled yourself up to the top. It was almost like those builders didn't want me to get in there and develop my driving skills by hot-wiring bulldozers to smash up their tea huts, the inconsiderate cunts.

You didn't see a lot of film stars on the mean streets of Shepherd's Bush in those days, even though the BBC TV studios were just around the corner. So when Jack Wild – the kid who played the Artful Dodger in *Oliver!* – walked past the end of my road, one day in the late 1960s, that was always going to be something which caught my eye. I was already a bit of an artful dodger myself by that time – maybe not picking a pocket or two yet, but certainly giving the odd stolen bike or brand-new train set fresh from the Hamleys stockroom a good home. But I wasn't looking at Jack as a criminal role model. All that interested me was the fact that he was famous – if it'd been Elsie Tanner from *Coronation Street* walking down my road, I'd have been just as excited.

Me and a few other kids cottoned on to who he was and started following him. I suppose this wasn't anything too weird in itself, just the common reaction any thirteen-year-old might have to someone they recognised from a film or off the TV – wanting to be as close to him as possible in the hope that some of the magic might rub off. But I always had to push things one stage further. One by one, all my mates dropped away, but I carried on trailing him, like he was Peter Pan or something. I'm not sure why now. I guess I was just more strongly drawn than they were to that special quality stardom gave to him.

Jack Wild was a couple of years older than me, but he wasn't much bigger than I was. He didn't look nothing special – he wasn't wearing his top hat or anything. It's just that when you're one of those kids who has that sense of yourself as being trapped and maybe a bit lonely, if you see someone who seems like they've got it all sorted, you think if you can just be close to them everything will be all right and all the pain you feel will just go away.

I don't know what he thought about me following him. I guess it freaked him out a bit, especially with all that corrugated iron along the sides of the road that he'd never have been able to escape over. At that time my mates and I were part of the first wave of skinheads; listening to Motown, Ska and Blue Beat, loving the music of people like Prince Buster who we'd picked up on from the West Indian kids who lived around us. So if Jack had turned round to sneak a glance at me – trying to look casual while he did it – he'd have seen me bowling along behind him in my oxblood Dr Marten boots with the space-age soles you could see through. I polished the shit out of my first pair of those. I'd have probably been wearing some nice Sta-Prest or Prince of Wales check trousers as well, and one of the crisp Ben Sherman shirts I'd go all the way to Richmond to nick from a shop called Ivy League.

He probably felt quite relieved when I finally gave up the pursuit about a mile further on. In later years I'd cross a lot of lines to get close to people I thought could fix me, but I hadn't started boozing yet by this time, so I still had a few boundaries left. Jack Wild would be off to Hollywood a short while after, but I don't think his story ended too happily. A lot of those child stars seem to have tragic lives in the end, don't they? Fame fucks them up at an early age, but when you're busy envying someone you never think about the fact that they might have problems of their own.

As a kid I used to have fantasies where I would imagine having different parents. I'd see people in films or on TV shows and think, 'Why can't I be in their family?' Diana Dors, who was kind of the English Marilyn Monroe, she was one of them. I would spend ages thinking about how much better off I'd be if I was her kid: 'Let me be with Diana, instead of these parents I've got.' The funny thing is, I don't even think it was a sexual thing at the time, I just didn't like my shit life and I was looking for anything I could grab onto to get me away from the place I was in.

It's not like I had the worst childhood ever. You hear horrific stories of kids going through way worse abuse than I did, and I'd hate it to look like I'm trying to put myself on that level. What I do know is how much things that happened when I was a kid fucked me up – still now, to this day. Of course the chemistry of everyone's brain is different, so some people might deal with a lot worse and come out fine, and others could have it really easy and still feel very hard done by. All I can tell you about is my own experiences, and given how dodgy my memory is, I can't even be too sure about some of them.

I ain't got a clue what my story is gonna look like once it's all set down on paper. I haven't got any kind of agenda at the outset, beyond a few things I want to set straight, and maybe hoping I'll be able to make a bit more sense of how different stages of my life fit together. One thing I'm pretty sure of is that I'm not going to come out of the whole thing smelling of roses.

You know that bit in *A Clockwork Orange*, where the main guy has his eyes forced open to make him feel like shit every time he remembers what a rotten cunt he was? That's pretty much how writing this book is going to feel for me. Obviously no one's forcing me to do it, and I've had my share of good times as well, but now I can't be doing with my old shenanigans any more it does sometimes make me feel almost physically sick to think of some of the horrible shit I used to get up to.

Even though it's been half my life since I first stopped drinking and taking drugs, I still wake up in a cold sweat sometimes, thinking about all the things I've done that I'm not proud of. But if I made a big song and dance about holding myself accountable for every new crime against humanity as I commit it, this book would get very boring very quickly. So I'm going to have to ask you to take it on trust from the kick-off that I'm trying to be a less despicable person these days, and then anyone who wants to judge me can do so at the full-time whistle.

One thing I can promise you is that I won't be pontificating about how everyone else needs to get sober. I don't give a fuck if other people wanna get high. I've had my go and now it's your turn – knock yourself out if that's what you wanna do. Of course if someone else can relate to my experiences and by some miracle that helps them to be less of an arsehole than I was, then that's all well and good. But I don't want to be that cunt where it's like, 'Oh, he was a rock and roller, but now he's telling everyone else how to live.' Fuck that preachy guy. He's the last person I want to be. Just because I eventually ended up following Jack Wild to

Hollywood, that doesn't mean I bought a one-way ticket to La-La Land as well.

It'd be a few more years after bumping into the Artful Dodger till I met my own Fagin, aka Malcolm McLaren (who loved all that Dickensian shit). Once that happened, it was like ol' Jack had passed on the baton, and it wasn't long before our merry band of musical outlaws started picking record companies' pockets like there was no tomorrow. But by the time we'd realised that our light-fingered Svengali had spent all the loot on *The Great Rock 'n' Roll Swindle* – a film explaining how the whole punk thing was his idea and we were just a bunch of suckers who couldn't play – it turned out the joke was on us.

And as for the annoying little brat with the great bone structure who's always asking for more . . . well, let's leave Johnny Rotten out of this for a while, shall we? He's had his say a few times. Maybe enough times. It's my turn now. Because much as the Sex Pistols couldn't have existed without John – or Malcolm, or Cookie, or Glen, or even Sid – it was my shit upbringing that got the ball rolling. That's not me showing off, it's just a fact.

2. MY NICOTINE RAG

I was born in 1955 – around the same time as rock 'n' roll. I got my sense of rhythm from my mum, Mary Jones, who was a Teddy girl, so I was in her fucking womb when she was jiving down the Hammersmith Palais.

Teddy girls – and Teddy boys, which is what my dad was – were the first in the long line of British youth cults which would brighten up the post-war years. Their name was shortened from the Edwardian style of clothes they favoured (like drainpipe trousers and long, drape jackets) and they were the ones who started rioting to 'Rock Around the Clock' when the film *Blackboard Jungle* came out. It's no wonder I've got such a strong connection to all those old rockers from the early days – Eddie Cochran for sure, but not just him.

Up until the age of about six years old, my childhood was going pretty smoothly. OK, so my dad had fucked off without hanging around long enough to say hello to me, and at that time it was a bit of a no-no to be what was still technically known as 'a bastard'. But you couldn't really blame him, as I don't think he and my mum had been together that long when she got pregnant. And the household I lived in felt like quite a normal – even loving – home. You might say, 'How does a kid know what normal is, when they've got nothing else to compare it to?' But I think they just know. I certainly did.

My mum and I lived with my nan Edith and grandad Fred in a third-floor flat in Riverside Gardens, Hammersmith. It's that big brick Peabody buildings estate, near the bridge. If you were heading out of London towards Heathrow airport, you'd see the Hammersmith Odeon – or Apollo, as it is now – on your left as you drove west over the flyover, then our flats would be on the right as you come down off the flyover and the main road levels out. I say that as if it's changed, but they were still there last time I looked (although admittedly that was in 2008).

It wasn't just the four of us. My gran and grandad's three other children lived there too. I slept in a cot at the bottom of the bed my mum shared with her sister Frances. My gran and grandad had their own room, and my uncles, Barry and Martin, shared the last bedroom. The flat ran between two corners of the block, so one main window looked out over the flyover towards the Odeon (the scene of a few memorable adventures later on in my life) and the other faced the opposite way. There were no lifts, so you had to walk up the stairs to get there, but this was nobody's shithole. It was a proper Victorian housing estate – decent accommodation for decent working-class people who were getting by OK.

I'm not sure how the Joneses were keeping up with everyone else, though, because my grandad was a lazy cunt. The story was he'd avoided having to fight in World War II by putting his foot under a tram to mangle his leg. I don't know if that was true, but he certainly never worked the whole time I was there, maybe because of the same injury that kept him out of the army.

He just used to sit there in his chair all day smoking roll-ups while my nan went out to work cleaning other people's houses. He'd still managed to buy himself some wheels, though – an Austin A40 which started with a crank. Having a car parked in the square down below the flats was quite a status symbol at that time, even if it did always break down when he tried to drive us down to Brighton in it. Come to think of it, his leg couldn't have been that bad if he could still drive. I remember him sitting me in his lap sometimes and letting me steer when he'd take the car for a turn around the square – my first underage driving experience; maybe that's where I got the bug from.

Most of my memories of those times are happy ones. Like my nan giving me a bath in the sink, or making those amazing old-fashioned steamed suet puddings where she'd stretch a cloth over the top of the bowl and tie it with a piece of string. She'd fill the bowl with raisins and then cover the whole thing in treacle from a green and gold Tate & Lyle tin. There's some things which happened last week that I don't remember too well, but fifty-five years on I can feel how good that pudding tasted on my tongue as if I'm eating it right now.

My nan wasn't spoiling me, she was just doing what any normal grandparent (or parent, come to that) would've done – nurturing, I suppose, is what you'd call it. I don't remember my mum so much at this time, even though she was there. The flat was pretty crowded, so it was easy to lose track of people, but it's my nan I remember doing all the cleaning up and making the dinners and checking everyone was all right. She was great.

I got the feeling that my nan had always preferred boys to girls, and as a result her sons had probably got the lion's share of her attention. Maybe that was part of what my mum didn't like about my nan being so warm and loving towards me when I was little. It made her quite cold towards me when I was growing up.

All I knew about my dad (apart from the fact that he was a Teddy boy, which was how he and my mum had met) was that his name was Don Jarvis and he was an amateur boxer from Fulham. That was the only information my mum gave me then. I think I'd picked up that it wasn't a subject she was too keen to talk about, though I do remember going down to some kind of court at a very early age where my mum was hoping to get money off him. I don't think she had any luck, because they'd never been married and she was definitely having a good old moan outside the court after.

My family did like to complain, but there was a lot of laughter, too. My grandad was a grumpy old sod, but he was funny with it. He would sit me on his lap – there was no weird shit there, nothing noncey – and he had this rag that he used to blow cigarette smoke into and then hold it over my face. I fucking loved the smell of those cigarettes. Breathing in the smoke from that rag was one of the best and most comforting feelings I've ever known. When it got put back in the drawer I'd be shouting, 'Where's me rag? Where's me rag?' It wasn't just for special occasions, it was for all occasions.

I can see now that this was probably the start of my first addiction. I don't think it was just the nicotine I loved, it was the fact that my grandad cared enough to blow smoke into the rag just because he knew I wanted him to. Either way, I really craved that rag when I didn't have it, and it certainly didn't take me long to progress to a pack of Players No. 6 as soon as I was old enough to buy my own fags (although I did get into Gauloises for ten minutes at one point because I heard Ronnie Wood smoked them; they were a good strong smoke). A few years later, when I was on heroin, I'd be on five packs a day. You smoke a lot more once you're on dope. As if it's not fucking unhealthy enough already.

Obviously you don't see the nicotine pacifier recommended by too many parenting manuals these days, but to me it was part and parcel of what I look back on as really good times. Even though she wasn't exactly the maternal type, I think my mum and I got on OK at that stage. Once she got me a brand-new pair of Tesco bombers – just shit jeans – and plimsolls that were like Converse but weren't Converse. I used to love it if ever I got new clothes: I'd be on top of the world the minute I had a bit of fresh clobber on, and I felt like I could walk tall through the squares that linked up the different Peabody buildings.

There was a real sense of community on that estate. There was a boozer on the corner with an off-licence next to it, and when we'd take back the R. White's lemonade bottles to get the deposits, I'd sit outside the pub listening to the guy who played the piano. That's one of my first conscious musical memories, although there'd be plenty more to come (and a few unconscious ones to go with them).

I also loved going to the matinees at the ABC cinema, just round the corner on King Street, to see *Commando Cody* and all those shit Saturday serials. I preferred sitting in the back row, because I didn't want to be close to all the other kids, and for some reason I loved it when the geezer would come out between the films and go, 'Hey, kids, what do you think?' Then everyone would go home and you'd have to come back next week to see the spaceship with a little bit of string holding it up.

Looking back on them, these were some of the happiest days of my life. I'd made a few friends on the estate and started primary school at Flora Gardens in Ravenscourt Park down the road. My grandparents loved me. It was all good.

I think I'd still have ended up being an alcoholic even if I'd had more of a charmed upbringing and stayed with my nan and her steak and kidney pies till I was old enough to leave home. There were quite a few big drinkers among the men in my family, and I just had that obsessive–compulsive alcoholic gene from day one. That's nothing to do with scenarios that have unfolded in my life, it's just who I am, or that's what I believe, anyway. But I don't think the Sex Pistols would've ever existed – at least, not with me in them – if it wasn't for what happened to me next. Apart from anything else, the urge to look for a better life wouldn't have been there, because I'd already have had one.

3. THAT PLACE STANK OF RUBBER

So there I was, having a great old time in the shadow of the Hammersmith flyover, when all of a sudden this guy comes along and my life takes a turn to the dark side. Ron Dambagella his name was, and I think my mum met him at work. She'd had a few part-time jobs. I remember one as a 'telephone girl' – that meant cleaning other people's spit off the telephones in offices, which can't have been a barrel of laughs. But then she got something a bit more permanent at this factory making rubber components, I'm not sure if they were for shoes, or cookers, maybe both.

Anyway, after a while she got moved to a smaller workshop under the arches, right next to Flora Gardens, my first school. I think he was in charge of that place, and I always remember the two of them working there alone, because once they'd got together she used to tell me proudly, 'Ron's the boss,' and I used to think, 'You're the only ones there!' But when I asked my auntie Frances about this, which I had to do, because my mum and I haven't spoken for a few years and I wanted to make sure I've got everything as accurate as possible, she told me there were other employees as well. Apparently old Ron (and he was old – a good ten years older than my mum, anyway) had a reputation of being 'very flirtatious' with the female workers.

I'll have to go into a lot of detail about things that happened over the next few years, some of which will probably be quite difficult for anyone who was involved to read. But I want to say from the outset that I'm not doing this to make my mum look bad. I've absolutely no interest in coating her off (though my stepfather is a different matter). I understand that her life wasn't easy. She had me too young – when she was about twenty – my dad had left her, and she maybe didn't feel like she had too many options, so I can see why she might have lowered her standards a bit. She probably thought, 'Well, I've got this kid, which is baggage to a lot of men, and I ain't gonna get anyone better.' My mum was not a square, in fact she was kind of hip – she bleach-blonded her hair and had massive knockers – so I bet Ron couldn't believe his luck.

The first time I sensed something was going on was when my mum was walking me along King Street to school – she'd drop me off there on the way to work – and we stopped at a crossing. I can't be sure if this actually happened or if I've elaborated on my mental picture over time, but I do have a memory of the wind catching my mum's coat and blowing it open, and me thinking she didn't have anything on underneath – well, maybe stockings, but not a skirt. That momentary flash kind of spun me a bit, and when I was older I'd wonder if they were maybe up to some kinky shit at work. For the moment, though, I was only six years old, and my whole world was about to go down the toilet.

The next thing I know, this Dambagalla guy's in the picture. He never came up to visit at my nan's, but I guess part of the deal for my mum in getting a new geezer in tow was so she could get her own place. So we waved goodbye to happy times with my nice, nurturing nan and grandad, and began our shit new life in a one-bedroom basement flat at

15 Benbow Road, Shepherd's Bush. It wasn't much more than a mile away from where we'd lived before – I even stayed at the same school – but it might as well have been on the other side of the world.

Fuck, that place was grim. It was dark and damp and horrible and I was sleeping on a fucking camp bed at the bottom of what was now my mum and Ron's bed. The khazi was outside, and when the tin bath came out in the front room, I'd be the last one into the dirty water after he'd gone first and then my mum had followed.

When I've talked to Americans over the years about what being poor meant in Britain at that time, they've never quite seemed to get it. I don't remember having a fridge or a TV, no one ever had showers, and for hot water there was the sink with the Ascot heater above it. You'd put money in the meter to get the radiator on and most people would knock the lock off and keep putting the same 10p in. I remember when I first went to America in the late Seventies, even poor people who were near the bottom of the ladder seemed to take things for granted that I'd always seen as luxuries.

Where I grew up, it was fairly normal to turn a blind eye to the odd bit of opportunist thievery. If people were struggling to get by and could get away with nicking something every now and again to make ends meet, that was maybe frowned on a little bit but no one was really going to hold it against them. We were all living at subsistence level – in short, none of us had a pot to piss in – so I can understand now why when families went to the Tesco supermarket on King Street together I'd sometimes see them putting stuff under their overcoats. Maybe there was nothing left in the house for dinner and it was their only way to put food on the table. At the time, though, I didn't really get it. Maybe because it wasn't really talked about afterwards, I'd be thinking, 'What's going on here?'

Another time they had some kind of competition in Tesco's where they would read out a number over the PA and if it was your number you could win a prize. I don't know how it happened, but my mum or Ron must have known someone on the inside, because their number came up and they won something, but for some reason it was obvious that the whole thing wasn't legit and they got rumbled. It was all a bit of a farce and quite humiliating, but again because nothing was ever really explained to me, I found it all very confusing.

A similar thing happened at school at Flora Gardens when we had an assignment to draw a picture and bring it back to class the next day. One of my mum's brothers – I think it was my uncle Barry – drew something and it looked good, so he said, "'Ere you are – try that,' but when I took it into class the next day, the teacher caught on straight away. He just asked me to draw the same thing again, and of course I couldn't do it. Barry was no master draughtsman, but I couldn't match him. I suppose looking back the feeling that incident gave me was shame, but at the time it just felt like I was worth a bit less than everyone else.

It was the same at home, too. I was second fiddle, I was put in the back, while my mum did everything she could to keep Ron happy. It felt like I was in a competition – with my stepdad, for my mum's attention – that I couldn't possibly win. I'm not saying my mum got off on the power this gave her, but sometimes it felt like she did. When you're a kid, you don't think of your mum the same way you think of other people. You don't think she's entitled to have character defects or do shitty things or just generally fuck up like everyone else does. So when that does happen, it can be hard to deal with.

It's only recently that I've started to look at her as a person like any other and not just my mum. I would love to know what her motivation was and what her life was like when she was growing up, but I don't think she would know where to start when it came to that conversation. I tapped on the window of it a few times when we were still talking but the curtains got drawn very quickly. If I tried to ask her about what my nan and grandad were like as parents it just seemed to make her really uncomfortable, almost as if something bad went on there. You'd think if nothing did she'd gladly talk about it, wouldn't you? But there's no knowing with my mum.

She'd say, 'Make sure you wipe your arse and put clean underwear on when you leave the house . . . in case you have an accident. I don't want the doctors thinking your mum doesn't look after you.' It was like that was all she cared about – not whether you've had an accident and 'Are you OK?' but would your arse be clean enough to reflect a positive light on her?

A lot of it was that classic English thing of 'What will the neighbours think?' My response to that has always been, 'Who gives a fuck what the neighbours think?!' But it was part and parcel of a working-class upbringing in Britain in those days that you got brainwashed into apologising for living in shit. 'Just shut up and get on with it, let the rich be rich and the poor be poor, Henry the Eighth is up there in his castle and everyone else is down below in their little mud huts.'

In a way, the Sex Pistols would be the end of that way of thinking, but even now I lapse into it every so often. Sometimes when I know I am selling myself short I feel that old lack of self-esteem reflex stirring within me – 'Oh, that's OK, I'll make do with this thing I don't really want because I haven't got the right to ask for anything better.' The programming is deeply rooted.

My mum didn't tell me much more about Ron than she had about my real dad – and she never had any good words for him, only that he was a cunt who never made any paternity payments. I think Ron had lived in East London before they met, and I had a feeling that maybe he had a daughter, although I never met her. I found out later that he was still married when he and my mum got together, which might explain why the two of them never got hitched, although they stayed together till he died a few years back, so they must've loved each other in their own way.

From his dark skin, jet black hair and foreign-sounding name, I got the impression that maybe Ron had originally come from Italy, or maybe Turkey, or Greece – there could easily have been a bit of Bubble (bubble and squeak = Greek) in there – but this wasn't talked about much either. In fact, nothing was. Without ever saying much, Ron made it pretty clear that he'd have preferred it if I wasn't there so he could have my mum all to himself. I quickly learnt not to ask too many questions, because curiosity seemed to be frowned upon. It's only over the past few years that I've started to find some of the answers that a person who'd grown up in a normal family would've known all along.

I'd often wondered what my nan and my uncles thought of Ron, because I got the vibe that maybe he wasn't popular with the rest of the family. So I asked my auntie Frances if this was because the family disapproved of the way my mum and Ron got together, and she said it was more likely because the brothers and sisters weren't close. She also said my grandad was a grumpy old sod who wouldn't leave the house, but if a trip to 15 Benbow Road was all that was on offer, I don't really blame him.

No one would've been going back to that dingy gaff voluntarily, that's for sure. The whole time I lived with my mum and Ron as a kid – after a few years in the basement in Benbow Road we'd move to an upstairs flat in the same house, and then later my mum got a council flat in Battersea – I never remember them having friends or family over. I found that weird at the time and I still do now. I'm not saying my mum and stepdad were like the Moors Murderers, but Ian Brady and Myra Hindley probably had more visitors.

The workshop under the railway arches where Ron was supervisor was even worse. Obviously this wasn't my mum and Ron's fault – they weren't hanging out there for fun – but I hated it when I had to go there. That whole place stank of rubber, the curved roof and bare brick walls made it really claustrophobic, and there was this one big fucking machine with steam coming out of it that stamped out rubber rings all day long. It made so much noise you couldn't hear what anyone was saying. It was like something out of the movie *Eraserhead*.

The one glimmer of sunshine that came into my life during this dark and depressing time was when I got a dog. He was only a little mutt but his name was Brucie and I got very close to him very quickly. That dog was fucking great and he really loved me, but one day I came home from school and he wasn't there any more. My mum just told me, 'Oh, Brucie's gone.'

She never explained what had happened to him, so I assumed they'd just got rid of him because he was too much work. It felt like the same thing might happen to me at any time when I was living in Benbow Road, and at a couple of points, it did.

This is where the gaps in my memory really start to widen – presumably because I was so upset by some of the things that were going on that my mind just tried to close them down. Auntie Frances can't help either because, as I've already mentioned, she kind of lost touch with us once we moved to Shepherd's Bush. Later on, as a teenager, I'd be sent to several different institutions for a variety of reasons (mostly connected with getting nicked), which I can generally recall quite well, but there's one place I half remember getting carted off to soon after we got to Benbow Road and I've just got no fucking idea what – or where – it was, or why I had to go there.

All I'm sure of is that it was out in the country and I was only there for about a week. I don't think it was a punishment, I think it was some kind of children's home, so maybe my mum couldn't look after me and no one else was willing to take me cos I was too much trouble. It's not like I was a total hooligan by that stage, though – I was only a little kid when I got sent there.

The only clear memory I have is that when I arrived they had a litter of kittens in a basket in the hallway. All you cat-lovers out there should look away now – I don't want to turn the cat people against me at this early stage, the pussy's going to be in enough jeopardy later – but I was so fucking angry about having to be there that I started trying to strangle them. These poor little fuckers have only been born a few days and already they've got my traumatised child's hands closing round their throats. I'm glad to say I didn't go through with it, but I sure as fucking hell did miss Brucie.

Your brain's still developing when you're young, and when you're quite isolated and you make a close attachment like that – even if it's only to an animal – and that contact gets taken away, it can mark you. All of a sudden this thing that made you feel like you mattered has fucking disappeared, and you don't get the hope of that back. When the scar heals over, it gets kind of hard. No wonder I can't have a proper fucking relationship with a woman . . . but let's not go down that road just yet.

For the moment, the main side effect of how fucking miserable I felt was that I started to fall even more behind at school. I couldn't read or write that well from the beginning, anyway. When it came to all the kids' comics with little stories in them like *The Hurricane* and *The Topper*, it was only really the pictures I was looking at. But the more unhappy I was, the more I fucked about, until eventually I got put back a year for not learning enough.

If I was a kid at school now, I'd probably get diagnosed pretty quickly as being dyslexic and/or having ADHD, but there was no 'special needs' teaching in those days. Or at least, none that applied to me in the schools I went to. I guess I seemed like a normal kid, just a bit more loony than the others. My problem was I just couldn't keep words in my head as they came off the page. Even now in later life, when I've taken steps to sort myself out on the literacy front, I still struggle to focus – it's like I'm not listening in my head to what I'm reading, because my mind is already away thinking about a pair of socks or something.

I've never been the sort of person who'd show off about not having once read a book all the way through. This was always a source of embarrassment to me, and another reason I never paid attention in school for one fucking second. It was the first of a series of situations where it became easier to find a way of blocking out the reality than to face up to it. No one was saying, 'Maybe this kid could be dyslexic.' Not at school, and certainly not at home, where no one had anything but the worst expectations of me, academically. Teachers assumed it was my destiny to fuck around and get in trouble, and so I did. It wasn't like I felt they had it in for me, just that what they were teaching didn't really have anything to do with me.

4. THE NONCE IN THE UNDERPASS

A couple of strange things happened to me just before we moved to Benbow Road which I forgot to tell you about. Anyone out there thinking this book has all been a bit Mary Poppins so far, well, this is where the David Lynch hits the fan.

Alongside the more celebrated landmarks of the Hammersmith area – the Odeon, the Palais, the flyover, the bridge, the Broadway – the local paedophile was another neighbourhood fixture. Every area has one (or usually a lot more than one, more's the pity). I guess they have a range that they cover, the same way urban foxes do, and this one's territory stretched all the way over to Shepherd's Bush, which would become significant a few years later . . . so just file that away for the moment in the part of your memory marked 'ominous facts'.

Once, and it was when I was still living in Riverside Gardens so I know I wasn't more than six years old, this guy tried to lure me down into the underpass beneath the Hammersmith flyover. He didn't do it with sweets or chocolates like it said he should in the 'stranger danger' adverts, but by tearing out pages from a lingerie catalogue and dropping them in front of me to leave a trail – like the fucking breadcrumbs in 'Hansel and Gretel'.

The question I've asked myself a lot is: 'How did he know this would work?' You've got to bear in mind that I was living happily at my nan's. Nothing bad had happened to me yet, and I had only just started school. Technically, I was still a pure and innocent kid. And yet somehow he knew that, if he did this, I would follow him. I think maybe some kids just give off more of a sexual energy than others, and they're the ones who are vulnerable to predators. It's like you're marked in a way that only they can see.

For whatever reason, I was one of those kids. I should've been thinking, 'Why's that creepy guy tearing pages out of that magazine and laying them on the stairs?' But instead of that, because I'm this prematurely sexual being, I'm interested. I can see exactly where this happened very clearly in my mind's eye: it was the steps down under the Chiswick side of the flyover, the way you'd go if you were heading for the river. He was trying to draw me off my usual turf and away from safety.

I didn't want to go with him, but I did want to get my hands on those pictures of birds which were getting me excited for reasons I didn't understand. I followed him down the stairs and into the darkness to a point where – and I remember this very clearly – I could see the light behind him from the exit at the far end. It wasn't a long tunnel, just under the road, but I could see him making his way up the stairs and I just thought, 'Fuck this, I'm going home.' For the time being at least I was going to stay on my own territory, which, I hardly need to add, was very much the right decision.

Another weird thing happened around then. Again we were still living with my nan, so things hadn't really started to get dark yet. But one day I was playing around the squares with some other kids when this girl – not much older than me and I didn't really know her – pulled her knickers down. Maybe things weren't right in her own home or maybe this kind of exhibitionism is quite normal for some kids of six years old. I don't know. One thing I'll tell you for sure is that my reaction wasn't the same as the other kids'. She pulled her knickers down and there was her little shitty arse. All the other kids kind of ran off laughing, but I just stood there staring at her. I was totally transfixed – it was just so fucking sexual. She never moved either. We didn't touch each other, but I was standing there in a trance for so long that by the time I'd snapped out of if some cheeky little cunt had had the time to nick my bike.

Later on, when I was reflecting on my life and trying to work how the fuck I came to connect stealing with sexual feelings, this incident was obviously hard to get past. But that kind of stuff is really deep and once you get down there trying to figure things out you've got to be careful not to leap to the obvious conclusions. Therapists love to jump on something like this and say it's the reason for everything, but life just isn't that simple. One fucking chancer even suggested that maybe I nicked so much stuff over the years that followed because I was trying to make up for the loss of my bicycle!

There's no shortage of evidence to go through for anyone trying to work out why I ended up the way I did. Another time I was on the swings in the playground at school in Flora Gardens and there were girls standing around laughing at me. Girls tended to like me because I was cute, even though I was quite shy around them until I discovered alcohol. But I was still definitely one of the cooler kids, so I wasn't used to people taking the piss. I didn't know why they were all laughing at me until I realised my cock was hanging out of my shorts. I got so ashamed and embarrassed because I didn't know how to make them stop. Of course I'd find out in the end, but that wouldn't be for a few years yet.

There's one other incident of this kind I probably can't get away without mentioning, even though I'd like to. But if I'm trying to be honest about my past, it's got to be all or nothing. My mum was walking with me along the main street in Hammersmith. It felt late at night but maybe it was just early evening in the winter, as I was probably only seven or eight at the time. Either way, the shops were closed. But somewhere along King Street, my mum stopped by this lingerie store to look at the stuff in the window. Not really thinking about what she was doing, she gave the front door a push and found that they'd left it open when they went home. No one was in there and so all this stuff she couldn't normally have afforded was free to a good home. She was really surprised and excited – I remember her saying, 'Fuck me!' – not your usual window shopping.

You don't need to be that psychiatrist bird in *The Sopranos* to see that the combination of having my mum's attention, her swearing, the lingerie in the window and the excitement of getting away with something might have had some kind of impact on my sexual development. But when it comes to those murky waters there's a big pike in the fishpond that I've not got to yet.

Never mind the paedophile in the underpass, more often than not it's the one who lives in the same house as you that you really need to worry about. At least, that was how it worked out in my case. We'd been in Benbow Road a few years by the time my stepdad fiddled with me. I must've been ten or eleven, because by then we'd moved upstairs to a slightly bigger flat in the same house that had an actual toilet and a bathroom. Technically we were going up in the world, but it didn't feel that way.

My mum was in hospital when it happened. The way I remember it, she had a miscarriage and had to stay in hospital for a while afterwards. I'm not 100 per cent sure that's what happened but that's what I remember. I don't know how long I was in the house on my own with him. Frances said she thought this was a time I was sent to a children's home for a while, but if that did happen, it didn't happen quick enough to save me from getting fucked with.

One night, Ron's in bed in Benbow Road when he calls me in to see him. He doesn't generally acknowledge my existence unless he absolutely has to, but when he does address me directly, there's usually a bit of intimidation going on. So I wasn't going to say no, even though I'd have had no reason to think anything good was going to come of it (and it fucking didn't). Anyway, I've not been in the bedroom long before he starts bullying me into jerking him off. I'm only a kid. What do I fucking know? I haven't got a clue what's going on, but I'm there on my own with him and there doesn't seem to be any other option other than to go along with what he wants. So that's exactly what I do – fiddle with his cock until he cums, with him looming over me all the while telling me what I've got to do.

All I remember feeling immediately afterwards was a bit bewildered – just thinking, 'That was . . . odd.' But the consequences of what happened are still with me half a fucking century later. I never told anyone about it for years afterwards, and it feels quite strange putting this in a book even now. But knowing the damage all the confusion I felt did to me over the intervening years makes me want to do all I can to let anyone who's been in a similar situation know they're not alone.

Obviously Ron would have to be a bit of a sicko to do what he did to a ten-year-old kid. I certainly never got the impression that he felt any conscience about it afterwards. I used to wonder if he'd done it to other children, but my instinct said probably not. It felt more like part of the power play around my mum – one of those alpha male things, like something that would happen in prison, where he had his chance to put his mark on me and so he did. He never tried it again, but if his objective was just to fuck me up he'd already achieved that goal, so why would he bother?

He'd always wanted to get rid of me so he could have my mum to himself, and now he'd pretty much got his way. From that point on, I never wanted to be at home. I didn't feel safe there. I wasn't actively in danger – I just felt threatened by his presence, and he seemed to revel in that. I guess when an adult who's meant to be looking after you does something like that, it changes the way you feel about people in general.

An abused kid with no one to talk to will often think what's happened is their fault, even though at some level they know it isn't. That was certainly true of me. Another common response is to get angry and act out, and I did that too, if not necessarily in the way you'd expect.

Remember that local nonce I mentioned at the start of the chapter? Well, four or five years on he was still hanging around the area like a bad smell, and my confusion was his opportunity. I ran into him in the street not long after the thing with my stepdad happened, he started spinning me a line, and I went for it and let him suck my cock for some money. Isn't that weird? I'm living in a different postcode to where he tried it on before, but this same fucking paedophile still manages to find me. This cunt must've had some kind of nonce super-sense which told him I was confused and vulnerable enough for him to blag me into getting what he wanted.

It's not like I was wearing a badge that said, 'I have just been molested by my stepdad,' but something like that fucks with your idea of normality. Once it's happened the first time I guess it's more likely to happen again, because from then on there's a little voice in your head that thinks this is what normal is.

I was no more than eleven years old by that time, maybe only ten, but either way, I was definitely still at primary school in Flora Gardens. It happened in a stairwell by a petrol station off Goldhawk Road in Shepherd's Bush. The paedophile was trying to suck me off and having a pedal (and crank) while he was at it. Obviously it was a sexual transaction from his point of view, but not from mine. I was definitely not old enough to ejaculate even if I had felt the inclination.

I don't know what happened to the guy afterwards – whether or not he ever got put away for doing shit like this – but everyone in the area knew who he was. Later on, when I became friends with Paul Cook, he knew about him too, though I never told him what had happened. In fact, I've never mentioned it in public before – and barely ever in private. It's what you'd classify as breaking news.

This was quite a lot of secrets to be carrying around in my head at only eleven years old. Factor in not really being able to read or write properly and it was no wonder my secondary school career did not get off to the best of starts. I arrived at Sir Christopher Wren boys comprehensive school on Bloemfontein Avenue in White City and was put straight into the nutters' class.

My biggest worry at this point in my life was in my pants. For some reason I became overwhelmed with humiliation at the idea that I had a little cock with no hairs around it. It was the time when everyone's bodies developed at their own pace. I wasn't the first one out of the blocks when it came to puberty, that's for sure, and the fact that I knew I was a year older probably put a bit of extra pressure on – I'd see these kids with big cocks and hair everywhere and it just turned me into a basket case. This became such a fucking issue for me that I used to spend all my time torturing myself about the fact that I was going to have to get in the showers with everyone after playing sports. I was obsessed with not wanting anyone to see my cock, to the extent that I would keep my underwear on in the shower and tell everyone I had some weird thing wrong with me rather than face the imaginary music.

Of course it was all in my head. If I'd just got in the shower with my inadequately garnished meat and two veg on display like everyone else, no one would've said, 'Ha ha, look at you.' But I guess it was a sign of how much I was struggling that I fixated on these details in such a self-destructive way. It's not like I was one of the nerdy kids. My fellow swimmers in the bottom stream would've probably thought I was hip, and if you were here with me now, I'd happily show you my cock to reassure you that it is at the very least of normal size, if not quite magnificent.

I can see now that at least some of the sense of shame I had about my body probably came from what had happened with my stepdad and then the nonce. But that didn't occur to me then. Either way, it ruined my schooling. I'd go in there on a Monday thinking, 'Oh fuck, I'm going to have to get in that shower in five days from now,' and any slim chance of concentrating on what was meant to be happening in class would go straight out the window.

What it all came down to was me not feeling comfortable with myself. These experiences of molestation had knocked me out of alignment with the world. There didn't seem to be any escape from feeling like this, not at school and certainly not at home, and all the shit I started getting into from then onwards – thieving, drinking, drugs, with birds – was basically about trying to leave that sense of discomfort behind. I was just looking for a way to feel all right, and I wasn't too bothered about who got hurt in the process.

Would I have been a real goody two-shoes without my stepdad's helping hand? (Well, technically it was my hand doing the helping, but you know what I mean.) Probably not. I don't think I was that bad a kid prior to that, though. If I'd ever tea-leafed before it would just have been the occasional one-off – far from the one-teenager West London crime wave that I was about to become.

I've often wondered if things would've worked out differently if I'd been able to tell anyone what had happened at the time. My mum had no way of knowing – Ron certainly wasn't going to tell her, and it's not like I tried to talk to her about it and she shut me down. She probably would've done, but I can't really hold that against her when I didn't give her the chance to prove me wrong. I know she noticed a change in my behaviour from then on, because she mentioned it in an interview she did for a Sex Pistols book a few years later, but all she said was I 'seemed to be very upset' about her having a miscarriage. She didn't know the half of it!

I can't deny I've carried a lot of anger towards both of them over the years, but I don't feel so much towards my mum now. If it hadn't been for me getting in the way, she'd probably have been able to get someone better than Ron anyway. When you're single with a kid you're not going to get the pick of the litter as far as geezers are concerned, are you? So this cunt came along and she made do with him – I can't really blame her for that. And if I'd had a safe place to retreat to and lick my wounds, I wouldn't have had the motivation to go off in search of the kind of adventures that would help me forget them.

When it comes to what defines me as a person, a lot of the best things in my life have come about because of the worst things, which is a weird one when you try and think about divine intervention and all that bollocks. It would be a pretty twisted kind of God who would say, 'Let's abuse that child so he can go off the rails and form a band.' But looking back, I do feel like someone or something – God, destiny, whatever you want to call it – definitely threw me a lifeline in giving me music to hang on to. Without that I was in serious danger of getting swept away by a tide of fucked-up shit.

Right in the middle of my darkest time in Benbow Road I heard a noise I liked coming from our neighbours' window. The bloke next door had one of those little Dansette record players and he was playing the '45 of Jimi Hendrix' 'Purple Haze' on it. As tinny as it must have sounded, it really spoke to me. Not so much the words of the song – I've never been too bothered about lyrics, even to this day – just the feel of the whole thing and the way it fitted together.

There was a catchiness about it as well as the power, and I loved the syncopation, the way Hendrix' guitar would kind of go 'Clunk' and then 'Weeeoh!' I loved it so much that I wouldn't let them stop playing it. I stood in the street outside their window shouting up 'Play it again! Play it again!' till I drove them half crazy. At this point I wouldn't have dreamed of ever trying to become a guitar hero myself, but one thing was for sure: I needed a fucking outlet, and music would give me one.

5. SKINHEAD MOONSTOMP

The overwhelming reality of my life at that time was that I did not want to be in the same house as my stepdad. This probably gave me a head start over other kids my age in terms of how far afield I was willing to go in search of excitement. Effectively I was running away, but once I started getting on buses or tube trains and heading up to the West End, I found it exciting to explore the city on my own.

I was pretty green and given my seemingly irresistible allure as far as the paedophile fraternity was concerned, I was probably lucky I didn't end up getting chucked in the back of a van and whisked off to Dolphin Square to get rumped and killed by some fucking evil Tory MP. Whether you're talking about that establishment side of it – and even if the police don't believe it, some people still reckon kids got killed in that place but it was all covered up after – or Jimmy Savile terrorising the *Top of the Pops* dressing room, it's taken years for the truth to come out about how much VIP paedophile shit was going on in London at that time. I still don't think they've done more than scratch the surface.

As it turned out, the worst thing that happened to me on my first few trips up to the West End was getting ripped off by some street conmen playing Three-card Monte (or whatever you call that when it's dice under cups). You know those geezers with the orange-boxes who are all working together to make you put your money down so they can have it off you, but if you're really naive like I was you don't realise? I've still got such a clear memory of how certain I was about which cup it was under – I swore blind I was going to win and when these cunts took my money off me the only word to describe how I felt is 'violated'.

I guess it's odd that word should spring to mind when I'd been in other situations that seemed to suit it better. But thinking about it, maybe that's actually not weird at all, because sometimes the only way to deal with those sort of things is to keep them at a safe distance. And I was genuinely fucking devastated about the money. It could have been as much as a tenner – which was a lot then – and the probability that I'd come by it dishonestly did not make me feel any better about losing it.

Would it have occurred to me that this was how all the people I nicked stuff off probably felt? Not for a second. All I cared about was making sure I never fell for such an obvious trick again. I was only a young dude then, still a long way from the hardened criminal of later years, but that was a big learner for me – walking away from the situation, knowing I'd been royally done.

You could tell by the kinds of things I was nicking what a kid I still was. Hornby model railway accessories were one of my first stops on the branch line of larceny. I'd go up to Hamleys, the big toy store on Regent Street, and come back with all this stuff for the amazing train set I'd sometimes be allowed to lay out on the floor of the living room in the upstairs flat at Benbow Road. I was obsessed with the detail of the engines, and the great thing about them was you just opened the packet and there they were. Not like with Airfix kits, where I would've loved the finished product of a World War II fighter or a bomber, but because of the attention deficit thing I just didn't have the patience to make them. Well, I tried a couple of times, but mine came out looking more like train wrecks.

Not being able to read the instructions probably didn't help, but the main thing was I just did not get the concept of delayed gratification. Why would I want to spend weeks and months painstakingly making one when I could go out and steal something else that would have the same level of detail and all the work already done?

Instant gratification was also the name of the game in my other main criminal speciality, which in the early days of my reign of terror was nicking bikes. There was a proper bike shop on Putney Road, just south of the river – I think it was called Holdsworth's. I used to walk across Hammersmith Bridge, turn left along the towpath towards Putney, then go right off this one road and come out near the bike shop. I'd stand there waiting till some geezer would get off his amazing Tour de France racer to go in there, then if he didn't lock his bike up properly I'd be off down the towpath on it before anyone knew it'd gone.

I got some pretty tasty bikes that way. I used to stash them in the coal chute of the Benbow Road basement. And it wasn't long till I progressed from nicking bikes to nicking mopeds. They were easy to get going – you just had to pedal them and they'd pretty much start. I had some good runs up and down that towpath. I remember getting chased by the Old Bill down there once with someone on the back – I can't remember who.

Early on in my thieving career I had a decent track record of not getting caught. One time when I was still no more than twelve, I was shoplifting in Selfridges department store – one of my other favourite West End haunts – when this geezer goes, 'Oi!' I thought he'd collared me, but gradually I realised he just wanted a sweet, excited kid to demonstrate a toy for a story in the paper. It was called a Johnny Astro and was essentially a balloon you had to land on the surface of the moon using the air from a fan. You can see the suspicious look on my face in the photo they took, cos I still can't quite believe I'm not nicked. The fact that this photo appeared in the *Sun* was just the icing on the cake. This was my first appearance in the tabloid press, but it wouldn't be my last.

The guy who took the picture had no idea what a little crook he was dealing with. I guess people who aren't hardened thieves can be a bit naive when it comes to realising kids are up to no good. I can tell when someone's at it in two seconds – there really are few truer sayings than 'it takes one to know one'. And that doesn't just apply to thieves: the same goes for junkies. If you're high on dope, I can smell it on you, because I was that guy. It's actually a pain in the arse, because even though I'm not doing those things any more, my head's still full of them. You can't relax because you've constantly got the antennae on – like I would never leave anything lying around backstage at a gig, in case there's a Steve Jones around. I suppose there's a kind of justice to that in a way.

The first thing my friend Paul Cook – Cookie for the rest of this book, no point standing on ceremony after all these years – says he remembers noticing about me once we became friends was that I was always 'doing furtive things with bikes in the basement'. Our paths had crossed a few times before that when we were a bit younger, walking to our different primary schools. I think our mums vaguely knew each other for some reason I never quite understood, because they used to wave at each other across the road. It never went much further than a quick hello, though.

It took us a little while to get to know each other once we'd both started at secondary school because we were in different classes. I was in the one with all the thick cunts and he was in the top stream. It was both being skinheads that brought us together.

A few people over the years have said that our personalities complement each other, and I guess that's so. He's a Cancer and I'm a Virgo, for a start. Not that we'd have given a shit about that bollocks when we were at school, but it basically means he's quite secure and laid-back whereas I'm more of a loon. When it came to getting in trouble I was always the instigator and he was the one who came along for the ride. He wasn't a criminal like I was. He didn't always need to be thieving like I did – he didn't have that drive – but he liked a laugh enough to tag along and see what would happen.

Some parents would've seen their kid becoming friendly with a troublemaker like me and tried to put a lid on it, but Paul's mum and dad weren't like that. I never got that from them. They took me into their house and showed me what a normal home life could be. The Cooks were a loving family – his dad, his mum, his sister, they were all good people who enjoyed each other's company. They even had friends who would come over to their house to watch TV sometimes: that's how sociable they were.

Apart from Cookie's house, another place where I found a bit of sanctuary was going to see Queens Park Rangers play football on a Saturday afternoon. It took me five minutes to walk up to their ground at Loftus Road. A load of other kids from Christopher Wren went and I just followed suit. If there was an away game I'd sometimes go to Fulham or Chelsea – and they're my team now. I guess that's a King's Road thing.

There was a phase when I was really young when I would watch the game, but once the skinhead thing took over, it was all about going to the ground for a bit of a rampage afterwards. I remember a few times when we all went into a shop on Shepherd's Bush Market and nicked Ben Sherman shirts. I was proud of the number of those I'd managed to get my hands on by fair means or foul over the years. I think I topped out at thirteen, which was a lot for a kid of my age – certainly more than any of my friends had.

The buzz of it was all about feeling part of something. I liked the camaraderie of being with a bunch of blokes, even blokes you didn't know but only saw at the game. I was so used to being on my own that it was a relief to be part of a group. I'd go with mates from school, too. Cookie, Stephen Hayes, Jimmy Macken and Alex Hall – that was our little crew. The violence side of it wasn't for me, though. I might've bullshitted myself that it was for five minutes, but that's not really my nature. There was plenty of shit going on at the time but when you're only twelve you're not in the front rank and no one's really expecting you to be – it's more about being one of the kids at the back going, 'Come on, let's 'ave 'em!'

I had no ambitions to be the leader of any hooligan firm, but I always wanted to dress like the top dog. This was why I was happy to go miles out of town to that Ivy League place in Richmond. Even as a twelve-year-old, I'd travel to the ends of the earth (that's officially where Richmond is, right?) to get the best clobber. I'd still do that now, almost fifty years later. As its name suggests, Ivy League was an American shop selling what I suppose you'd call preppie stuff – clothes like the Beach Boys would wear, nice short-sleeved checked shirts with Levi's Sta-Prest and the proper fucking brogues. Even if the only shoe sizes they had were too big for me, I'd rather put up with the blisters on my feet than not look the part.

I had all the good shit. A lot of skinheads didn't have a fucking clue; they'd wear some horrible old tat. I was a snob when it came to clothes. If you didn't have the right stuff, I didn't want nothing to do with you – if you wore a Brutus shirt, or jeans that weren't Levi's, or had sideburns (though that last one may've been because I was too young and couldn't grow 'em yet), then forget about it. By the same token, if you saw another guy with the right gear you'd kind of bond with them straight away, just because you knew they had that little something special about them.

Of course not everyone's like that. In fact, the vast majority of people don't really give a shit about these things, and the longer any kind of youth movement goes on, the more the kids who don't really care tend to get involved. That certainly happened with the skinheads, and it went the same way with the punk thing later on. At the start it was all about making an effort to look distinctive and stand out, but then it became just the uniform of leather jacket and jeans, with no thought or care going into it any more.

That was especially true when the Americans got involved. I think there's something specifically English about caring so much about these kinds of fashion details. I've never been able to quite put my finger on what, but I think it started with the Teddy boys and then got even stricter with the mods and the skinheads. And it carried on into the Eighties with the casuals – the football hooligans who dressed really smart when Margaret Thatcher was on her throne. There's almost a queer element to the whole peacocking side of it – the idea of 'who's the face?' where you have to dress and do your hair a certain really detailed way and you're a cunt if you don't look as good. But in the end I think this mentality is more of a class thing than a sex thing.

The way people were brought up in the British class system must have had something to do with it. If you were working class you were raised with the feeling that you had to know your place, and one way of escaping that was to subscribe to a different set of values which allowed you to become part of your own fashion aristocracy. That's why Americans never tended to quite get it when they tried to transfer our subcultures over there, because they didn't have that conditioning to push back against.

For me, having the proper sheepskin coat or the genuine cashmere

Crombie was a way to feel good about myself. It was your own little thing that marked out a space you could be successful in. The two-tone suits were the perfect example of that. Not many of us were heading for the kind of jobs where you'd need a whistle (and flute), but we could go down to a place called Stewart's on Uxbridge Road – he was this little Jewish tailor who saw an opportunity – and get him to make us one for £10. Every kid that was a skinhead from my area had to go through that rite of passage. You'd go down there to get measured up and he'd go, 'Come in, my boy . . .' I bet he couldn't believe his luck.

In later times, skinheads would come to be seen as very narrow-minded and racist, but it wasn't like that for us. After all, what brought us together was that we all loved Jamaican and black American music. Even in the 1960s, Shepherd's Bush and White City were very mixed areas – a lot of Irish people lived there, but also a few Asians and increasing numbers of black kids. And in the early days there was none of that Nazi shit going on. Being a skinhead had nothing to do with racism as far as we were concerned. There was a black kid from school called Cecil who was one of our mates and he was a skinhead without anyone saying anything about it.

As time went on, 'Paki-bashing' and 'queer-bashing' did become more and more part of skinhead culture. I don't know how that happened; I think maybe the National Front involved themselves and managed to twist it all in more of a fascist direction. And that side of things got really warped and full-on anti-Semitic once it went over to America. By the time I crossed the Atlantic for the first time in the late Seventies, the Nazi element had really crept in, until no one was really thinking about dancing to *Tighten Up* compilations any more. Maybe Americans just took the whole thing out of context, the same way they did with punk.

6. THE STEVE JONES CLOAK OF INVISIBILITY

My career as a heterosexual started with a bang. When I lost my virginity at the age of thirteen I'd never even jerked off before, so my first ejaculation didn't come from playing with myself, it was from rumping a bird. Well, sort of rumping her. I had my cock pushed in between her legs, but I'm not sure if there was time to get fully inside her before I fucking shot my load. Still, it definitely counted. Or at least, it did as far as I was concerned.

The setting for this once-in-a-lifetime event was the shed where they stored the *Flying Scotsman* train for the Battersea funfair's miniature railway. It had that special streamlined shape at the front, kind of like the Japanese bullet train, and my first non-nonce sexual partner was lying back against the metal curve. In retrospect, the choice of location was quite funny (given my obsession with nicking train sets) and I certainly got to my destination at express pace.

After it happened, I was stunned. My mind was spinning – 'What the fuck was that?' I ran home to the Battersea council block we'd recently moved to when my mum's name finally got to the top of the housing list, bolted upstairs to the bathroom and inspected my cock for signs of damage. I thought it was bleeding or something. For someone who'd already found himself in the situations I had, I was embarrassingly innocent. But after that first nut, I loved the feeling of cumming so much that I just couldn't stop myself. I was jerking off five times a day – with toilet rolls, vacuum cleaners, all kinds of weird fucking things.

At least, I presumed they were weird, but maybe some of them would count as the usual kinky experiments any regular teenage boy would get up to. Either way, I remember I had this obsession with putting toilet rolls on my cock and jerking off – because it almost felt like it wasn't me doing it, I think that was the concept. I was so fixated on doing this that sometimes I'd get a fucking rash from the roughness of the cardboard.

I suppose I was still trying to figure shit out, and at least I was actually inside something – even if it was only a toilet roll, so it wasn't that big a step forward. One result of your sexual life getting off to the kind of fucked-up start mine did is that even though you're doing something which might be fairly normal, you don't always know that, so you assume it's as deviant and wrong as all your other impulses. Of course the other side of that coin is that some very strange shit can all too easily become normal to you. It certainly did to me.

The ejaculation thing happened prior to any significant drinking or drug-taking on my part (gasping on a Players No. 6 excepted), and it was my first major fix. Something that got me out of my head for a while, so I didn't have to deal with all the shit that was in there. Given half a chance, it still works like that for me today, even now I've kicked all my other addictions except sugar . . . I guess you never forget your first loves.

Chasing that sexual high would take me into pretty dark territory in the years ahead. For the moment, it was a good job I finally had my own room, even if there was no way its concrete walls were going to hold me and my exploding teenage libido. I couldn't sit still for a fucking minute at that age.

The flat we'd moved to in Battersea was in one of those really long, brutal-looking boxes. It had only just been built, and they'd interspersed three of these new blocks with the older, Peabody-type places that remained. Our block bordered on a big patch of waste ground where I think a gasworks used to be, and there was a shaggers' alley over the other side that I got quite fixated on. People would pull up in their cars and I'd be over the other side of the wall, having a wank while watching them shag – that was a real turn-on for me.

Peeping Tom-ing became a big part of my life over the next few years. I was ashamed of it, but I suppose that shame was part of what was driving me on. It certainly didn't stop me. Later on, the whole thing would get even more obsessive. I'd find another shaggers' alley down near the railway lines in Battersea, and I'd be up on the bridge looking down at people fucking in their cars. I'd be so angry that some other guy was getting pussy and I wasn't that sometimes I'd find a big fucking rock and slam it down on the bonnet from above. Can you imagine being in that car getting your end away when a fucking boulder crashes down onto you? You'd think it was Judgement Day. Not that I'd hang around to see the chaos my handi-work caused. I wasn't that stupid. I'd leg it and live to wank another day.

There's not a shelf in the library high enough for this shit, is there? This is the good stuff you just don't get from the guy from Nickelback (at least, not so far as I know).

Battersea was a rough place to live in those days, but the flat itself was all right. It was a relief to have my own room for the first time in my life, and I was happy to leave behind Benbow Road and its bad memories. The part of it that was a major nause was having to travel all the way from Battersea to Shepherd's Bush to go to school.

It wasn't just that we'd moved south of the river – it took me four fucking buses to get there. The weird thing was (given how not into school I was) it was my idea to stay at Christopher Wren when I could've easily gone somewhere nearer. My mum wasn't bothered either way, and I doubt the school authorities were exactly overjoyed to keep me – 'Thank fuck for that, lads, Steve Jones is staying!' – but I didn't want to leave my mates behind and have to make new ones.

As it turned out, the fact that I now had to get up at seven in the morning if I wanted to make it to Christopher Wren on time was probably the final nail in the coffin of my school career, but it's not like I was bound for glory in that direction anyway. What moving to Battersea definitely did do was push me a bit further away from the kind of normal life Cookie would've probably been having without my intervention. I'd already got used to heading off into the city on my own in search of any kind of mischief to distract me from having to live with my stepdad. Now I had a whole new territory to explore. This is where the Steve Jones Cloak of Invisibility really started to come into play.

My secret weapon when I went out thieving had always been to convince myself that, wherever I was, I was meant to be there legally. Like in Hamleys, I wouldn't be nicking train sets off the shop floor. Oh no, that was a mug's game – I'd sneak into the stockroom. People who actually did work there would see this twelve- or thirteen-year-old skinhead looking furtive among the expensive toys and do . . . absolutely fuck all about it. It was a bizarre concept, but so long as I'd convinced myself what I was doing was perfectly normal, it seemed that people would accept this by sheer force of my will. I don't know how it worked, only that it did. It was almost as if I'd made myself invisible. Like a fantasy of having a superpower, except you came out the other end with actual free stuff.

The confidence this gave me would take me anywhere I wanted to go.

If there was a door, I'd walk straight through it. No matter where it was – the grandest shops in the West End, or the run-down changing rooms of the St Paul's School playing fields in Barnes, just the other side of Hammersmith Bridge, by the towpath I used to ride stolen bikes and mopeds down. While the normal people were outside in the fresh air playing football or rugby or cricket, I'd haunt those changing rooms, nicking their wallets. I used to do that a lot. It was a great distraction from all the things I'd otherwise have to be thinking about.

Was I technically a kleptomaniac? Well, there wasn't a day that went by when I didn't wake up and think, 'What am I gonna pilfer today?' If you substitute drinking or getting high or shagging for the thieving, you've got a pretty straightforward picture of what addiction is. The fact that what I was doing made victims of strangers never bothered me, even as I was thinking, 'Who's going to be the unlucky soul today?'

I certainly got a sense of satisfaction if I got home with a good haul, but I'd still be back at it again the next day. My thievery wasn't goal-driven; it wasn't about getting enough money together to do some particular thing, it was about excitement for its own sake, seeing what I could get away with. Well, that and having something I could focus on that would distract me from myself. Plus, it was something I was good at. I stole for the love of it, I tells ya.

The Cloak of Invisibility wasn't only useful for nicking stuff – it was a multi-purpose garment. I used to put it on to sneak into Battersea Power Station as well. Pink Floyd hadn't done *Animals* yet, but you didn't need a flying pig to show you how those fucking huge chimneys dominated the landscape around my new home. I had to find a way in, which wasn't hard, and once I was in there it was easy to find stairwells and other little cubbyholes I could sneak off and hide in if any of the geezers working there got suspicious. Which they never did, obviously, because I had the Cloak on.

That place was massive inside. There was this giant open room with these huge fucking turbines – one for each of the chimneys – which you could see them working on even at night-time. You didn't have to tiptoe around, really, because it was so loud in there no one could hear themselves think. The heat from the burning coal certainly kept it hot enough, but I soon figured out a way to get up to the top of the building so I could go out on the roof. It was fantastic up there – the views along the river were incredible. Years later when that film *Brazil* came out, with all the scenes filmed inside power stations, the whole thing felt very familiar to me – I knew I'd been there before.

Once you were out on the roof, the four giant chimneys had little ladders on that you could climb up. I went most of the way up one, but not all the way because I fucking bottled it. I was very agile when I was young – it was one of my many gifts – and I had no fear of heights, but I'm telling you it was scary up there. Someone told me Glen Matlock's book has a dramatic description in it of me getting chased right up to the top of one of the chimneys by the police, but I don't remember that actually happening (what was I going to do when they caught me – jump off?) so maybe I embellished the story a little bit. Either that, or Glen's got my real life mixed up with the ending of a film.

There was a real thrill to the cold night air hitting your face when you climbed out of that giant furnace room and onto the roof. It's a fucking shame some idiot developers have been allowed to rip the guts out of that place to make a quick buck. Those chimneys are the only thing anyone remembers about that part of London. Well, that and the dogs' home.

The view from the top of the power station wasn't the only excitement that Battersea had to offer. As I mentioned at the start of this chapter, wonderful things also happened at the fairground in Battersea Park. I used to love going there, and I had another of those landmark musical moments – epiphanies, I suppose you'd call them – by the waltzer, where the Fairground Ted stands on the back to impress the girls and try and nick money out of people's pockets. They were playing the hit songs of the day and Otis Redding's '(Sittin' on) The Dock of the Bay' came on. It was the same basic MO as with 'Purple Haze'. Boom! The song doesn't just stick in your head, it rewires your brain.

I must have stood there for a full two hours, hoping to hear it again, but obviously they weren't gonna play the same song twice. Eventually it got to about nine o'clock at night, the fair shut down and I went home with 'Dock of the Bay' still reverberating round the old noggin. Maybe it's the whistling. I do a thing now on my radio show, *Jonesy's Jukebox*, where I whistle a song over the guitar chords and people have to guess what it is: it drives them nuts when they can't get it. So I suppose Battersea Funfair could be where that started, but it's more likely it was just something about the song as a whole that resonated with me as a thirteen-year-old kid.

I don't know why I was so desperate to hear it again. I suppose you could look at the lyrics and say, 'Well, it's someone stuck somewhere near the water who is trying to imagine a better life,' but as I said before, I've never really listened to the words of songs, although maybe I've just taken them in without really noticing. I hate admitting that because it makes me sound like a fucking dumbass, but it's true – the melody and the over-all vibe were what mattered to me more than anything else. Thinking about the lyrics would've reminded me of school. Of course things can take root in your mind in a way that you don't understand, but however that song spoke to me, it wasn't through me thinking about what Otis Redding was singing.

One thing I've realised about myself when I was growing up is that I never asked questions the way other kids did. I think I'd have felt like

I was bothering someone, so rather than just ask 'Why?' if there was something I didn't understand, I just let it go and glossed it over. It wasn't that I wasn't curious or didn't notice what was going on around me, but if I was confused about something I never expected anyone would want to help me.

When you grow up like I did, with the world and even your own family constantly giving you the message that you're a piece of shit who is never going to amount to anything, it's hard not to start believing that yourself. It wasn't that my mum and stepdad were directly telling me, 'You're nothing, you'll never get anywhere,' all the time – although once I started to get in trouble with the police I would hear that kind of thing more and more; it was just a general feeling of not being supported.

The sad reality of my Cloak of Invisibility was that it was double-sided. The beginning of it was just being ignored. Then I took that painful reality of not feeling wanted in my own home and flipped it around – 'Well, if no one's gonna notice me, maybe that means I can just wander into places and nick stuff. At least that way I'll get something out of it.' It was almost as if not feeling I had the right to belong anywhere gave me the impulse to go everywhere. Some of these issues were just too painful to think about, and so long as I was on the move from one crime scene to the next, I knew I could ignore them. The Cloak could protect me.

It didn't occur to me at the time, but I think there were two sides to how my mates saw me as well. On the one hand, I was the chosen one – Jimmy Macken used to say I 'could fall down in cow-shit and come up smelling of roses'. On the other, even though this – and especially not the thing with my stepdad – wasn't something we'd ever have talked about, they must have clocked that things weren't right at home. It's not something you really want other people to know, is it? You want everyone to think you come from a normal family so you don't have to be the odd one out. But why else did I always want to stay over at Cookie's or Hayesy's or Jimmy Macken's?

I was that kid who never stopped wanting to hang around and stay over. I was probably a right pain in the arse, but I think my friends' parents must've felt sorry for me, because I don't remember any of them ever letting me know that I was surplus to requirements. They could see that I was trouble, but they did their best to look out for me anyway. I guess some people are just warm-hearted like that.

7. SILVER MACHINE

Our next musical move after being skinheads was not an obvious one on paper. It normally takes a few steps to get from Ska to Sabbath, but we did it in a single bound. As anyone who listens to my radio show will tell you, I still love to make a leap of faith when it comes to musical genres, and this one felt pretty logical at the time. When Stephen Hayes' older brother played us Black Sabbath and *Led Zep II* with 'Whole Lotta Love' on it for the first time, we were instantly hooked.

Stephen's brother's real name was Tony – although we called him Dick to get on his nerves – and the Hayes family lived on the White City estate. It was a tough place, where most of the cool kids from Christopher Wren tended to live. All the streets seemed to have South African names, which I thought at the time was because of it being White City, but it turns out to be something to do with the exhibitions they used to have on the site before the stadium got built.

I've got a very clear memory of sitting on a bed in the Hayeses' house listening to 'Dow dow . . . dow, dow dowwww'. I'm sure you've already guessed what song that is – any fool could recognise it's Black Sabbath's 'Sweet Leaf'. I hadn't picked up a guitar in anger yet, but if any song's going to make you fancy having a go yourself, it's that one. The funny thing is, we were very innocent and didn't know that the lyrics were about weed. Unless of course I've got it wrong and 'Sweet Leaf' is actually a song about the coming of autumn . . .

It's not like drugs were unknown to us at the time. I was only fourteen years old the first time I took a Mandrax. I did it outside a QPR game – it was just a little white tablet that was meant to be a sleeping pill, like an aspirin except maybe a bit fatter – and on top of a couple of pints it had me falling all over the place at around one or two in the afternoon. I remember the older guys all laughing at me and me thinking the tingling feeling the Mandy gave me was the tits. They must've been quite easy to get at the time, because I managed to get one and I didn't know anybody.

I did LSD a couple of times as well, but I fucking hated that. Once was at a friend's house, which was right on the Westway. Acid is a bit like that road: once you're on it, you can't stop, and you've not got much control about where you come off. His mum and dad were in one room – with no idea of what we were doing – and the two of us were in another. When I got up to go for a piss at one point I looked in the mirror and all I saw was this black skeleton. Fuck that for a game of soldiers! I don't think I got a wink of sleep till the sun came up – it felt like the night was never going to end.

I understand that LSD is good for some people's heads, but it didn't work for mine. Weed was kind of similar, I'd just get too paranoid and freak out. Some people find it helps them relax but I can't enjoy it – maybe I'm just too controlling.

One impulse I had no chance of controlling was my addiction to cumming. To that end, my activities as a peeping Tom probably peaked at the ages of fourteen to fifteen. If you ever wondered who it was making little holes in the wall of public toilets in the late 1960s and early 1970s, well, that would have been me. (Not just me, obviously, but if West London had staged a regional championship, I definitely would have been seeded, in more ways than one.)

I used to wait and watch for a bird to go in one and then go in next door and look through the hole. Part of the excitement was knowing how wrong it was – the excitement and shame of sneaking into the lav, just full-blown wanting to nut because I knew that instant gratification was the quickest way to feel good . . . Normal people aren't out doing that kind of thing every night, are they? It was like I'd become the local nonce, only in a different form. This was the world I'd been drawn into. That shit was like a virus.

I got nicked when I was out peeping Tom-ing once. I was looking through the window of this block of flats where some toffs lived in Hammersmith and someone must've seen me and called the Old Bill. The police caught me and said, 'What are you doing?' At first I answered, 'Nothing,' but they weren't having that.

I was too embarrassed by the fact that I was trying to have a pedal to tell them the truth, so I pretended I was planning a break-in. That turned out to be a pretty good move, as since I hadn't actually got in there, they couldn't do me for it. But I didn't get off so lightly the time a couple of bouncers at the Hammersmith Palais caught me up on the roof peeping down into the women's toilets. They hung me over the edge of the roof by my fucking ankles and threatened to drop me.

No one would've really blamed them if they'd done it. As you can imagine, being the kid in that particular picture was not a good feeling. It was a time in my life – and not the last one, either – when listening to music was as close as I could get to making things feel all right. I got myself a decent stereo with the proceeds of my thieving and I used to buy some weird records to play on it. I remember this band The Groundhogs who had a great song called 'Cherry Red'. I knew nothing about them, I just saw the cover of their album *Split* in a record shop on the King's Road and liked the way it looked.

Someone else in that same kind of bluesy area who doesn't get a lot of love these days is Paul Kossoff, the guitarist out of Free. I loved that flat sound they had. Their songs had a real strut about them, but also an elegance. You could still hear the black influences in there, but they were doing their own thing with them. This was the kind of music I'd be listening to in that Battersea bedroom when I was bunking off school and my mum and stepdad were out at work. I'd sit in there feeling lonely and looking out of the window at the huge expanse of waste ground.

Covent Garden Market has been been moved there now, but in those days it was just a big patch of emptiness with a Securicor depot in the distance. The void where the old gasworks used to be was a place of opportunity, and not just for peeping Toms. There was also a big Carlsberg warehouse over the far side, where I could sneak in, climb up to the top and sit on giant crates of Special Brew getting drunk on my own. Sexual deviants, trainee alcoholics – this place had something for everyone. All it needed was a free outdoor driving school for teenage joyriders . . .

In the course of long hours spent staring out of my window, I'd started to notice how many large earth-moving vehicles were left lying about on the wasteland – dumper trucks, lorries, bulldozers and so on. The weird thing about them was they didn't seem to be anyone's responsibility; no one was looking after them and even in broad daylight I never saw any bods over there. It would be bad manners not to make the most of this kind of opportunity. Apart from my grandad letting me hold the steering wheel of his Austin A40 as a little kid, I'd never come close to driving anything, but now here I was at fourteen, manoeuvring these huge fucking lorries around the dump.

It's a great way to learn to drive, borrowing a fucking big lorry, and I would recommend it to anyone. They were easy to get into – they were never locked, and you could start them with the handle of a comb. I was quite systematic about teaching myself to drive, learning how to shift the gears and use reverse. It turned out that when there was something I really wanted to learn, I could apply myself after all. It just came naturally to me. No one taught me – I figured it out for myself.

Years later I'd find out that my real dad worked for many years as a lorry driver, so maybe there was a genetic element. In the meantime, it was a good feeling, picking it up so quickly. I must have looked fucking ridiculous – a fourteen-year-old kid at the wheel of a giant earth-mover – but no one ever stopped me. Of course I had my Cloak on, but sometimes a mate called Alex Hall joined me and he didn't have one, so fuck knows how he got away with it.

I didn't go crazy at first. I was more interested in figuring the whole thing out. But as time went on, I got more ambitious – progressing from the back-loading lorries that they fill up with dirt, to diggers and bulldozers. And once I'd got the basics of driving, we could start to really enjoy ourselves, knocking down wooden tea huts and generally having a riot. Just the simple action of smashing stuff up made me feel a hell of a lot fucking better. No thought of consequences ever came into the equation – we were too busy having fun.

I was lucky to be young in the golden age of car crime. If I'd come of age in the CCTV era, I'd probably still be stuck in Brixton prison now. As it was, there were no cameras, no alarms, no deadlocks, and you could nick just about anything on wheels. Once I'd sussed out how to drive on the building sites, I could take my joyriding skills out into the wider world. Minis were the easiest to get into because of the two little windows. The swankier motors tended to be harder because they'd have a bit more going on, as far as where the key would go was concerned. We did get a Jag once but not till a bit later on so maybe I'll save that story.

All the time my early adventures in not-so-grand theft auto were going on, my mates were still at Christopher Wren. Sometimes I'd travel over to meet them outside the school gates after a hard day's bunking off, and once I went up there in a nicked car and was being a jack-the-lad up and down the road outside to impress everybody when I smashed straight into another car this woman was driving her kid home in. Luckily no one was hurt, but it was right outside the school and pretty much a head-on collision. Everyone saw me. I legged it, thinking, 'Fucking hell, I'm in trouble now.' And I should've got in trouble, but I didn't. The knock on my mum's door never came. I don't know why – maybe the other car was stolen as well.

Given the extent of my criminal activities at the time, it was inevitable I'd wear a hole in my Cloak of Invisibility, but I never expected that what I'd ultimately get nicked for would be nicking a Lambretta. I'd had it for so long that I felt like it was mine, and I'd taken the side panels and the front off it to turn it into a 'skeleton' – essentially just two wheels and an engine – which is what all the fashion-conscious scooter thieves were doing in West London in the early Seventies. I was riding it round Battersea Park when the police stopped me, and I ended up getting sent to an 'approved school' called Banstead Hall.

If I was doing a public information film for teenage criminals, like the old Alvin Stardust one for the Green Cross Code, my advice would be: 'So, all you young kids, don't turn your stolen scooters into skeletons because you will get nicked.' But getting sent to Banstead Hall didn't work out too badly for me. It was a beautiful old Victorian building down in Surrey – right out in the country – and I actually liked it much better than being at home.

Approved schools were one step short of borstals. They were places where they sent kids they still thought had some chance of turning a corner, and Banstead Hall was run in a pretty decent way. There weren't a lot of us there – probably twenty kids at the most – and you slept in big rooms that had four beds in each. The staff were all right. They knew we were wayward boys, but it felt more like they were giving us another chance. It wasn't like a proper nick where they'd just treat you like shit.

This was the first time I'd been in the countryside for longer than a day trip, and it took me a while to adjust to not living in a big block of flats with all sorts of other bullshit going on the whole time. Once I got used to it, though, I started to really enjoy myself. It wasn't quite the Famous Five, maybe more like when kids from London got evacuated in the war. After you'd been there a while they'd put you out to work in the gardens. That was a beautiful experience to have as a kid – being out in the fresh air, surrounded by nature. It definitely planted a seed – and that's why these days I'm always banging on about wanting to move out of LA and up to northern California.

I liked being at Banstead Hall so much that when it got to the point where they'd let us go home at weekends, I didn't always want to. Nearly all the others would be off except me and maybe a couple more kids with fucked-up home lives. We decided we'd rather stay where we were. Being in the countryside gave us a kind of comfort; the only drawback was, there was nothing to nick.

Of course I had no interest in giving up thievery – and that was where the whole rehabilitation process broke down. In fact, one of the funny things about being there was that the times I did go home to London for the weekend, I'd often end up nicking a motor to drive back to Surrey on a Sunday night. This was prior to computerised licensing and everyone knowing what was nicked and what wasn't, so it never felt like anything I was going to get done for.

You'd think someone might have clocked all the stolen cars parked in the field out the back after a while, but they never did. And I can't take the piss out of them too much for being unobservant, since I'd somehow managed not to notice that the whole point of me being at Banstead Hall was to stop me thieving. I just didn't connect those dots at all. The way I lived my life back then – and for a good few years afterwards – was that I was just in a place, and whatever happened was just another experience. That attitude would become a big part of what punk was (or at least was meant to be) but it got me in a hell of a lot of trouble.

One of the best things about life at Banstead Hall was being able to watch *Top of the Pops* on a Thursday night. I was sitting in front of that approved school TV when two of the biggest events in my musical education took place. The first, in June 1972 (that's definitely right, cos I looked it up on YouTube), was Hawkwind's 'Silver Machine'. Obviously I didn't know then that I'd end up buying speed off Lemmy in Notting Hill a few years after, or that we'd be friends for years in LA later on. What I did know was that I fucking loved that song. If there was a soundtrack for my car and bulldozer and moped stealing exploits, 'Silver Machine' was it.

Two months later (thanks, YouTube), an even bigger musical bomb went off in my brain: Roxy Music's 'Virginia Plain'. It was the way they looked combined with the sound that really did the damage with this one. Of course you only saw it once, cos there were no video recorders with pause and rewind buttons yet, but that just made the memory of it even more special. Brian Eno looked like he came from outer space with his green feathers, and Bryan Ferry was so dandified he'd become a bit of a fantasy figure for me in the years to come.

He was kind of like James Brown and Prince Charles rolled into one, and I used to imagine him living in a penthouse in Knightsbridge and think about how much I wanted that kind of glamorous existence. My mum had a part-time job washing people's hair in Knightsbridge around this time, and that seemed about as close as I was gonna get to the international jet set.

Even though I'd still not picked up a guitar and had no technical knowledge of music at all, I already had a very clear sense of what was good and what was shit. It was the same as with clothes, knowing the difference between Levi's and Brutus. For example, even though Sweet and Gary Glitter and all that were put under the same 'glam rock' umbrella as Roxy Music, I knew theirs was shit music designed for teenagers who didn't have a brain, whereas Roxy Music had an intellect and depth to them and were just generally more stylish.

Well, Ferry and Andy Mackay and Brian Eno were. Phil Manzanera was a good guitar player but he didn't go the whole hog with the image, that's for sure. He seemed more like an old prog guy who was trying to go along for the ride – he still had a beard and all that shit. OK, he made an effort to fit in with something a bit more avant-garde, but you could tell he didn't really want to.

I loved those first two Roxy Music albums so much when they came out – the self-titled one and *For Your Pleasure*. I still love them now. The third and fourth albums are great too, but it was the first two that changed everything for me. I've got the intro of 'Beauty Queen' as my mobile ringtone even now.

I don't know why – maybe because he seemed the most approachable of the three, and he was also really odd and out there doing his own little fucking thing – but Andy Mackay was the one I'd end up latching onto. A few months later (and it was only nine months between the first and second albums coming out – fuck me, they didn't hang around in those days, did they? That Chris Thomas must've been a real slave-driver), l got myself a pair of those brothel creepers with glitter all over them you can see him wearing with a boiler suit in the gatefold sleeve of *For Your Pleasure.*

Andy Mackay even inspired a bit of a hair experiment when I dyed the front of my hair with household bleach in his honour. Unfortunately, I have that fucking thick hair which won't conform to whatever you want to do with it. This untrainable barnet would cause me a lot of problems over the next few years. It's probably the thing about myself I've been most consistently disappointed by.

The unsuccessful attempt to bleach the front of my hair to look like Andy Mackay's was not the only daring glam experiment of my Banstead Hall era. One time when me and this other kid were getting the train back to London at the weekend, I got him to suck me off in one of the closed-off railway compartments that all manner of shit used to go on in, and then gave him 50p for his trouble. I know what you're thinking – 'the last of the big spenders' – but 50p was a lot of money back then. You could buy a single with that.

Given the men-only nature of my sexual initiations, it was weird that as a kid I'd never worried that I might be gay, but from an early age I was always very confident about my sexuality. I knew I loved birds and, as a general rule, didn't want nothing to do with geezers. I'm not saying this through embarrassment. If I'd been into geezers that would've been another thing. But my Banstead blowjob was the first of a handful – if that is the right word, and sometimes it would be – of exceptions that proved this rule over the years to come.

At the root of all my shit over the years has been the same thing: loneliness and a desire to feel OK in my body, which at that age I never seemed to be able to manage unless I was acting out in some way. In that context, it doesn't feel like the fact that in the absence of female company I was occasionally willing to broaden my catchment area a bit was actually that big a deal. I can't know how the child abuse affected me. I've no fucking idea if these things would have happened without it, but at the end of the day, does it really fucking matter?

Obviously not everyone feels the same, and in some ways it would have been easier for me to keep schtum about the tiny portion of my bulging back catalogue of sexual experience that was what is technically known as 'geezer-on-geezer'. The reason I thought it was important to 'go there' in this book was that a lot of guys – and probably girls – have the occasional queer moment and end up beating themselves up about it for years.

Some people will take their feelings of guilt and anxiety to their grave, and the other thing is that when you see a gay guy getting beaten up in a film, you can be 90 per cent sure that the guy who's doing it will be either gay themselves, or at the very least unsure of their sexuality. People often attack others for something they're worried about in themselves. I never went that way, because it's never been a big deal to me. I'm not saying me telling all is going to change anybody's life – 'Oh, Steve admitted it and now I feel OK about what I did.' I don't really care what anyone else does, but I do think the world would probably be a better place if people were less embarrassed about this stuff.

8. IN ROD WE TRUST

After I'd been at Banstead Hall a few months, they started trying to introduce us to the world of work. You know when you have to meet someone, and it takes precisely ten seconds to realise you're gonna hate 'em? Well, that was pretty much how it was with me and normal paid employment. I just never thought it was something I was meant to do, and my early experiences in the labour market did nothing to change my mind.

The first job they sent me to out in the local area was as a plumber's mate in a children's hospital. It was one of those places where all the kids had massive heads; encephalitis, I think that's what they call it. I was carrying this geezer's tools through wards full of kids who looked like aliens and it kind of freaked me out. There had to be easier ways of making a buck, and I already knew several. What I needed was someone from a similar background to me to look up to as a role model. Luckily, I already had a steadying influence who could help give me an appropriate set of aspirations for a working-class boy made good. That man was Rod Stewart.

In Britain at that time there weren't many examples of people like me who things had worked out for. Rod certainly fitted the bill, though. He was a normal bloke whose destiny fell into place just because he had the hair and raspy voice and the long legs. I used to think that rock stars fell from the sky. In real life they probably came offstage at *Top of the Pops*, took their gear off and went home to watch TV like everyone else, but as far as I was concerned, they lived on Mars and came down by spaceship to perform for us. I didn't think it was possible for anyone like me to become one. But I saw a bit of myself in Rod (no, not that bit) and I felt like I had his back from the beginning.

I was never one of the kids who preferred it if the music they liked was not successful. I wanted all my favourite songs to go to the top of the charts to show everyone how fucking good they were. I remember going up to HMV in Oxford Street to buy Rod's 1971 album *Every Picture Tells a Story* as soon as it came out – before anyone else knew how big it was going to be. I was so proud of myself afterwards when it went to number one in Britain and America at the same time. I remember thinking, 'I knew it! I fucking showed you!'

I was already convinced Rod was a star cos his previous album *Gasoline Alley* was so fucking good – it was almost like I worked for him. I loved *First Step* and *Long Player*, the two Faces albums that came out either side of it, too. I think there was some legal complication which meant it's basically the Faces who play on Rod's solo records as well, although Micky Waller is on a bunch of the drum tracks. I know the Faces got pissed off with it in the end, but the great thing about the whole arrangement from my point of view was that you got twice as many albums to listen to. If you count the third Faces LP, *A Nod Is As Good As a Wink . . . to a Blind Horse* and Rod's next solo record, *Never a Dull Moment* – which I certainly did, as they were just as good – that's five brilliant albums Rod released in the space of about two years.

Although there were a lot of things I struggled to focus on, I was very attentive to the music I liked. I would listen to it over and over again till it drove people fucking crazy, and if no one else was around I'm not ashamed to say (well, maybe a bit) that lonely teenage Steve might even be found miming to 'Maggie May' in the mirror, perfecting the old hairbrush microphone technique. It wasn't that I particularly fancied the idea of myself as a singer, but you can't really be miming guitar or drums in the mirror or you'll look a complete tool.

The look of things always meant as much to me as the sound. I loved staring at the sleeve of *Never a Dull Moment* and then opening out the gatefold to all the pictures of what he was wearing. I've got to give Rod kudos for how obsessed I was with him as a teenager – especially as spearhead of the Faces – but the couple of times that I've met him in LA in recent years I didn't really want to let on. I knew he had some idea when his daughter got him to sign a picture for me, though, because he signed it 'To Steve Jones, you've got a big knob'. He's got a funny sense of humour, Rod, plus on top of that he is very observant.

The reason I ended up bleaching my hair like Andy Mackay of Roxy Music's was that I'd already tried and failed to make it look like Rod's. The thick hairdresser's fucking do that would later save me from becoming a cartoon spiky-haired punk character like Johnny or Sid (much as I wanted to be one) was never going to allow me to tease it up the way Rod did. I had to spray a gallon of Aqua Net on my head to get it to stand up even a little bit. If someone had lit a match near me I'd have gone up like a human torch. It must've looked fucking ridiculous.

Luckily I could do a better job with the clothes. I used to find out where Rod had got all the gear that he was wearing on the album covers, then head off up over Chelsea Bridge and nick it from the shops on the King's Road where he'd bought it. I'd usually get the 137 bus, my getaway vehicle of choice. Take 6 was the place working-class people who were doing all right would go to buy the little slim suits with the big kipper ties like the normal cunts dancing on *Top of the Pops* would wear. It was called Take 6 but I always used to Take 7. Dave Brubeck would've stopped at 5.

That place wasn't really flash enough for Rod. The main shops the rock stars went to were Alkasura – I saw Marc Bolan wearing something from there – and especially Granny Takes a Trip. Granny's, as the cognoscenti called it, was a fantastic place with a Cadillac sticking out of the front window. It changed a lot over the years but it was fucking cool when I started going there. I didn't realise it at the time but the reason you could literally walk out of there with a velvet rhinestone suit you hadn't paid for was that the guys who were meant to be front of house were nodding out on smack out the back.

I'd go to any lengths to get the details right. There was a shop down Old Church Street called Zapata's which I found out stocked this amazing pair of white shoes with an orange bit in the middle and a beige crepe sole that I'd seen Rod Stewart wearing. By the time I got there they only had one pair left, which were way too small for me, but I bought them anyway (obviously shoe shops aren't great for nicking from, unless you've only got one leg). The only way I could wear them was to buckle my feet right over inside, which was fucking painful, but it was worth it, though I wasn't going to be climbing the Battersea Power Station chimneys in those.

Around the peak of my Rod Stewart fixation I remember coming out of my Battersea flats and walking up the main road where the dogs' home is. It was about five in the evening on a Sunday, so there weren't many people about. In my own mind I would've been cutting a bit of a dash with my carefully tousled hair and Rod-inspired wardrobe, although I may have been hobbling slightly on account of my determination to wear the same shoes as him even though they didn't actually fit.

Anyway, as I staggered on, I heard the roar of a powerful engine behind me. I turned round and of course there was Rod and some fucking beautiful bird driving by in a Lamborghini. At the time I didn't even think of this as embarrassing – that's how shameless I was. It felt more like he was showing me the missing pieces in the jigsaw; you've got the look, now all you need is the car and the girl. Either way, it was more like a dream than real life, but it did definitely happen.

There were also a couple of times where we saw him and Ronnie Wood in the Roebuck – one of the pubs on the King's Road that we used to go to. I'd go all weak at those moments, because Rod in particular and the Faces in general were my idols then. I think I knew that if I was even going to begin to think about trying to get anywhere with music it would have to be as part of a group: not really being able to sing or play an instrument would definitely be a problem as far as a solo career was concerned. And there was something about the way the Faces interacted with each other – the way it all seemed to be about good times and girls and booze and football and the lads in the band – that was irresistibly attractive. They were kind of a yobs' band, but stylish with it, wearing nice shirts and trousers, not clogs and flares and moustaches like the hippies did.

We – that's my little crew of me and Cookie and Hayesy and Jim Macken – went to see them at the Roundhouse in the summer of 1972. It was funny that we found out, years after, that John Lydon was there too with his mates and so was Glen Matlock, even though we didn't know who either of them were yet. Later on, when people were thinking about who influenced the Sex Pistols, they would never really say the Faces, because it wouldn't be considered cool enough, but we took a lot from them, not just at the beginning when we were trying to find our way, but all the way through the band. Like the pace of the songs, for a start. Because me and

Cookie were the ones who set the tempos, and the music we liked best was them and early Roxy Music, that's who we tried to emulate. In my weird mind, it was almost like we *were* the Faces, which was the main reason we never played that fast, and also why the idea that we'd copy the Ramones is so ridiculous.

One of the most important things about the Faces was that at a time when music was getting more and more distant, they were approachable. That gig at the Roundhouse, it felt like the audience and the band were all at one big party together, where if you saw Led Zep or Pink Floyd or any of the really big bands, you couldn't get near the stage.

I was so close to the front – down below, looking up – that when Ian McLagan threw his tambourine out into the crowd at the end of the show, it was me that caught it. Everyone else was trying to get it off me but they were never going to prise my fingers off it. I just thought, 'No, no, I'm having this.' When the band came back on for the encore, Ian came across to the front of the stage and said, 'Sorry, but I need that tambourine.' I didn't want to give it to him, but he promised I could have it back at the end of the song, so I gave in. And the magical moment was when he found me before going offstage and handed it over. Good luck getting John Paul Jones to do that!

Looking back, it's easy to see how things escalated in terms of me not respecting the Faces' personal space. You can't give me that kind of message, because I don't have any boundaries. A few months later, when the Faces played Wembley in October 1972, I removed a door panel so a few of us could get in round the back of the Empire Pool, and we sneaked into their dressing room. We were drinking their champagne and having a chat with Ronnie Wood – it was great. I don't think just any old fans could have waltzed in there like that and got away with it: it was all down to the fact that we looked the part in the finest stolen clobber King's Road could offer. The security guys probably thought we were another band. Either that, or the spoiled sons of the geezer that owned Warner Brothers.

That was a great night for me for another reason, because the support act were the New York Dolls, who very few people in Britain had heard of then as it was still a year before their first album came out. The funny thing was, pretty much everyone else there seemed to hate the trashy way they looked and sounded – loads of the Faces' fans were shouting 'Faggots!' and really giving them some stick. But I fucking loved them – they'd end up as one of my four biggest influences, alongside Bowie, Roxy Music and that night's headliners.

If you'd told me then that in a couple of years' time I'd be playing Sylvain Sylvain's guitar in a band managed by the Dolls' ex-manager, that would've probably gone beyond even my most unrealistic fantasies. Obviously that tour didn't end too well for the Dolls themselves, as a few days after that gig their original drummer, Billy Murcia, died in a bathtub when someone tried to revive him by force-feeding him black coffee after an accidental Mandrax and champagne overdose. Don't try that one at home, kids.

It was around this time that the four of us – me, Hayesy, Jimmy Macken and Cookie – decided that since we already looked like a band, we might as well become one. I'm not sure if we ever got as far as an actual rehearsal, let alone writing any songs, but we certainly had some fucking great-looking instruments. Jim had a job in a petrol station which he worked hard enough at to actually buy himself a Farfisa organ. He even taught himself to play a few keyboard riffs by copying Jon Lord, the geezer in Deep Purple. Stephen Hayes was going to be on bass – he had a Hofner like Paul McCartney (though that was where the resemblance ended). Cookie had got himself one of those blue sparkle Premier drum kits, and I – in theory at least – was gonna sing and play a stolen Gibson guitar. Everyone had name brand gear, none of that Chad Valley or Woolworth's shit – only the best for the worst.

We might not have been making much headway in terms of actually playing together, but my love of music in general and the Faces in particular was giving me a new-found focus when it came to thieving. That's how I ended up getting my hands on Ronnie Wood's coat. Well, it turned out to be Keith Richards' coat, but I thought it was Ronnie's at the time. The portable TV was definitely Ron's, though.

The Wick was a big grand house on top of Richmond Hill that once belonged to John Mills the actor (the actress Hayley was his daughter). Ronnie Wood had got it off him somehow, I don't know if he'd bought it or rented it, but when the four of us found out that was where he lived, we were such massive fans that we would drive up there in Jimmy Macken's Bedford van (which he'd bought for the band to go on tour in, even though we'd not done any gigs yet) and park outside his house. Sometimes he'd look out through his living room window and wave to us and we'd wave back and get all excited. We were obsessed; just like the kids that would hang around a rock star's hotel, really, only a little more street-wise.

Of course a normal full-on fan might've left it there, but I couldn't let it go. I had to push it one step further. I started going back there to lurk about on my own. A little lane went off the main road and down the side of the garden, then at the end of it there was another entrance to what I suppose now was a guest house, but at the time I just thought was part of the same property. Anyway, I figured out a way to get in there. I can't remember if I jumped over the wall or the door was open but, either way, I sneaked in there and had a look around.

Luckily for me, no one was in, but even so I didn't go too crazy. All I took was a little portable TV and the coat which I thought was Ronnie's.

(I later found out it was Keith Richards', because apparently he heard about me admitting I'd nicked it and took offence.) As far as I was concerned at the time, I wasn't doing anything that wrong. Obviously I broke in and went sneaking around the house, which I shouldn't have done, but I was a fan who wanted something of theirs as a trophy and my only way of doing that was to thieve – just like the screaming girls trying to tear the jackets off The Beatles' backs.

I don't know what I did with that coat in the end – probably sold it – but I wish I still had it because it was a beautiful herringbone Crombie. Years later I saw a picture in a book of Mick Jagger wearing it, so Keith could've nicked it off him first, for all I know, but it's more likely they just swapped clothes around between themselves, the way bands do.

You might think stealing something is a weird way of showing that you love someone, and I suppose in a way it is, but when you look at the background I came from, it kind've makes sense. My stepdad, who was meant to be looking after me, decided to fuck about with me instead as soon as my mum wasn't around, so that was the kind of example I'd been given. Not that I ever looked at this geezer as any kind of father figure. He didn't want me there from the beginning – I was just in the way.

The one time I remember us doing anything good together was on Christmas Day in 1972, when we went out to the boozer for a drink while my mum was cooking the dinner. I got really drunk – probably because I was so uncomfortable around the cunt – and when I got back, the room was doing that spinning-round thing when you close your eyes and you know you're going to have to throw up. I hugged the base of the toilet for a while – happy fucking Christmas – and came downstairs to see that *Top of the Pops* had started. Then I got all excited because Rod Stewart was on doing 'You Wear It Well', and I remember drunkenly pushing my face up close to the black-and-white screen, trying to work out what colour his jacket was.

9. THE GUY WITH THE PRONG

Around the time I came back to Battersea from Banstead Hall, my mum and Ron got themselves a budgie. Maybe they'd missed me more than I thought and needed a replacement, but when I remembered what had probably happened to Brucie, it seemed weird that they'd want to get another pet. That budgie was funny, though. He'd sit in his cage in the living room, and he hadn't been with us long before he started swearing so much my mum had to put him upstairs when my probation officer came round. There wasn't a lot of laughter in that flat, but we did have a chuckle about that. And a few years later I'd get to try the budgie's act out on Bill Grundy . . .

For the moment, though, music was one of the only things in my life that felt clean. Everything else was pretty much shit. Don't get me wrong, I was getting more than my share of teenage kicks. There was a pub we used to go to a lot called the Bird's Nest (appropriately enough, given how many birds we pulled there) down at the west end of King's Road. A road next to it went to the Albert Bridge, and about fifty yards down that was the Chelsea Drugstore where they had a disco at the weekend. Even though we were going in there from the age of fifteen or sixteen, they were pretty lenient on the door. I don't ever remember any of us getting asked for a driving licence or anything (good job too). You'd just say you were eighteen and that was it.

I wasn't looking for a relationship at that time. There was this one girl, when I was maybe fifteen, I got really lovey feelings for, but she wasn't available because she already had a geezer. Not long after, she broke up with him, but the minute I knew I could have her, all the lust I'd felt instantly disappeared. I've always been attracted to birds like that – the ones who aren't available. That's the turn-on. With normal birds, the ones who love me, I'm bored shitless straight away. I didn't understand why at the time, but I realise now it probably all went back to how things were with my mum. She never really seemed available either, and then the situation with my stepdad warped the whole thing even further.

Whatever the reason, going up to Piccadilly for a prostitute was something that was quite normal to me from the age of about fifteen onwards. The sex thing was still new to me, then, and it was totally exciting – looking to see if the red light was on, then walking up the stairs thinking, 'I'm gonna get laid right now and all I've got to do is give her this £10 in my hand, I don't even have to talk her into it.' It was scary walking round Soho at night, then, because there were a lot of dodgy characters lurking about and no end of criminal noncey shit was going on. Even if you didn't know exactly what it was, because those kinds of thing weren't as exposed then as they are now, you knew you were taking a risk, and that only added to the excitement. I got the clap a few times because I never wore condoms back then. I still don't now, but that's another story – it's enough trouble to get a hard-on at sixty, never mind putting a fucking balloon over it.

Whether or not using brasses from such an early age affected my attitude to women is not for me to say. But by the time I was sixteen or seventeen I was all about a quick shag and see you later. That was my MO. It's what the whole glam thing was about to us. Me and Cookie would shag a lot of birds together – not at the same time (well, not usually). But we weren't your stereotypical lads about town either. We were always on the lookout for something a bit different. That was how we ended up knocking about with this pair of drag queens called the Dumb Belles.

This was some time before we met Malcolm McLaren, and I can't remember how it happened. We might've been in a boozer where they were performing and started hanging about with them afterwards. Either way, I know me and Cookie went round their gaff for parties a few times, which was pretty broad-minded for a couple of straight working-class kids. They were fun, though, and I don't remember anyone trying anything. I think they were just happy to have a couple of young studs around.

Drag acts were very popular in London in the early Seventies – they brought a bit of colour to what was a very fucking grim and Dickensian landscape. It was almost like a family thing that mums and dads would go to together for a laugh, and kids would look through the pub curtains to see what was going on. When I dress up as this very camp character Fabian Fontaine of Earls Court on my Instagram now, it all comes from this time – that's when that whole way of talking was planted in my head. Obviously it could've gone the other way after what had happened to me as a kid, but I never hated gay people; in fact I was very comfortable hanging out with them. They were like the underground crowd, which was always where I felt closest to being at home.

I was in Battersea at the age of about fifteen when they were shooting the last scene of the movie *Villain*, which Richard Burton played a gay gangster in. That was pretty controversial at the time, and I don't think it did his career any good in the long run, but I was cool with it. They filmed it down by the railway line, under the arches – near where I'd throw those boulders down off the bridge – and I was there in the background, watching while it was being shot.

I never knew if my mum or stepdad had any idea of the kind of shit I was up to at that point, or if they'd have had any concern if they had found out. I know I used to get a clump if they got called out by the police; the Cloak of Invisibility was still basically working but the edges were fraying a bit, especially when I'd had a drink. The impression I got was basically that they were waiting for me to fuck off. Even so, when I was still in my Rod Stewart phase in Battersea I do remember thinking, 'I'm gonna become a rock star and get my mum a good house.' So there was still a part of me that was what you'd call normal in terms of ambitions.

A lot of people who are alcoholics will tell you they were off and running from the moment they had their first drink. It's the same only more so with junkies and heroin. But it didn't work that way with me on either count. When I started going down the King's Road with the boys – Cookie, Jim, Hayesy and Cecil, the usual gang – we'd drink pints of lager or vodka and lime. But it wasn't like I was thinking about having a drink from the moment I got up in the morning. Tea-leafing was still definitely my first concern, with cumming a close second.

OK, I'd make the odd trip over to the Carlsberg warehouse, but that was more of an occasional thing. I wasn't really caning it yet. But I definitely noticed a difference in the way I felt when I put alcohol in my system. It made me feel OK with myself. When I was sober I was pretty shy, but once I had some booze in me I would do anything. Jimmy Macken was the same. He came from a bad background, the same as I did – in his case with a horrible, violent dad who'd beat the shit out of him but then fucked off. I think this made us both more prone to instigating trouble – we simply had less to lose than the others. Always being the one that starts things is sometimes a good way to hide from that.

I know Jimmy had a few issues with Paul, because he thought he played things too safe. Jimmy was basically a good kid who loved the Faces, but he became a heavy drinker quite quickly and he also liked to fight. His whole thing was hitting someone so hard the fight would be over after one punch – he was a real tough nut. I was less into violence but I did have that same impulse to keep drinking till I got plastered and then I would have to do something else to keep the buzz going. For him it might be punching somebody, but for me it would be to maybe take a Mandrax and nick a car.

Obviously combining Mandrax with drink-driving isn't really a good idea, because it's a sleeping pill. They give you this amazing tingling feeling, but you're supposed to take them at night, to help you kip, not when you're going out partying or driving stolen cars at high speed through the streets of London. But when you're a kid you're fearless and you don't see the fucking consequences of what you're doing – at least, I didn't.

I don't remember smashing into other vehicles deliberately but when I was driving on Mandrax I did sometimes swipe the edge of other parked cars. How I never got stopped is a mystery to me, given that I wasn't old enough to drive legally and was usually drunk and in a stolen car. The Cloak seemed to work OK when I was driving, too. But there was one time when the police nearly got me. I only remembered it recently because I was talking to the bloke who fixes my motorbikes and he's got the same kind of old Austin Healey 3000 that I was driving on the occasion of this run-in with the law (the difference being that he actually owns his).

They're lovely cars, which is the main reason I'd nicked one. I was coming round Shepherd's Bush Green, where the Empire is, with a friend when the police tried to pull us over. They were in a little Morris Minor – it's a Noddy car, really – and there I was, probably sixteen years old, driving this beautiful red convertible with the top down. It was fast as fuck, and at first when they chased us down Wood Lane towards the BBC and flashed to pull us over, I was kind of going along with it.

There's a thing in England with the Old Bill – at least there was, I don't know if they still do it – where instead of parking behind you when they pull you over, you have to let them overtake you and then stop. Of course, the moment the two coppers got out of their car in front of us – it was right by White City tube station – I fucking freaked out. I put the Austin Healey in gear and I meant to go round them but I was accelerating so fast that I clipped the back of their car before zooming off down the road almost to the White City estates. Then, without really saying anything, we just knew we had more chance of getting away if we split up; the two of us jumped out and went our separate ways.

I ran down and along the railway lines and my unnamed partner in crime, well, I'm not sure where he went because I wasn't with him, but I know he never got nicked. Putting one over on the Old Bill was the ultimate excitement. If they'd caught us they would have beaten the shit out of us as well – not just for smashing into them, but also for having a better car than they did. Afterwards it seemed unbelievable that we'd both got away. I knew running down the tracks was risky, as a lot of people get killed that way, but those people are morons. The secret is don't fucking run along the middle of the tracks, and if you hear a train coming, get out of the way. It's not rocket science.

I wasn't quite as good at avoiding accidents in the workplace. My few abortive attempts at legitimate employment usually ended in a smash-up of some kind. There was a brief flirtation with helping out a milkman where I smashed a fucking cart up at the depot. I don't know why I was even driving it; they should never have let me behind the wheel that early in the morning. Maybe the guy just asked me to bring it over to him but, either way, he should've known better. I was too fast to live, too young to die in those days, even at the wheel of a milk float.

Give me a stolen bulldozer and I was fine, but anything vaguely legitimate and I went to pieces. I just had no attention span for any kind of normal, responsible job. There was a cab company too, down near Shepherd's Bush, where I briefly used to wash the cars, but I think something that happened there maybe ended with a taxi getting smashed up. When you put all these incidents together a pattern does begin to emerge. I don't think I fucked up deliberately, but it might have been my subconscious mind's way of telling me (and the world) that this kind of mundane menial work was not for me, and I certainly wasn't qualified for anything more executive. Except being a rock star, of course.

I've seen interviews I did when the Sex Pistols were happening where I said I'd been a window cleaner before, but I think I was talking out of my arse. The bullshit I was spouting about all my sexual adventures sounded more like the storyline of *Confessions of a Window Cleaner* than anything that would actually happen, anyway. I may have carried some geezer's bucket a few times, but as far as getting round to cleaning a fucking window was concerned, forget about it.

The closest I came to an actual job was another spell as a plumber's mate – this time for a heating and ventilation company called Benham's. I'd got the job through an employment agency called Manpower. Maybe the name was a clue to the fact that one of the plumbers would try and get hold of me inside a giant fucking industrial boiler. He was another one that wanted to wank me off – he wasn't trying to fuck me – and the way my memory goes blank when I try and recall exactly what happened suggests I might've let him give me a pedal. It certainly wouldn't have been out of the question.

Some people give off this fucking energy. Maybe once you've been down the road of doing things that aren't normal, others who are on that road themselves can almost smell it on you. It's not just about being fucked with and then people spotting you as a target. Some people are just born more sexual than others, and I was definitely at the front of the queue when that shit was being handed out. I did have one happier memory of that job, which will show you what I mean even more clearly. I think it was at lunch break when the guy I was working with went off to get something to eat and I stayed behind and tried out this big industrial vacuum cleaner on my cock. It actually worked pretty well as far as I remember; at least, there was no need for a trip to casualty to get it removed.

When I wasn't conducting deviant sexual experiments with high-powered vacuum cleaners, the work with Benham's usually involved servicing boiler rooms up in the West End. But the one job which stood out from the others involved heading north into the wilds of Willesden. There was a Wall's sausage factory up there, and I remember having to see them slaughtering the fucking pigs. These weird dudes with aprons covered in claret were doing the deed. The strange faces these guys had – they looked like lunatics. But wouldn't you, if all you had to do all day was kill frightened animals?

I don't know what we were supposed to be doing, or what the geezer I was meant to be helping was up to, but he left me alone long enough for me to wander off and watch the whole grim process. The pigs came in off a lorry and got shuffled into these little pens, then the geezer would put the big electric prong on them. Before there was time to see if they were dead or not, they'd get hooked up by their hooves and sent whizzing up this fucking conveyor belt with their back feet at the top and their heads hanging down.

First they went through this furnace which would burn all the skin off, then they'd be washed clean with jets of water. The poor cunts didn't stop on the conveyor belt till they were in a packet. I remember watching up to the point where the geezer with his big knife slit open the stomach and all the fucking claret came out the middle of it – then I had to look away. That place was just a fucking hellhole and I'd never seen anything like it. Not even when Chelsea played Leeds. As far as me and work were concerned, that was pretty much the final nail in the coffin. It certainly was for the pigs.

The worst part of it was that you could see some of the pigs were really smart and didn't want to get off the truck. The geezer with the prong just got on there and pronged them off and they'd make that horrible squeaky squealing noise that tells you how scared they are. Anyone who tells you that farm animals don't fucking suffer has never been inside one of those places, I'm telling you. Did it stop me eating sausages? Did it fuck. But it did teach me one thing.

I was never going to be one of those people who just go along with what everyone else thinks you should do, cos that's how you end up getting your guts ripped out and your arse wrapped in plastic. I'd done a normal job for ten minutes: that was more than enough. If this was someone else's book, they might try and blag you into thinking that what went on in that factory was some kind of prophecy of what was going to happen to them when they got sucked into the machinery of the music industry. But things would not work out that way for me. If anything, I was the guy with the prong.

10. THE FURNITURE CAVE

When I was young I sometimes felt that if I wanted something badly enough, I could get it through sheer force of will. I can't do it any more. Maybe the drive to make stuff happen was a reaction to how little control I had over other areas of my life. Cookie remembers sending me letters for a while when I was stuck in a place called Earlsfield House in Wandsworth that I have absolutely no memory of whatsoever. He says it was during the glam times and I was really pissed off to be missing out on all the weekend action at the Chelsea Drugstore – which sounds like me – plus he had a clear picture of writing the address on the envelope. I hope he didn't spend too long on the contents cos I wouldn't have been able to read 'em anyway. But as for what I was doing in there, that is a complete fucking mystery.

If it was a prison, I could've understood it. The old Cloak had taken a bit of punishment by this time and some of the things I was getting nicked for were just downright stupid. One time on King Street when I was drunk I put a brick through the music shop window thinking I was gonna have a load of guitars away, but there was a shutter inside the glass. So I'm standing there trying to work out what to do next – paralytic, on my own – when the Old Bill pull up and ask me what I'm doing. The best response I can come up with is something totally lame like: 'Oh, here you are! . . . I don't know.' It's not exactly the Pink fucking Panther, is it?

I think I might have got let off with a warning for that one – like they thought the embarrassment was punishment enough. And when I looked that Earlsfield House place up online, it seemed it used to be a Victorian workhouse. By the time I was meant to have been in there it had turned into something called a 'Receiving School', which sounds like a kind of halfway house between a borstal and being in care. There's black-and-white photos of lines of beds and nothing's ringing any kind of bell at all. Googling shit for your own peace of mind never really works, does it? But if I wasn't in there for being a bad boy, presumably it was just because my mum and Ron didn't want to deal with me.

Maybe I just checked out mentally because I found it all so painful, and that's why I don't remember it. It's the best explanation I can come up with, anyway. All this does is verify again that I did have quite a shitty upbringing – my credentials are solid in that area. Sometimes in the back of your mind you tell yourself, 'Oh, it wasn't that bad – maybe you're just making a fuss,' but then something will come up which puts you in some gaff in Wandsworth you can't even remember and then you think, 'No, I was right: it was fucking shit.'

Even though it took us a while to get the whole thing going, the idea of having a band at least gave me something to hold on to. There was this kid we'd known from school called Warwick Nightingale – 'Wally', we called him, because he was one – but he could actually play the guitar a bit. He had an amp and a Gibson Les Paul copy, and given that the first line-up of the band never really made it as far as a proper rehearsal because Macken and Hayesy weren't really that bothered, it seemed like Wally might be ready to take the whole thing more seriously. He used to tell us,

'You've nicked all the equipment, you might as well do something with it,' and he was right.

We weren't doing things on a schoolboy whim any more, and there was no point in fucking about. We could have managed without Wally's miserable boat-race, but our natural good looks were enough to carry him – or so we thought, at first. Wally's mum and dad had a little house with a garden on Hemlock Road in East Acton and they didn't mind us hanging out there, so that kind of became our first base. There's a picture of us in Kew Gardens with these weird outfits on. It's the original line-up, which is me, Cookie, Wally, Jimmy Macken and Stephen Hayes.

We got our original name – The Strand – from 'Do the Strand', the first track on the second Roxy Music album. In the lyrics Bryan Ferry was telling people to 'Do the Strandski' – the idea being that this was the dance that all the cool kids would want to do, so that worked OK. And going up to the Rainbow in Finsbury Park to see Roxy Music on the *For Your Pleasure* tour in the spring of 1973 was a really big deal for me and Cookie.

Another big gig for us around that time – well, a couple of months later – was on our old Christopher Wren turf at the White City stadium. That place was usually a greyhound-racing track, which had no appeal to me whatsoever (although, thinking back, I suppose there would've been some fat wallets there), but every now and then they'd put a big gig on. I remember this one as being headlined by Humble Pie, but Cookie assures me it was The Kinks. Apparently Ray Davies' wife had left him and he had a bit of a tantrum onstage and retired from music at the end.

It bothers me a bit that I have no fucking recollection of this whatsoever – or of Sly and the Family Stone, who were on the same bill. Maybe I was pissed. Blackouts seem to have been a feature for me at those White City stadium shows, as Cookie also insists we were there for

David Cassidy the next year, when a little girl got crushed to death at the front. What the fuck we'd have been doing at a David Cassidy show I have no idea, so maybe he could be taking the piss with that one. But maybe when there was a local event we felt duty-bound to sneak in for nothing.

Either way, the one bit of that big Kinks gig which did stick in my mind was when the guitarist Rick Derringer came out with the Edgar Winter Group and played the solo in that song, 'Rock and Roll, Hoochie Koo'. It was so fucking slick it completely blew my mind. I wasn't even thinking of myself as a guitarist at that time, but I guess looking back the writing was already on the wall for poor old Wally.

We'd been practising together for a while by then. Our first rehearsal space was in the basement of a shop called the Furniture Cave, down the bottom end of the King's Road – about a mile west of World's End, on the way to Parsons Green. A load of furniture shops were gathered there round a little hump-backed bridge. We'd set up our stuff in this dingy room with the amps facing outwards to make it feel like a proper gig. Me and Cookie were on a bit of a mod trip at that time – taking lots of speed and trying to re-enact what it was like to be in the Small Faces or The Who.

Obviously some of that stuff would carry on to the Pistols when we'd do 'Substitute' and 'What'cha Gonna Do About It?' but it would have to go through more of a filter before it actually worked. The fact that John didn't like that kind of music as much as we did probably helped give the vocals an extra kick. Me trying to sing like Rod Stewart wasn't going to start a musical revolution any time soon, and we were probably too straight and sincere in the way we approached things at that time. Basic-ally we were the mod revival six years too early.

Of course I wasn't as reverent towards other bands' equipment as I was towards our own musical source material. I did nick the odd guitar from that place when other bands were in. I went down there on my own one day to have a wander round – as was my habit – and found all the lights on with a load of gear set up. It was like the band had just finished a song and then all gone outside to have a fag. Even someone with the capacity to resist temptation might've struggled to do the right thing in this situation, but for me it was a no-brainer, and I took the opportunity to make off with a really nice Sunbird Special.

I feel a bit bad about this one because I've not had the chance to make amends to the guy who owned it yet, and he was in one of my favourite bands. He wasn't rehearsing with them at that time, but had his own group going. It's silly giving clues without saying his name, though, isn't it? No point being coy about my victims at this late stage in the game. Come on down, Ariel Bender from Mott the Hoople – I owe you a fuck-ing guitar. Ariel's real name was Luther Grosvenor. But apparently, at least according to Ian Hunter in the Mott documentary, Lynsey de Paul came up with his memorable stage-name after seeing the band's lead guitarist, Mick Ralphs, walk down a German street bending all the car aerials to express how pissed off he was. I think we've all bent a few aerials in our time – I know I have.

Not long after this – I don't think we were copping any heat for my light fingers, it was just a better deal – we moved round the corner to a place called Sumer in Lots Road. I think the guy there was trying to build a studio he couldn't really afford and if I helped him out a bit we'd be allowed to used the place for next to nothing. Chris Spedding's band the Sharks, who supported Roxy Music a few times, were rehearsing there too. I don't think I nicked anything from him then, although our paths would cross again in the very near future.

By this time Hayesy and Jimmy Macken had kind of fallen away, and we'd got Cookie's brother-in-law Del Noones in to play bass and slimmed down to a four-piece. Del was another White City boy who used to go to Christopher Wren. He was two or three years older than us, but I'd known him from a very young age because we'd been skinheads together, and I saw him a lot when I stayed over at Cookie's house and he was going out with Paul's sister. The only problem with Del was, he couldn't really play.

Of course this was at a point when none of us, with the partial exception of Wally, knew what we were doing. I wasn't playing the guitar then, just singing, but both Paul and I knew we had tons to learn and were happy to put the work in. Cookie was getting better on the drums but Wally used to say I was better at playing them than him and to be honest – although I doubt Paul would agree with me – I think I still am. We're very different people and he plays more with his head – not literally, I mean in his mind – whereas with me it's more of a feel thing. I suppose he'd be the Charlie Watts type whereas to me the ultimate drummer of all time is John Bonham, with Keith Moon a few steps behind.

I met Moonie once at Malcolm and Vivienne's shop, very early on when it was still called Let It Rock. He came out of there dressed as a country squire and said 'Good evening, gentlemen' in that exaggerated posh voice he used to hide behind for comic effect. It was an exciting moment, because he was a real icon to me. The way he used to do drum fills over the vocal parts was all over the shop (not Malcolm's shop, the shop in general) but somehow it always sounded fantastic. Moon's nickname was on the money – he was a total loon. They don't make them like him and Bonzo any more, that's for sure.

Although I've never actually got to do it on an album, I find it very satisfying playing the drums even now, and I've often fancied making a whole record myself the way Prince did – starting with the drums and then seeing what happens. It wouldn't be an egotistical thing (well, not entirely), but when you've spent a lot of your life explaining what you want to drummers and it never sounding quite the same as it did in your head, it would be exciting to see if I could actually deliver the beat exactly the way I want it. I'm not having a go at Paul here, because what he did totally worked on *Never Mind the Bollocks* . . . and someone drumming the way I would've might have ruined it.

The differences between me and Cookie could have easily taken our lives in opposite directions at this time. There'd always been a contrast where he'd be busy doing something normal like playing football after school while I'd be off peeping Tom-ing or nicking from the Harrods warehouse down near St Paul's School playing fields, on the same towpath of opportunity that used to take me to the bike shop in Putney – I murdered that gaff! Once we got to that time after leaving school when respectable kids are trying to get jobs, Paul picked up an apprentice-ship as an electrician at Watney's brewery. But it didn't matter how hard he worked, I always seemed to have a bit more money than him from the proceeds of my nefarious doings – nice one!

A lot of kids like me who leave school without qualifications take that attitude out into the world with them. When it feels like the whole economic and educational structure is designed to keep you at the bot-tom, it's only natural to try and find a way to turn the whole thing upside down, and the obvious way to do that is either by direct thieving or finding some other way to scam the system. I think there's probably more of that shit going on in England now than ever, because the system has got even more entrenched, so a lot of the little highways and byways there used to be for people to improve their situations by legal means have been closed down. Now the odds are even more stacked in favour of tax-dodging businessmen with a public school education, and against people working hard to try and do things the right way. I can say this without being accused of political bias, because I was never part of either group.

One subsection of the community I did sadly get to belong to was people who have got nicked because their partner in crime gave his sister a stolen Afghan coat. We were quite the aristocracy of one, I can tell you.

There was a place on King's Road called Antiquarius which was one of those mini-arcades that have lots of different shops. As well as a load of antiques stalls, there was a clothes shop called the Great Gear Trading Company that I had my eye on. I figured out a way of getting in there when it was closed on a Sunday afternoon and went back three times to empty the gaff out. I never got caught in the act, but where it went wrong was that one of the guys I knew from Battersea came with me and afterwards we gave some of the stuff to his younger sister. Unfortunately, she stood out from the crowd so much in her smart new Afghan coat that she got stopped by the Old Bill.

This shows you how poor it was round there, then. Never mind *Cathy Come Home*, it would've been *Cathy Fucked Off & Never Came Back*, if Cathy had any sense. They pulled this kid and asked, 'Where did you get that?' She said, 'Oh, off him,' and grassed her brother up – she wasn't old enough to know any better. He then did the same to me, even though he didn't have that excuse, and it ended up being one of the more serious of the thirteen times I got nicked. (I know exactly how many there were because the number of my criminal convictions would nearly stop the Pistols going to America a few years later when we were trying to get visas.)

Luckily for me, I still wasn't quite eighteen, so instead of going to adult prison I got put in the juvenile remand home at Stamford Brook, just off Goldhawk Road. Me and Cookie go back there to talk about that in the special features of our 2008 reunion tour DVD. Because it was near where he lived, he used to come round and shout up to say hello and

I'd wave at him out of the window. The only other thing I remember about that place is that one night I was a-kip when some horrible cunt came and pissed on me for no reason.

I woke up feeling something wet all over my skin and then saw him running off. It was this big black dude. I don't know what his problem was with me cos we hadn't had any run-ins. I suppose he was just being a dick for the sake of it, but it was quite weird because I wasn't generally one of the guys who got picked on. I wasn't one of the bullies, but I wouldn't usually get bullied either. I don't remember going to fight him afterwards or anything, like my mate Ray Winstone's character did in *Scum*. I just thought, 'Fuck it, let's not get involved.' If life's pissing on you anyway, there's no point hitting it with your umbrella.

Scum didn't come out till a few years later, but one film I've already mentioned which did have a big influence on me at this time was *A Clockwork Orange*. It was just a brilliant movie for teenagers. I think I saw it with Cookie in Shepherd's Bush when it first came out. It was withdrawn not long afterwards after a lot of copy-cat violence – they thought it was going to inspire youngsters, and it certainly inspired me. Not so much to commit acts of inhuman cruelty as in terms of my taste in home decor. It wasn't just the outside of my block in Battersea that looked a bit like the place in the film where they're walking by the water; the inside of my bedroom looked like somewhere Alex DeLarge would feel at home.

First off, I had a really good stereo (though I wasn't listening to much classical music on it). There was also a leopardskin rug that still had the head on it. Everything in there was top of the fucking range, whereas everything else in the flat was pretty much tuppence. Given that my mum and stepdad (who as far as I knew were doing their best to be law-abiding citizens by that stage) didn't really have two baked beans to rub together,

I can see in retrospect why me living it up on the proceeds of a life of crime would've pissed them off.

I certainly used to get a clump off Ron when they'd have to come and pick me from the cop-shop. He definitely had a resentment about the fact that they'd be out working hard all day when all I was doing was nicking stuff and then either getting caught or not.

The whole thing came to a head one night when I got home late and they'd locked me out so I woke them up. Ron didn't like that, but I was getting too grown up to be pushed around by him any more so we had one of those kind of bullshit fights like Phil Daniels' dad has with him in *Quadrophenia*. (I found out recently that Lydon was up for the part Daniels played – thank fuck he didn't get it as the film would've been ruined.) Ron told me to get a job and I said, 'I don't want some shit job like you've got,' then a few punches may have been thrown, but no one got fully done over.

I don't like confrontation, so it felt like my best option was just to fuck off and never go back, which is pretty much what I ended up doing. The fact that I didn't have anywhere else lined up to live didn't really bother me.

PART II: DURING

11. LET IT ROCK

The shop assistants of the King's Road never seemed all that pleased to see me. They must have had some kind of unreasonable prejudice against people who were only coming into their retail outlets to nick stuff. As a result, when I went in Granny's or Alkasura or any of those classier gaffs, I never really felt like I had the right to be there. There was one place, however, where reprobates like me seemed assured of a slightly warmer welcome.

The first time I went into Let It Rock must have been late 1971 or early 1972. There'd been another slightly cool shop there before, but I think the owner fucked off to America, leaving Malcolm McLaren and Vivienne Westwood with a foothold in 430 King's Road. By the time he got back they'd taken the whole thing over, like an infestation of high fashion moths.

Let It Rock had a totally different vibe to the 'buy something then get the fuck out of here' mentality of somewhere like Take 6, and I was very attracted to it. There was a couch and a jukebox and it felt like you could hang out there. The jukebox didn't just have any old shit from the charts on like the ones in pubs did, it was full of cool stuff like Billy Fury and the Flamin' Groovies. And the people who worked in there weren't cunts, either. That didn't just apply to Malcolm and Vivienne, but to the staff they got in to cover when they weren't there as well. If you had a bit of time to kill, which I usually did while my mates were at school or out working for a living, then you could sit around and have a chat with them.

The shop started out selling an updated version of the Teddy boy gear my mum and my real dad would've been wearing when they got together in the mid-1950s – big brothel creeper shoes, peg trousers, drape jackets – with the odd zoot suit thrown in as time went on. It felt like the opposite of the flowing flares and ethnic prints of the hippie era, and I think that was pretty much the idea. I didn't consider it to be old-fashioned, I just thought of it as cool.

I was so impressed by the atmosphere of the place that I even began dressing like a Teddy boy myself. The first thing I actually bought from there was a pair of pink peg trousers, which was a pretty bold choice in 1972, but I told you I lived on the edge. Eventually I got myself the shoes and the drape as well, though I don't ever remember wearing them all together. I never went full-on Edwardian. I was kind of half Teddy boy, half fucking idiot from Battersea. I even went to a Teddy boy club in Liverpool Street a few times. It was at a pub called the Black Raven – what other fucking colour do ravens come in? – where Teds would pose around looking at each other and listening to Eddie Cochran.

It wasn't so much the music for me as that need to feel like I was part of a group – to connect with another little gang. Man, I wanted to belong so badly; whether it was to QPR, or the skinheads, or the Teddy boys didn't even matter too much. I just had to be *something*. You could see how desperate I was by the fact that I even tried to be a hippie for a while – around the time I was breaking into all the other shops down

King's Road, you'd often see me bowling along there in patched leather flares with platform boots and a big hairy Afghan coat.

As far as British teen subcultures of the Sixties and Seventies were concerned, I was just about all of them at one time or another. There really weren't too many that passed me by. On one level, this was just what young people did at that point – experimenting with shit to do with their identities – but because I didn't really have anything holding me back in terms of a stable background or a sense of self-worth, I was free to take it much further than the normies did.

Of course I didn't realise this at the time, but now I can see that trying on all these different youth cults for size was almost like the apprenticeship I had to serve before helping to start a new one of my own. There were limits, though, even for me. I was lucky that Jimmy Macken shut down my hippie phase before it could get out of control. He hated it when I started trying to act like a prog-rock guy. He'd ask me something and I'd say, 'I don't know, man, it's just not progressive enough.' Then he'd get the hump with me and call me a cunt. Basically he'd busted me on the fact that it was all just a pose, and I couldn't have that – I needed to find people who really understood me.

This was where Malcolm and Vivienne came in. I don't specifically remember the first time I met Malcolm, but he'd definitely have been dressed as a Teddy boy (with Vivienne as a Teddy girl). We got chatting, and I started coming back to Let It Rock regularly – once a week at first, but then more and more often till it was virtually every day. I felt pretty blank to everything at that time, but something was pushing me to go in there. As I've said, it wasn't just about Vivienne and Malcolm either. When they weren't in the shop I was just as happy chatting to the other people who worked there.

This was before Glen Matlock or Chrissie Hynde were hanging

around. I remember this good-looking black kid called Stuart who worked there who was very queeny but kind of tough, too. Once I'd left home and was needing a place to stay I would kip over at his house sometimes, in the same bed but with nothing sexual going on. He definitely wanted to suck my cock – who wouldn't? But I wasn't having it.

There was never anything happening sexually between me and my mates. The handful of times when I trespassed to the other side were all at weird random moments when I was by myself. I know there was the odd rumour about me and Paul but I can definitely tell you that never happened. When we slept in the same bed – which we did often over the years – it would always be top to toe, with his head at one end and mine at the other. That said, there was one time when he woke me up and said, 'What the fuck are you doing?' So I guess I must've been rubbing his leg or something, but I was totally a-kip. I bet he still thinks I was trying to get hold of him. Don't flatter yourself, Cookie, I was only touching you in my dreams.

I'm trying to imagine what Malcolm must have thought of me when I started hanging out in the shop. He obviously didn't think I was one of the regular run-of-the-mill kids who would walk up and down King's Road at that time wearing tight suits and kipper ties and platform boots, although I did go through a phase of doing that. Cookie calls it the 'Adam Faith in *Budgie*' look, but I reckon that was more denim. There was a bit of *Hunky Dory*-era Bowie going on too, with all the tank tops and stuff, but I wasn't so into that. *Ziggy Stardust* and *Aladdin Sane* were the two big Bowie albums for me – the earlier records when he still had curly hair gave off more of a folky kind of vibe, which wasn't really for me. It felt more like something people in squats on Portobello Road would be listening to.

Anyway, back to Malcolm. I guess he would've noticed the energy that I had, the way that music and fashion mattered to me, and the element of fucked-up-ness that meant I didn't give too much of a shit about anything else. They liked damaged goods, Malcolm and Vivienne, but I don't think it was because they were looking for people they could use to put their ideas into practice. I think it was because they were quite damaged too.

Maybe not so much Vivienne – the vibe I got from her was more that she was terrified of being some normal Northern lass (maybe she'd had a taste of that with her first husband and so now she was going the other way) – but definitely with Malcolm. It was easy to see that he'd had a very confused upbringing. I never found out exactly what it was, but some weird shit definitely went on with his mum and his gran, and he left home really young, just like I did.

Later on, when John came into the picture, he would never give Malcolm credit for that. Because Lydon had come from quite a loving family background himself, he didn't make allowances for people with a less secure foundation in life. He tried to make McLaren out to be some kind of middle-class hippie idiot, whereas me and Paul saw him as more of a chameleon, which might sound like a good thing – but when you think about it, trying to fit in with everyone around you instead of just being yourself is actually really hard work. We noticed how when he was hanging out with poncey types Malcolm would put on a front to try and sound more posh than he was. But when he'd come out with me and Cookie, he'd go all jack-the-lad and cockneyish.

I never minded that. I thought it was funny the way Malcolm would echo people back to fit in with them, as that would only make it more obvious how different he was. I understood why he was doing it, because I was always trying to find a way to fit in as well. This is why in later years the idea of me, and to a certain extent Cookie (although it was more true of him), being the no-nonsense engine-room of the Sex Pistols would be so far off the mark. Because I was probably the biggest poser out of all of us. Well, maybe not as big as Malcolm, who when he was selling the peg trousers came up with a special way of standing at an angle where he'd bend his leg at the knee to show them off. He was fucking hilarious.

The other thing about the early years of the Sex Pistols people have really got wrong is to think of everything that happened as being planned out by Malcolm from the start. He tried to paint it that way once he started believing his own publicity, but McLaren was actually doing himself a disservice by making himself out to be this kind of old-school Svengali figure who controlled everything, like Larry Parnes or Colonel Tom Parker.

The great thing about Malcolm in the early days wasn't that he had everything all worked out, it was how open he was to picking up on what was going on around him and twisting it into a new dimension. The direction wasn't dictated from the top down, it came up from down below. Even in the way he and Vivienne changed the shop – first to Too Fast To Live, Too Young To Die, which had more of a biker element, and then later to Sex – that wasn't about them thinking, 'Right, we're gonna make these idiots buy whatever we want them to.' What they did was pick up on our energy and transform it into something no one was expecting.

If you even think about me and Cookie – normal kids who were into birds and football but were also totally at ease hanging out with gay guys and drag queens and going to all these weird places in Earls Court – that was kind of something new and unusual. I guess a lot of it overlapped with glam. The upfrontness of Sex would partly come out of that. Not saying it was all down to us (I didn't even like all the bondage stuff – that wasn't my cup of tea at all), but we were all plugged into the same electricity.

Malcolm and Vivienne were like a bright light in the darkness I'd come from, and I think they got a kick out of me because as art school types they had been trained to find the working classes exotic. And not only was I a real 'erbert, but I had a sense of avant-garde style. So we both had the same attention to detail, but it came from different perspectives. I definitely behaved myself around them when it came to nicking stuff from the shop. Well, I did once I got to know them. Viv might've got the hump with me a couple of times early on, but I think even from the start she knew that I wasn't stealing stuff in a bad way, it was just because I wanted to look the part.

As time passed, I started to run little errands around the place. That made it easier for me to blag clothes off them without having to resort to thieving. Malcolm couldn't drive, so I'd take him round all the tailors in East London picking up samples in Viv's olive-green Mini. It wasn't one of the classic *Italian Job* ones, but the newer shape from the early Seventies. Of course I was a traffic violation on wheels, cos I had no licence or insurance, but that never seemed to worry them.

Their flat was a really nice council gaff in Clapham – one of those Simon Templar blocks from the Sixties with only a few floors. I think maybe Viv had got it when she had her first son, Ben, with the bloke she was married to before she met Malcolm. Then she and Malcolm had another son together, Joe, and the two boys shared a room with bunk beds in it. Sometimes, when Ben was away, I'd tag along home with his mum and stepdad after the shop closed to get something to eat and stay over in the spare bunk. Joe and I got along well – he seemed like a normal kid and we'd have a laugh together.

I really enjoyed staying there. I was kipping anywhere I could get a bed at this point, and their place was something a bit different to staying at Hayesy's or Cookie's. It felt more like a workshop – a sweatshop, even – than a normal home, because they had all the sewing machines laid out in the front room. Instead of lounging on couches round a TV, they'd be cutting patterns on the table. I was interested in fashion, so I liked watching the process all the way from the designs till the clothes were pieced together. Because those kinds of details mattered to me, it was exciting to be in the place where the decisions were made. The funny thing was, I don't remember hearing any music in that flat, maybe because you couldn't have heard it over the noise of the sewing machines. I guess the sewing machines were the music.

The staying over started when the shop was still Let It Rock, so they weren't making the rubber stuff yet, and this became a really good time for me; before the Pistols were really happening. I didn't know anything about the world Malcolm and Vivienne lived in – toffs, health food, it was the opposite of everything I'd known. Being in their orbit I felt as close as I was gonna get to a London version of the Factory – the Warhol scene that surrounded The Velvet Underground – and I really gravitated towards that. It meant a lot to me that I was made to feel welcome there, treated like an equal, and even given a bit of encouragement. It gave me confidence.

I can see that from the outside Malcolm and Vivienne dressing in the clothes my mum and dad would have worn makes them look like the parents I'd always wanted. There was a bit of that with Viv, to be honest, because she was quite maternal in her own way. She would do things like turning me on to decent toothpaste, which I really appreci-ated. I never fancied her – not that she wasn't attractive, she just wasn't my type – so I suppose that helped. Vivienne's vibe was kind of asexual. In a funny way, I suppose the feelings I had towards her were more like what you have towards a mum.

There wasn't so much of a surrogate dad thing with Malcolm,

though. He was more like a clever older brother that had gone to college. Even though he was almost ten years older than me, it was like he was having his teenage years late. He certainly looked like a kid who'd been in the dressing-up box. In any case, my relationship with my stepdad had been so fucked up that I wasn't really in the market for a father figure. I think 'mentor' would probably be a better word for what Malcolm was to me.

That said, he and Viv did kind of adopt me for a few years when I was out in the streets on my own and needed someone to point me in the right direction. They opened my eyes up to a new world that was a lot more colourful and exciting, and I was eager to explore it. I wasn't stubborn or ignorant – I was very open to bettering myself.

For example, we used to go out to eat at that vegetarian gaff round the back of Carnaby Street where the name was just one word – Cranks, that was it. There weren't many places like that around in the early 1970s and sitting down in there with them to order food I hadn't eaten before was very exciting. I didn't just want fish and chips or a curry, I wanted to try something new. I'm still like that with food now. OK, the grub in there might not have looked quite as appealing as pie and mash at first, but it was really tasty when you ate it. It wasn't vegan, just vegetarian – quiches and salad, stuff like that.

I'd always known there was a better fucking place than the one I'd come from, but before I started hanging out at Let It Rock, I had no way into it. As a homeless tea-leaf, the closest I could get was by breaking into famous people's houses and nicking their stuff, and that just wasn't close enough. I'm still grateful to Malcolm for giving me the chance to tag along with him and not just see that other world but actually become part of it. Whether he was introducing me to avant-garde art-world chicks who were happy for me to fuck them, or taking me to the Speakeasy to hang out with the rock aristocracy, it was all brand new, and I think he got a kick out of what a thrill it was for me too. There was a generosity about Malcolm at that time. He had his fucking issues, same as we all do, but I couldn't help but like him, and I got a lot out of our friendship – probably more than he knew.

12. THE PHANTOM OF THE ODEON

The two places I loved going best with Malcolm were the Speakeasy and the Roebuck. The Roebuck was just a regular boozer around the corner from the shop, but you'd get some good faces in there, even the actual Faces. The Markham was more the hippie pub in the area – that was where the longhairs would go – but the Roebuck was where the classic Chelsea characters and the people who owned the shops down the King's Road tended to hang out. We were in there with John Bindon a few times, the actor/gangster who shagged Princess Margaret. He was famous for his massive knob, which he was always whipping out to impress everyone, and he didn't disappoint us, though I never saw him do his party trick with the full beer glasses.

The real highlight for me was when Malcolm would sneak me into the Speakeasy. It wasn't easy to get in there, especially if you were still underage like I was, because that was where the who's who of everyone who was anyone would go to drink after hours. Not just rock stars – footballers, actors, everyone. That gaff was on a little road parallel to Oxford Street on the north side, and I was always pestering Malcolm to go on a Friday or Saturday. We'd have the odd run-in there once the Pistols were up and running till it all got a bit awkward, but for the moment that was my favoured weekend destination.

What was our conveyance of choice? There was still the odd stolen motor going on. One time I nicked a Jag and took it up the West End. The memory is a bit foggy, but that could've been the time the Mandrax really kicked in, this poor fucker pulled out in front of us into the main road and I just fucking sideswiped him – knocked his car right out of the way. We just kept going with everyone thinking it was hilarious. I'm pretty sure he wasn't hurt but it could've been horrendous. Mandrax, booze and stolen cars is just not a good combination, cos everything's a fucking joke when you're on that stuff.

For a change I experimented with driving vehicles that were actually mine. I remember buying a car off Wally Nightingale's dad's mate for £50, but the cunt completely turned me over. That motor broke down so fast that I was sure they'd done that classic thing of putting sawdust in the petrol tank so the car runs for a few miles and then just dies. That was the first car I'd ever technically owned, but getting ripped off just made me more determined to get something decent, and I had a nice blue Mini Cooper S for a while after that.

I also got hold of a minivan, which was not only very useful for transporting stolen goods, but also gave me an option of somewhere to kip if I was desperate. A fair few lucky young women got the chance to help me test out the mattress I'd put in the back – it was a proper British Leyland love-wagon, like the last scene of a Bond film, but on a toy car budget.

Even owning my own cars wasn't going to persuade me to try and take an actual driving test. It was just one of those things that seemed like an impossibility, so I never bothered doing it. And I remember Cookie saying it was a nightmare because all the studying was so difficult. It's a bit of a trigger word for me, 'studying' – so I just thought, 'Fuck me, that's never gonna happen.' I didn't think I had the patience or the intelligence to do anything the right way. The message I'd got from my upbringing and education was that I was a piece of shit who was never going to amount to anything, and that kind of negative view of yourself can very easily become a self-fulfilling prophecy.

I wouldn't be legal on the roads till more than ten years later, after I'd moved to California. The driving test in America is a piece of cake: you just have to answer a few questions and get round the block without killing anyone. Basically, a chimpanzee could pass it. In fact, I think it was specifically designed by the American automobile industry to ensure that morons would still be able to buy cars.

I don't remember ever getting done for driving stolen cars or having no licence, road tax or insurance. Again, the early Seventies was a golden age for that kind of low-level car crime, especially with the old Cloak of Invisibility in operation. Nowadays with all the computer-linked CCTV cameras they have in London, I'd be up before the beak before I'd even got into second gear.

The one misdemeanour that the Cloak did not allow me to get away with was fucking my mates' girlfriends. I kept doing this and I kept getting caught red-handed (and not just handed) as well. Stephen Hayes, Jimmy Macken – even Cookie. No one was safe. It was awful, really. I must've known it was wrong, because I didn't want to own up afterwards, but that never made me pause for a second while I was doing it. I don't know what was driving me – I never felt like I was being competitive, just that if and when the opportunity arose, I couldn't help myself.

It was a miracle any of my mates were still talking to me, let alone still letting me kip over at their gaffs. I don't remember anyone really confronting me about this at the time – I certainly never got the punch in the mouth I probably deserved, though sometimes even now someone (usually Cookie) will mention something that shows me he hasn't forgotten. And there was one weird time when I was kipping round Stephen Hayes' mum's house not long after everyone knew I'd shagged his girlfriend of the time, when a load of his mates came round and started slagging me off.

For about an hour they were standing right in front of the bed I was lying in, telling me what an arsehole I'd been, and I just couldn't face dealing with it, so I pretended not to have woken up. It was pretty weird and horrible. I was in his brother's bed making out I was asleep, while Hayesy lay in his bed on the other side of the room not saying anything because he didn't know how to deal with it either. He didn't join in even though he'd have been more than entitled to – in a weird way I think he even felt sorry for me. And I think that made his mates even more angry, so they just carried on cunting me off and saying I should own up to what I'd done, while I just lay there squeezing my eyes shut. That was my approach to a lot of my life back then: fucking people over and then pretending to sleep through the consequences.

The exception to this rule – the one infamous act that I was happy to take the rap for in public – was the biggest coup in my whole career of rock 'n' roll thievery. It took place, fittingly enough, given how large this West London landmark loomed in the blighted landscape of my childhood, in the Hammersmith Odeon. (Everyone who is old enough to remember its glory days still calls it the Odeon.) When I was haunting its rafters like the Phantom of the fucking Opera, it was a beautiful old cinema that was one of London's premier rock venues.

It held about 3,500 people, and many of them (at least the ones with local knowledge) would've sneaked in round the back through the maze of tunnels and fire exits. I suppose the best comparison for American readers would be the Ritz Ballroom in New York. Not so much Mercer Hall, but maybe a little bit.

As I've said, the lyrics weren't usually the first aspect of a song that caught my attention, but there was one line in David Bowie's 'Hang Onto Yourself' on the *Ziggy Stardust* album that did really stick in my mind. That line was 'The bitter comes out better on a stolen guitar', and on the occasion of Bowie's famous Ziggy Stardust farewell shows at the Hammersmith Odeon (although no one knew that's what they were gonna be before they happened, as he only announced Ziggy's retirement at the end of 'Rock 'n' Roll Suicide' on the last night) I decided to put that theory to the test. Well, that's how I like to look back on it now. At the time it was probably a bit less of a scientific experiment and a bit more 'That's a nice amp . . . I'm having it'.

I was lucky enough to go to both those shows, and there was a fair amount of bullshit talked about them afterwards. They were good and everything, but all the stuff about loads of kids having sex everywhere while the gig was going on was bollocks – that was definitely something I would've noticed, but all I saw was a load of obsessed teens looking at Bowie like he was God and then getting very upset (but probably not as upset as Mick Ronson was) when he said he was going to knock things on the head with the Spiders from Mars.

I'm not sure which of the two closing nights I struck on. If it was the first night, that would help explain why D. A. Pennebaker's film of the event had such famously shit sound and picture quality – because we'd nicked most of their equipment ('we' being me and Wally, cos I don't think Cookie fancied it). It would make sense if it was the first night, because otherwise you'd think they'd have removed all the stuff rather than leaving it onstage for the Phantom of the Odeon to make off with.

Either way, after the gig, I had my minivan outside and I just went in

and got as much stuff off the stage as I could fit in the back: Trevor
Bolder's Sun bass amp was one of my best trophies, as well as a few cymbals and this little Electro Voice microphone that still had a smudge of
Bowie's lipstick on it. For some reason I remember Trevor always having
big sideburns to match his big thighs.

The security guard was snoring with his mouth open in the fourth or
fifth row, catching flies. I bet he wasn't too happy when he woke up. Well,
I know he wasn't, because I was there. I'd dropped the first vanload off
back at Wally's house and gone back to get all these Neumann radio
microphones that were being used for the recording, so I slung my hook
sharpish when I saw him start to come to. He didn't chase me out, but I
remember looking down at him from the stage as he shifted in his seat
and thinking, 'It's definitely time to go.' I don't recall feeling any com-
punction about nicking my idol's gear – only the full-on excitement,
especially when it was on the news on Capital Radio the next day.

I was chuffed when I heard that for sure. It was my first bit of fame
and I liked it. That's why I've got some understanding of what's going on
in the minds of these lunatics who go and shoot up a fucking school just
to get their fifteen minutes on the news. Or the fucking arsonist arsehole
who's set fire to a house and gets his kicks out of hearing the sound of the
sirens. It's that level of narcissism where you get excited because you've
made your mark on the world and no one knows it's you. You're so alien-
ated from humanity that you don't care how much damage you have to
do to get that feeling.

Although I'm happy – even proud – to admit to the Bowie heist, I
would like to take this opportunity to say that I did not nick two guitars
including a Gibson Les Paul from Rod Stewart's house in Windsor. I've
seen these thefts linked together in some accounts of the Pistols' early
days – which they easily could've been, I just didn't do it. Not out of any

special consideration for the feelings of my own Ace Face, but because Windsor was a bit too far out of town for me to be going on a thieving mission. If Rod had lived on the Gloucester Road, he'd have been fair game.

Those Neumann mics were probably worth five hundred quid each, but I didn't know their value at the time so I got stiffed on the sale. I went up to north Willesden or somewhere to palm them off on some mate of Bernie Rhodes' and he probably gave me a tenner for them. I liked Bernie – he was a laugh. He was hanging around the shop a fair bit at the time and when we all went out to eat together or met up at gigs I never used to think, 'Who's this cunt?' Obviously he'd end up having a fair bit of influence on some of the exciting musical events that were about to unfold. But fuck me, that man knew the value of a pound.

By this time – late summer and autumn of 1973 – in music it was getting towards what you might call the arse end of glam. Mott the Hoople's *Mott* – boot-boy music only with platform boots – and *Human Menagerie*, the first album by Steve Harley and Cockney Rebel, which was a bit lighter and more melodic with strings on, were big favourites of mine and Cookie's. I think Harley had a dodgy Scotch egg (i.e. leg) because he'd had polio or something, so he had to wear one of those built-up boots. Wally once mentioned me bringing the first Queen album and the single of Thin Lizzy's 'The Rocker' into rehearsals as well, which I don't remember but it sounds about right.

We saw Queen supporting Mott the Hoople at a famous gig at the Hammersmith Odeon where there was a riot. Both bands had to play two shows because the gig was over-sold, and for some reason – I think they tried to stop Mott's encore by bringing down the safety curtain – everyone suddenly started smashing the place up. It was fucking excellent. Queen were good then, too – more a glam hard-rock group than the weird kind of pop thing they'd turn into, but either way the Mercury was definitely still rising at that stage.

As for our band, the prospect of us taking our place at the forefront of rock was still looking distinctly fucking distant. I'd been trying to get Malcolm involved for a while because I thought he might be able to help us, but he didn't seem too bothered about us at first, and I don't think our name-change from 'Ihe Strand to Swankers did anything to convince him we were about to hit the big time. When he did finally pull his finger out and make a contribution, though, it was a big one.

Del Noones wasn't really cutting it as a bass player – he seemed to miss a lot of rehearsals and he wasn't learning as quickly as the rest of us. So Malcolm hooked us up with Glen Matlock. I already knew Glen, because he worked in the shop on Saturdays. He might've stopped me nicking something once, but I wasn't holding that against him. And Cookie may have played football against him at school. Anyway, Malcolm brought us together at a Thin Lizzy gig at the Marquee, and a few days later Glen came round to Wally's to audition. I think he played 'Miss Julie's Farm' and 'Three Button Hand Me Down' by the Faces. We had that connection of all having gone to the Roundhouse show, and the big plus was, Matlock didn't just limp through them – he could really fucking do it.

Now that we had one and a half (if you count Wally) members who could actually play their instruments, we might really start to do something. The only slight drawback with Glen was that he'd gone to Clement Danes, which was the grammar school on the other side of the Westway from Christopher Wren. From our point of view, that lot were the upper crust. They wore green and yellow uniforms for a start (ours were plain black), so they were obviously perfumed ponces.

Glen was all right, and both me and Cookie got on with him, but right from the start he had to carry that stigma of being the (relatively) posh one in the band. He wasn't exactly Stephen Fry, but he had a steady family background and was the kind of kid who's allowed to borrow his dad's car, which was a million miles away from how the rest of us – especially me – were living. He definitely came from the right side of the tracks (or the A40, in our case), which eventually turned out to be the wrong side as far as punk was concerned.

If we'd been starting a band like Yes, obviously Glen would have been an asset – we could've made him the leader and he could've pointed the stick like Jon Anderson used to. As it was, his art school contacts would later be very useful in getting the Sex Pistols off the ground. So it was no wonder he turned a bit sour for a while when he got pushed out a couple of years in.

13. 'SCARFACE, SCARFACE, SCARRED FROM EAR TO EAR'

Another way Malcolm showed he was starting to take an interest in the band was by sorting us out a bit of rehearsal time at Covent Garden community centre, soon after Glen joined. But it was a lot of hassle getting all the stuff up there, and the real breakthrough in getting somewhere regular to practise came from Wally's dad.

McLaren would be the one who'd get all the praise (and the blame) for being the Sex Pistols' Svengali, but Wally's dad was giving him a run for his money there for a while. OK, he'd mainly just pop his head round the door and ask if anyone wanted to go to the pub. But he did come up with some words for one of our first original songs, 'Scarface', which gave him more direct creative input into our music than Malcolm ever had. I can't remember the whole song – I think John took it over and changed the words to make it unrecognisable a little while later – but one line was definitely 'Scarface, Scarface, scarred from ear to ear'.

It wasn't exactly 'Bridge Over Troubled Water', but it was definitely up there with my one original songwriting effort at that point (which would later, with John's help, mutate into the Sex Pistols song some-times called 'Seventeen' and sometimes 'Lazy Sod'). Wally's dad's biggest contribution was to get us the stable rehearsal spot we needed if we were ever going to get up to speed for an actual gig. He was a bit of a wheeler-dealer who worked as an electrician and had contacts in both the union and the TV world. When his company got the contract to strip out the BBC's old Riverside Studios down by the river at Hammersmith – where the nonce was trying to lure me to – Swankers were in like Flynn.

It's great down there, right near the beautiful Hammersmith Bridge. If I was going to live in London now and I had the dough, that's defin-itely where I'd be. The studio was immaculate; in fact it was probably one of the best sound stages in Europe. All this amazing music had been made in there, and we were in clover. We could leave all our stolen equipment set up without any fear of someone like us coming along and nicking it, there were a few barrels of beer Cookie had liberated from his work at the brewery along the river, and Glen says (I don't actu-ally remember this, but I don't think he'd make it up) there was even a handy shaggers' alley for me to pop off to if I needed a quick peeping Tom break.

Hanging around with Malcolm was bringing me a better class of sexual opportunity. Now I was moving away from the boot-boy world into more arty circles – which were way more appealing to me – I was meeting women who knew nothing about where I'd come from and wouldn't have cared anyway. Judy Nylon was kind of an avant-garde American chick that Brian Eno once wrote a song about, and we were pretty into each other. She had a beautiful face. Later on, Judy formed a duo called Snatch with a woman called Patti Paladin. I think Eno produced their records, so he was definitely a fan.

Chrissie Hynde was another one who was a real tumbler, and I mean that as a compliment because that's what I was too (and still am, in my better moments). I've not read her book yet so I don't know how much space she gives me – half a page, a full page, even? Does she say anything good about us shagging?

When I had her on my radio show a few years back I thought she was planning to embarrass me by bringing up a few intimate details, so I got in first and put all our dirty washing on the table right from the off. There was no shortage of it, I can tell you. When Chrissie was working at the shop she'd shut the place up and we'd put Malcolm and Vivienne's gospel of Sex into practice. At that time I'd have been as surprised to find out she was going to have her own band and write a load of classic songs as she'd have been if you told her that one day I'd be an LA radio personality asking her about the time I had her over that bathtub at a party. But those kinds of surprises are what life is all about, aren't they? And Chrissie's been a good friend over the years. I hope she'd say the same of me.

So much action was going around then that even Glen was getting some. Once Malcolm brought John Cale's wife at the time (who's dead now, otherwise I'd just have had to say 'the wife of a leading rock star', which would have been a bit of a tease) along to see us rehearse at the Riverside. After the rehearsal, we decided to go down to Brighton for a laugh – all six of us crammed into my minivan (aka the shagmobile). For some reason, and this proves there's no accounting for tastes, Cale's wife only had eyes for Matlock. I think she gave him a blowjob at the Riverside Studios, which must have been a bit of an eye-opener for him, as I think he was still at school at the time and not as well versed in these matters as me and Cookie were. And by the time we got down to Brighton, she was on him like a viper.

We decided to stay at one of the big hotels on the seafront – not the

Grand, where the IRA tried to bomb Margaret Thatcher, but the Majestic, which was a step or two down the ladder in price terms, but still pretty fancy by our standards. It had those great balconies, like the hotel in *Quadrophenia*.

Malcolm had forgotten the combination to his wallet as usual (though he was quite good at remembering the combinations to other people's) so Cale's missus ended up stumping up for two rooms on the top floor: the lovebirds got one, and me, Malcolm, Cookie and Wally got the other. As you can imagine, being stuck in a room with those three was less than a barrel of laughs – livestock are transported in better conditions – so I decided to take a little constitutional along the window ledge to see what was going on in the room next door.

I didn't feel I was risking my life – it wasn't a narrow ledge, and I was like a mountain goat at that age, especially when there was a bit of sexual gratification by proxy at the end of the climb. I don't remember the possibility of falling ever occurring to me on my nocturnal rooftop excursions – except for that time the bouncers were holding me off the roof of the Hammersmith Palais.

What I was doing on this occasion would have looked impressive from down on the seafront – is it a bird? Is it a plane? No, it's the peeping Tom with no fear of heights. Did I have a pedal while I was peeping? A gentleman never tells . . . although he might ask for a couple of hundred similar offences to be taken into consideration.

Glen didn't know I was there, which was a good job as it would've probably put him off his stroke. Either that or he might have drawn the curtains. He'd never have found out he'd had an audience if I'd been able to resist the temptation to give him sex tips over breakfast the next morning. Once he'd asked me how I knew what he was up to, he took the news pretty well. The band that plays together stays together; well, for a while anyway.

The whole Cale's wife thing was very hush-hush at the time – I suppose The Velvet Underground's was one legacy even Malcolm felt quite respectful towards. Given that she'd been one of Frank Zappa's groupie group the GTOs, and I think she shagged Kevin Ayers at that big concert he and Cale did at the Rainbow with Eno and Nico, it wasn't like Mrs Cale was the conquest of the century. I didn't go to that gig in 1974 when it happened, but I've got the CD of it now. Apparently Cale was so pissed off about the Ayers cock episode that he wrote the song 'Guts' about it. Then again, he was such a miserable old fucking gringe when he came on my radio show a few years later that any bird he was with would probably have wanted to fuck someone else.

For music-lovers of taste and discernment, it was becoming more of a struggle to keep up standards by 1974. There was still some great stuff about; you just had to look a bit harder for it. The first Be-Bop Deluxe album, *Axe Victim*, and Sparks' *Kimono My House* were both big albums for me and Cookie – we'd sit in his bedroom for hours listening to them.

I didn't know this at the time, but Sparks were one of those bands who had to come over to the UK because no one in America got them. It's funny how that works – you couldn't necessarily guess the people it would happen to from their music. It certainly applied to Jimi Hendrix.

The main problem in the mid-Seventies was that the big bands – Led Zep, The Stones, Pink Floyd, maybe even The Who – had got too big, while the charts were full of two-bob cunts like Mud and Chicory Tip. These were people who probably got their clothes made by the guy at that funny shop Carnaby Cavern just round the back of Carnaby Street. Its motto was 'You name it, we'll make it' and that whole scene was tuppencery of the first order. No one was going to have their lives changed by seeing Dave Hill of Slade on *Top of the Pops* with that stupid comb stuck in his head.

The pub-rock thing would be a kind of reaction to this – trying to take things back to basics to make them more exciting again. It didn't have that name yet, but it was already starting to happen. We were going to a lot of gigs at the time, often at smaller venues. The Fulham Greyhound was a big haunt of mine, with all the wood inside. I saw so many bands there: Thin Lizzy, Mott the Hoople, The Groundhogs.

Obviously my criminal supersense had not deserted me. I still had my eyes open for a tasty bit of gear. Sometimes I'd go and see a band, decide not to nick their stuff beforehand because I wanted to hear them, and then regret it afterwards, because they were shit. Uriah Heep was one of those, and Genesis, who I saw with Peter Gabriel when he had all the make-up and whatnot, so they were still just about sneaking into the glam category. Imagine all the trouble I could have saved the world if I'd nicked all their stuff!

Just because I was behaving myself at Malcolm and Vivienne's shop didn't mean I was neglecting my thieving duties on the fashion side. Knowing them put me on the inside track to some of the good shops that not everyone knew about. There was a place in Covent Garden called City Lights which was run by a guy called Tommy Roberts, a kind of barrow boy/avant-garde type. He'd had other shops, and he may have been involved in the setting up of Let It Rock. He also went on to manage Kilburn and the High Roads, the superior pub-rock band Ian Dury was in before he got his Blockheads together.

Anyway, you could tell this City Lights place was an exclusive kind of deal because Roxy Music got some of their clothes there. I think it was where David Bowie's *Pin-Ups* suit came from as well. Also, you couldn't just walk in off the street, you had to ring the bell and be buzzed up. It was in this strange area round the back of Covent Garden and I can't remember how, but I worked out a way to get in there. Jimmy

Macken and Wally helped me push the door in and empty the gaff into Jimmy's van. I usually preferred to work alone on bigger jobs. I always felt other people were more likely to blow it because they didn't have the Cloak.

Just like that Bowie lyric which I could quote afterwards to justify nicking his microphones, Tommy had given a hostage to fortune by calling one of his previous shops Kleptomania. I bumped into him on the street in London years later and told him I was sorry and asked if there was anything I could do to make amends. He was kind enough to say that the insurance on that robbery had really helped him out because he was in a bit of financial trouble at the time, so all was well that ended well on that one.

While I'm on the subject of crimes against fashion, there is one more I probably can't get away without mentioning. This wasn't a theft but an actual look – my West Coast A&R guy phase, when I was on the hunt for new acts to go out on the road with Poco. I don't remember it being when I was mates with Malcolm, cos I think he'd have given it two thumbs down, the way Jimmy Macken did to my progressive experiment. Then again, McLaren was such a poser himself that he might've thought it was funny. And the fact that I associate this look with the band Ace and their song 'How Long' (which came out in 1974, when I was all over Malcolm's shop like an attack of genital warts) means maybe I tried it out while he was away in America persuading the New York Dolls to dress as communists.

I was just trying to convince people I was somebody. My strategy for doing this at that point was to wear my hair kind of long with a nice Hawaiian shirt, jeans, cowboy boots, and one of those beige slimline suit jackets with a big collar that places like Take 6 sold. I'd put on that get-up and stroll down King's Road carrying a stolen briefcase and hoping I looked like someone from a record company in LA. It was bizarre, really. I doubt there was even anything in the briefcase. Glen tells a story (which again I don't remember, but as I've said before he's not one for making things up – unlike almost everyone else in this book, except Cookie) about me once nicking a briefcase that had a load of cash in and buying us so much pie and mash with the proceeds that we could barely walk down Hammersmith Broadway, so maybe it was that one.

Either way, it was all was another blatant fantasy cooked up by me in a desperate attempt to get attention. I just twigged the look and thought, 'I'm gonna try that and see what happens.' The sad truth was, nothing much did. That whole vibe got quite fashionable for a while in the next century, so you could (though I wouldn't) say I was forty years ahead of my time. I think they call it 'yacht rock' now. I don't really like that name – it was never just about the yachts for me, it was more a way of life.

Given the number of risks I was taking, it was inevitable that my luck would run out one day. The fact that I can't remember exactly what I got done for is probably another example of my memory closing down when life gets too difficult, but I don't think it was the Fashion Police who finally put me away. Whatever the charge I was on, finding myself banged up in Ashford remand centre in the summer of 1974 was a rude fucking shock. Now I was over eighteen with a list of convictions as long as a basketball player's arm, I was in serious danger of getting put away for a long stretch in a grown-up prison. This wasn't some holiday camp for boy scouts like Banstead Hall had been: this was a proper Seventies nick like in the TV series *Porridge*.

I was a habitual criminal, so I did deserve to be there, but I didn't fucking want to be. It was a horrible place. I was only inside for about three weeks, but it felt like a year. Someone had a radio playing the top 20 and I remember putting my ear to the peephole in the big metal door to hear The Rolling Stones' 'It's Only Rock 'n' Roll But I Like It'. It wasn't their finest moment, but it sounded a hell of a lot more fun than I was having.

If I'd got the hefty sentence I probably should have, the band would've almost certainly broken up, as I was the one with nothing else to live for who was most committed to keeping it going. Happily – for me, if not for the music industry – this court appearance would be different to the many that had gone before, as now I had someone to speak up for me in front of the judge. Given what a turning point it was in my life, you'd think I'd have clearer recall of this courtroom drama. Knowing it happened, and thinking the hearing was probably at Marylebone Magistrates' Court . . . well, that's about it. Nothing.

I was lucky that there was someone around who was more tuned into what was happening than I was. That someone was Malcolm McLaren – the first person who'd ever cared enough about me to get involved in my life on this level. Malcolm gave the judge such a brilliant line of bullshit about what a bright future I had in front of me and what a great contribution I was going to make to British society that the guy in the wig let me off with a final warning. If he'd known what was really going to happen, he'd have locked me up and thrown away the key.

14. KUTIE JONES AND HIS SEX PISTOLS

After Malcolm got involved, we did just one gig with me singing. That was all it took to confirm that being the frontman was not my bag. It wasn't like this was some big pressure show, either, just a little party for some coke-taking rich kids at Salter's Cafe on the King's Road. But from how much I was shitting myself, you'd think it was the fucking Royal Albert Hall.

It can be a bit of a drag nowadays how everything gets filmed and documented from the very beginning, because it stops anything from developing on its own and you lose the mystery of someone who did see it telling you what happened. But I wish someone had filmed that gig, because watching how terrible I was would've been fucking hilarious. Afterwards Vivienne said I was 'singing in the back of my throat'. I'm not really sure what that meant – God bless her – but I think she was trying to be kind. The problem wasn't so much my singing (although that was bad enough) as the fact that I just had no idea what to do with myself onstage.

I wasn't wearing any punk clothes yet – I think the flash-hippie-Poco-A&R-man look was still operational – and we only did 'Scarface' and a couple of covers. But that was one hell of a long fucking ten minutes, certainly long enough for me to know that being the guy everyone was looking at was not for me. It just ain't my personality. Well, it is, because I do like attention, but only up to a point. I'm a strange mixture of an extrovert and an introvert like that – once the spotlight gets too bright, I just want to fuck off back into the shadows.

In a way, the same thing had happened at the shop, which had changed its name by then to plain old Sex. The whole point of that place was to be right up in everyone's face, and Malcolm and Vivienne were recruiting some very bold characters to help them get their message across. Obviously, I was one of them; at least, I was when I had a couple of drinks in me. But Pamela Rooke – also known as Jordan – who'd joined Chrissie on the Sex shop floor, she was something else, man.

It was like she was fully formed from the minute she arrived at the shop. Now, I liked Jordan. She was a good laugh, but how little of a shit she gave almost frightened me. She dressed so outrageously that I was almost embarrassed to walk down the street with her because everyone would be staring at us. It wasn't like she got changed to go to work, and no one had cars then, so at the end of her daily grind she'd totter off down the King's Road and get on a bus back to the countryside or wherever the fuck it was that she lived. She'd have her tits hanging out on the bus in all of this rubber gear! You could probably go to work in a bank looking like that now, but in early 1975 people had never seen anything like it. I guess she loved the attention, but I used to think, 'Fuck me! She's got some balls walking around like that.'

What Vivienne and Malcolm were doing with Sex was tapping into the sense a lot of people had at that time of just wanting something to happen – music had got so two-bob and Britain seemed so fucking grey and boring. If no one else was gonna do it, why shouldn't they get something going for themselves? The Sixties was yesterday's news by then, and with glam kind of dying away, what better way to cause a fucking stink than covering the walls with pornographic quotes and taking perverts' rubber gear out of the closet and putting it straight onto the fucking high street (or the King's Road, in this case)? Without people like Jordan around to put their ideas into action, Sex – and maybe punk too – would've been just another art school conspiracy. It would never have left the drawing board.

It did get pretty weird at the shop when all the bondage gear was in there. The rubber stuff wasn't my thing from a sexual point of view – it just did nothing for me. Even later on, when Linda the Dominatrix got involved with Sex and Sid and some of the other people around the band got into hanging out at her dungeon, I never really got into it.

As you may have noticed, I'm not a prude, but even I have my limits, and some of the shit that went on in Sex at that time shocked even me. I'd be in there with Chrissie or Jordan (I never shagged her, in case any-one was wondering – Adam Ant turned out to be more her type) and you'd get all these MP types in pinstripe suits sneaking in when they got off work. They'd go into the dressing room with some latex on and have a pedal in there. That was like a common thing with the pervy toffs. I guess they learnt it at public school. Glen was always moaning about hav-ing to clean up the bodily fluids.

Sex was designed to be a fashion statement, not a fetish shop, but I guess those cunts don't mind where they do it. If you build it, they will cum. I never knew who any of them were till people told me afterwards: they were just men with briefcases as far as I was concerned (unlike the one I carried up and down the King's Road, theirs actually had stuff in them, even if it was only Vaseline and a gimp mask), but I do remember the newsreader Reginald Bosanquet being around a few times. He was massively obsessed with Jordan, and sometimes when he was reading the news on TV in the evening he'd wink at the camera as a code to show her he was wearing rubber pants in her honour. In terms of what Malcolm was trying to achieve by showing the British establishment in its true colours, that was probably one of his proudest moments.

The one group of people who were even less into bondage than I was were the Teds. They used to love hanging out at Let It Rock, but they got really pissed off when it stopped being all about them. There were a few ugly scenes in the early days of Sex, and later on the whole Teds vs punks thing festered into real violence – several people in and around the Pistols, including Cookie, would get glassed or stabbed by Teds at one time or another. (I was lucky: I escaped injury with the help of the Cloak.) That violence tended to be seen as an old-fashioned mods vs rockers type of thing, but really it was more specific than that. The Teds hated the punks because they thought the punks had nicked their shop, and they also probably felt they'd been betrayed by Malcolm. Obviously they weren't the last people to feel that way.

I didn't have to model any of the rubber-wear once the band was in the public eye. Malcolm and Vivienne never told us to wear anything in particular, we just helped ourselves to what we wanted and they either charged us for it afterwards or didn't. I liked the T-shirts, though – the tits and the naked young boys smoking cigarettes and the Cambridge rapist mask and the cowboys with their cocks out. I got that the point of those was to shock people. Glen and Bernie Rhodes took offence at some of them, but I never did.

I didn't know what Malcolm's deal was, sexually. I got the feeling that he'd had some gay encounters, but I never felt that was what was driving him. He and Vivienne were like a proper couple, but the vibe between them wasn't very sexual. In theory McLaren liked all the earthy, elemental stuff, but it was mostly bravado. It wasn't about actual experience.

Sometimes when I did things he'd be shocked and get all giggly like a little schoolboy. I suppose that's why I never took him too seriously in that area. Even when he would fuck about with kiddie porn shit, which I suppose I could've related to experiences I'd been through and found upsetting, it never bothered me. Probably for the same reason I never thought twice about wearing the clothes with swastikas on them – because at the time it felt more important to shake things up a bit than to worry about hurting other people's feelings.

The first time the name 'Sex Pistols' appeared was on one of those T-shirts. I think Malcolm and Vivienne and Bernie designed it together and the idea was for it to be a kind of manifesto, so one side was 'Hates' and the other side was 'Loves' and the slogan at the top said, 'You're gonna wake up one morning and *know* what side of the bed you've been lying on . . .' There were long lists of things you were meant to like and not like – I hadn't heard of most of them, to be honest, and I think it was a matter of trying to get an 'Us against Them' vibe going more than anything specific. Anyway, there in the middle of the 'Loves' was 'Kutie Jones and his SEX PISTOLS'.

Obviously I was happy to be a Kutie, but I wasn't too sure about the SEX PISTOLS element. It just sounded a bit gay. It wasn't the idea of people thinking we were buckled that bothered me – as I've said, I had no anxieties about my sexuality, because I loved birds and at that time I was fucking so many of them I was like a walking dildo – it was more what choosing that name would say about the band. As I remember, the only one of us who really liked it at first was Wally, which was a bit cruel as he was on his way out by then.

Malcolm had been on at me for a while to take playing the guitar a bit more seriously. At first I think it was just to give me something to do with my hands so I wouldn't look such a knob onstage. But then I started picking it up quite quickly from watching what Wally was doing. I still had no idea that I was going to end up being the guitarist – I just got shoved in that direction and miraculously it worked out. I don't want to get all new-agey, but it is funny how things fall into place sometimes. Like with Iggy Pop – he was the drummer of his band at first, then all of a sudden he was the frontman because that was just how it was meant to be.

It was when Malcolm returned to England from his fucking car crash of trying to manage the New York Dolls in America that he really started to push me on the guitar front. He should've had his tail between his legs, but I think that failure made him keener to get involved with us, because now he had something to prove. He bought me Sylvain Sylvain's white Gibson Les Paul with the pin-up sticker on it – I think the band gave it to him in place of money they owed him, or maybe he nicked it, I'm not sure. Either way, even though I loved the New York Dolls, this didn't register with me as a big deal at the time. I knew a Les Paul was the best guitar for rock 'n' roll, and a few of them had already passed through my hands by then; I wasn't like, 'Oh, thank you, God – the sacred flame.'

This event probably got talked up a bit by Malcolm over the years because it made him look like Merlin getting the sword for King Arthur. The idea of him bringing someone over from America to be the new singer of the band – one of the Dolls, Richard Hell, Gladys Knight? I don't know who the fuck it was meant to be – was another of his imaginary managerial master strokes that got talked up out of all proportion. McLaren was notorious for changing the facts to fit his version of events afterwards; it was something he was really known for.

Another one who liked to edge a bit further into the spotlight every time he told a story was the *NME* journalist Nick Kent – I guess everyone wants a piece of the myth. Malcolm talked a good game about doing things a different way to other bands, but from the beginning he was always very keen to keep in with the music press, and when Nick Kent – who was a well-known rock writer at the time – came down to the Riverside Studios a couple of times, we assumed it was just to get him on-side. It was only years later that we'd learn how close we'd come to having one of the great musical geniuses of the twentieth century in our ranks.

Nick did know a few chords – I was quite impressed with an open tuning in G he showed me which made your guitar-playing sound a bit like Keith Richards'. The only problem was, Nick's Keith Richards addiction was totally out of control. He'd stand there doing his Keith Richards pose, his body all sloppy, just like his hero's. It was a joke. If Keith had wandered by and seen it he'd have said, 'What the fuck are you doing, man?' . . . shortly before asking me for his fucking coat back.

Nick Kent went out with Chrissie for a while. He was very jealous (probably with good reason, to be honest) and he came into Sex to be a cunt to her once. She stopped working there after that, which was a shame, as far as I was concerned, so there was a bit of 'what goes around comes around' about it when Sid had a go at him at the 100 Club a while later. All that was still way ahead of us at this point, though.

For the moment, our biggest problem was what to do about Wally. Before he went off to New York with the Dolls, Malcolm had already been telling us we should give him the push. It was harsh, but we had to do it. With hindsight, getting rid of Wally was absolutely the best thing to do. He didn't look right, for a start. I'm not saying he was an ugly geezer, but let's just say he lacked the classical bone structure of some other members of the band. Plus he wore glasses, which is just not accept-able in a rock 'n' roll guitarist. Don't blame me, I don't make the rules.

One thing I knew for sure was that the band wasn't going anywhere without me. I was pretty much homeless then, and music was all I had. It was the only thing in my life apart from stealing and sex that I'd ever invested any kind of consistent energy in. So if I wasn't going to sing, I was going to play the guitar – that was all there was to it. Something had to fucking happen for us, even if we didn't know exactly what it was yet.

There was stuff around for us to bounce off, like *Futurama*, the second Be-Bop Deluxe album, a big favourite with both me and Cookie by then. Bill Nelson was a great guitarist who really had the Bowie look down when we saw him live at the Fulham Greyhound. Pub rock was coming through more strongly by that time, too. I remember seeing Dr Feelgood at the Kensington – that place was just a boozer with a tiny little stage at the end. There was also a band called The Winkies who no one thinks about much any more that I thought were pretty good. They played on that Brian Eno song 'Seven Deadly Finns', and they had this guitarist who thought he was Keith Richards but had a little bit more to back that fantasy up than Nick Kent ever did. I remember looking up at him play-ing his black Les Paul through an Ampeg amp and thinking, 'Maybe I could do that.'

I must have liked them, because I didn't follow their Ford Transit after they loaded all their gear into it at the end of the gig and nick their equipment. Others weren't so lucky. All in all, when you looked around at the competition, there was nothing out there to really scare the shit out of anyone. That was going to be our job. All we needed now was a singer.

15. THE BOY LOOKED AT JOHNNY

Malcolm used to like exaggerating how close Richard Hell or Sylvain Sylvain came to joining the band, but there was one plan to import a vocalist that did almost happen. The source was a lot closer to home, but still just as unlikely as the gutter outside CBGB's. It was Scotland, where Midge Ure, who'd end up doing Band Aid nine years later, was singing with a second-division Bay-City-Rollers-style band called Slik.

Malcolm and Bernie convinced themselves Midge was the guy, to the extent of going all the way up to Glasgow to meet him, but when they arrived he'd just signed a record contract, so there was nothing doing. The joke was on him in the end, cos he ended up being in Matlock's band The Rich Kids before joining Ultravox. Good luck, Midge, and see you in the Rock & Roll Hall of Fame . . . or maybe not.

When it comes to the mechanics of how John Lydon finally came to fill our singer-shaped vacancy, that's another traumatic event in my life where my memory checks out a bit. So I've decided, since he's dead now and can't charge me for it (I reckon he still owes me, anyway), to use the account Malcolm gave when he came on my radio show in 2005. He was just hanging around in LA at the time – I'm not sure what he was up to, but I'd bumped into him a couple of times since the court case two decades before, and there'd never been any bad blood between the two of us, so the interview seemed a natural thing to do. To be honest, it didn't seem like too big a deal at the time. It was only after his death a few years later that it started to feel that way, and now I'm really glad we did it.

No one can deny Malcolm is a great storyteller, and while he should sometimes have had his poetic licence endorsed, this version of what happened does pretty much tally with the occasional fragments I can remember. I should add to anyone reading this out loud that he also did a pretty good impression of Vivienne – you can still hear it if you look the interview up on YouTube.

'So we were left with this name, Kutie Jones – that was you – and his Sex Pistols, that was the rest: Cook, Matlock, whoever else you could grab and put in the band. You weren't faring that well, so it was decided – I think at a certain point in the car going back from Brighton – that we would audition for a singer. I was going to stand in the shop every day and watch people come in, and various individuals were auditioned as a result. The guy who ended up being the lead singer of The Damned, and this group called The London SS which was the group Mick Jones was in before The Clash – they were looked at for possible singers, Chrissie Hynde at one point was considered . . .

'We didn't find anybody, at least I didn't. But Vivienne kept telling me, "Look out for this guy called John – he's very good-looking and he's very interesting in the way he wears his clothes." I sat in the store looking for him when in came a guy – a very, very obstreperous creature – who was looking for a pair of brothel creepers in white suede. I didn't have them in his size . . . but I could order them for

him the week after. I asked him, as I was asking everyone who came in the shop at that time, "Do you sing?" and he said, "Nah – only out of tune." I thought, "Alright, we'll test you." I told him, "If you want these shoes, I may even give them to you if you promise to head down to this pub round the corner called the Roebuck where you can meet the rest of the band tonight."

'He did, and typically of his character he turned up with a group of friends that even then he probably thought of as his bodyguards because he didn't want to arrive anywhere alone. I sat at the bar talking to a few of the local characters – fashion victims, drug victims – and let you get on with it. Then you came up and said, "Look Malcolm, if he keeps on 'ollering at me, I'm gonna beat the shit out of him. You've got to get him down to the shop now, cos I don't really know if we want to be involved with this guy."

'So I went over and dragged him down to the shop. At that point I became very officious and grabbed – I don't know why we had it – a broken shower-head device that could behave like a microphone. I gave it to John and told him to stand at the end of the shop. Then I put a song on the jukebox – I think it was Alice Cooper's "Eighteen" – and said, "Behave as if you're onstage and sing along to it, otherwise this guy that's sitting next to me now, Steve Jones, is going to beat the living daylights out of you." Then you and Paul Cook and I think Glen – the Saturday boy who'd become the bass player – stood back by the jukebox as we all watched John perform.

'I remember he began to look like the Hunchback of Notre Dame. He pulled out a handkerchief and blew his nose, he was spitting and coughing and talking about "sex in the grass is free", I don't know, God knows what he was talking about but he was trying to imitate and scream along. He was somewhat embarrassed and vulnerable

and strange. I laughed because I thought it was really funny and brilliant. Paul Cook said, "I'd better go back to the brewery and carry on with my job," but he was always like that. You went along with it. I think you just thought, "Why not?"

'Suddenly I put you all into a rehearsal room somewhere in Rotherhithe. That's what happened the following week, except he turned up and you guys didn't. Maybe you weren't certain about him, I don't know. Either way, then he was pissed off and he stayed at home . . . eventually we convinced him to come back to the band on the basis that you were going to get very serious and rehearse with him. That's when we dropped the Kutie Jones and it became just Sex Pistols . . . young, sexy assassins, that's what you were, and you were going to compete with the Bay City Rollers.

'That was the idea, cos they were on top of the charts at the time – they were the nubile, young, good-looking kids. You were coming in with a very different angle – far, far more cutting edge . . . less a pop sound but more something that was going to be completely new, more a sound that would really hurt and annoy people, a sound that would be stripped of all its slickness.'

I do remember Malcolm saying that about the Bay City Rollers. Tam Paton, the very sleazy geezer who managed the Rollers, got done for being a nonce a few years later, although he got off another set of charges when the rhythm guitarist Pat McGlynn accused him of rape. I don't think he fucked all of them, but whatever went on in that band certainly wasn't pretty – you could see it on their faces as they got older. The singer definitely didn't age gracefully, but then not everyone is lucky enough to have my classical good looks.

Fast-forward again back to us talking on my radio show. We stopped for a commercial break and Malcolm said he'd forgotten a bit, then added the following, which definitely had a grain of truth in it, although that grain was certainly no bigger than the pinch of salt you should probably take it with.

'What I forgot was when the Sex Pistols were finally formed I went back to see Vivienne and said, "I've found this John and he's gonna be all right – you were right, Vivienne." She said, "I'll come up to Chelsea and have a drink with him. I'd like to meet him because he's a very handsome boy." She arrived at the pub in the King's Road and came up to see me at the bar. She said, "That's not the John I thought I told you about – that's another John. You've got the wrong guy." I said, "He's OK, he's fine, he's got something." Then she replied, "You're gonna have a lot of trouble with him – you're never gonna hear the last of this. Oh well, you've made your bed so you're going to have to bloody lie in it!"

'At that point she walked out of the pub. The John she was talking about came into the shop a few weeks later. His name of course was John Simon Ritchie and he later became Sid Vicious. He wanted to join the group from the beginning – he said he could play the saxophone. I said, "We don't need a saxophone – we've got enough people in the group, it's fine." So instead he became the agent provocateur and invented the pogo.'

The way these things work out sometimes does make you wonder if God was a punk rocker, or do things just happen the way they happen? The timing certainly worked out pretty well with Matlock having crawled out of the 430 King's Road woodwork, me getting lobbed onto lead guitar and starting to learn really quickly, then John coming along, and it was like 'here's our guy'. The band was a great combination and the fact that none of us except me and Cookie got on too well was a big part of that, because the gaps between us were what the music sparked across. There's no formula for how these things happen. Look at The Beatles – they got rid of the good-looking drummer and got Ringo in, and that didn't work out too badly.

I was the one who ended up christening John 'Rotten' because of the terrible state of his teeth, and that kind of stuck, but I'd seen him coming into Sex a few times before the audition and I thought he looked fucking great. He was one of those guys who just have something. It was the same with Sid, who I'd also noticed hanging around the shop a few times before John joined the band – presumably that was when Vivienne had clocked him. He always looked fantastic, too. You'd see the two of them walking down the King's Road and they looked like they were stars already, even though no one knew who they were yet.

It wasn't just John's look that drew you to him – the dyed green hair and the safety pins (way before Vivienne started using them) and the 'I hate Pink Floyd' T-shirt he'd vandalised himself – he also had a great face. That set all the other elements off – his excellent bone structure. And a lot of the stuff that would later become the punk uniform, he did seem to do first. Obviously there'd been a bit of the spiky hair going on with Bowie, but that was more of a glamour thing, whereas with Rotten it was all on a do-it-yourself level, which was what made it really stand out.

Later on I'd see pictures of Richard Hell doing similar things a little bit earlier, but I don't think Rotten had seen those pictures, and I guarantee that if you asked him, he'd tell you he hadn't. Maybe if you were thinking a certain way about how the world was in the early 1970s, that was a natural style to start dressing in. Either way, it was a great look.

Americans claiming they started everything would get quite tedious as punk went on. The New York guys were definitely up to something, but it was different to what we were doing. Of course we'd been influenced by The Stooges and the New York Dolls, but no more than we had by Roxy Music or the Faces. And I remember us hearing the Ramones album for the first time when we were already rehearsing. We certainly didn't see them and think, 'Oh, we've got to be like this band now.' The funny thing was, I became friendly with Johnny Ramone a while later and I remember this one geezer, a journalist called Legs McNeil, who was the leader of the 'Oh, we Americans were here first' brigade – Johnny absolutely hated that geezer. He didn't want anything to do with him or his bullshit.

Back to the other John, though. Both Malcolm and Glen used to moan about how he always had to have his gang of mates with him, but the only ones I really remember him bringing around in the early days were a girl from his college whose name I can't recall and John Grey, who was more of an art school guy. Rotten never showed up with his Arsenal 'erbert mates, even though I knew he had some because that was what his brothers were into.

There was a bit of antagonism between me and him from the off, but not as much as Malcolm implied (he's still doing the divide-and-rule thing, even from beyond the grave). It was just the way he behaved at the audition that got on my wick. I thought he wasn't taking the whole thing seriously and it kind of bothered me that he wasn't trying to sing to get the gig. With hindsight, the fact that I wanted him to make an effort – 'OK, show us what you've got as far as being a singer is concerned' – was the reason I was the wrong man for the job and he was the right one. Because I was still from that school of trying to be like Rod Stewart, whereas he was right to be taking the piss, because that's Rotten in a nutshell, and that was exactly what the Sex Pistols needed.

On top of the fact that it was my band and he was coming into it from the outside, John was probably a bit intimidated by me being physically stronger. To compensate for that, he would use his intellect to put me down a lot, which he could do because he was very smart whereas I wasn't the brightest of kids and had never learnt anything at school. He still does that now, but luckily for me I've reached the point where I don't take offence any more. He says so many things that if it was someone else saying them it would probably hurt my feelings, but coming from John it's like, 'Oh, it's just him.'

I don't know if he and Malcolm ever really liked each other very much. John certainly didn't have the same kind of relationship with him that I did – I'd always be open to Malcolm's suggestions and wanting to know what we were doing next, whereas from the start he and John were more like rivals. I think they were possibly a bit too similar, and Rotten probably sussed him out early on as a bit of a bullshitter – which of course Malcolm was, but you know what they say: it takes one to know one.

However different their music might be, all bands are basically the fucking same. The reason I still – to this day – love watching documentaries about bands like the Eagles (I know they're technically just Eagles, but that looks stupid written down) is that I can totally relate to them. The personalities involved and the reasons for the tensions between them never seem to change.

The singer – because that job requires the kind of person who wants to be in the front going, 'Look at me, look at me' – will almost always be very insecure, and usually a bit of a cunt. Then there's the guitarist, who wants to get all the pussy, and there's always at least one weird introvert in the band. For me, in the Pistols, it was Cookie. It's quite unusual for that person to be the drummer, but that was good for us, because drummers are the ones who tend to come unstuck. I think it's cos no one really gives a shit about them and they're just sitting out the back. It gets to them after a while, the same way it does with goalkeepers in football.

One thing about our band that was unique was the way Malcolm and Vivienne's shop brought us all together. From me and to a lesser extent Cookie hanging out there because I didn't really have anywhere else to go, to Matlock being the Saturday boy, to John coming in there looking for his brothel creepers – Sex was the Mecca that drew everyone in. If we were going to take that vibe out into the world, we needed to find a place our music could call home in the same way.

Our first couple of attempts at finding rehearsal spaces were never going to fit that bill. First there was some hippie dump south of the river in Rotherhithe that Rotten has never stopped moaning about us not turning up to. Then there was the Rose and Crown in Wandsworth, just a pub that some chancer was pretending was a rehearsal studio. There wasn't any kind of soundproofing, so you'd get nothing but complaints, and it was on a roundabout – it felt like you were practising in the middle of the road. Everything about that place was depressing: getting there, setting all the gear up. It was awful and I hated it. In fact, it scarred me for life as far as rehearsing was concerned . . .

Well, that's my excuse anyway.

16. THE PRINCE OF DENMARK STREET

That first few weeks after Rotten joined the band in August 1975 were a real nause. We'd lost all the comfort and convenience of Riverside Studios the minute Wally got the boot, so any time we wanted to practise, we had to drive round everyone's houses and load up a rented van with all the gear I'd nicked – my shag-wagon wasn't big enough any more. Me and Glen and Cookie would have to spend a couple of hours setting it all up. If Rotten turned up for a couple of hours in the middle, that was as good as it got. Then we'd have to waste another couple of hours taking all the gear down, loading it back in the van and finally getting rid of the van again after driving the stuff back to wherever we were stashing it. The traffic in London wasn't as bad then as it is now, but it was still a fucking nightmare.

Luckily – probably in the nick of time, looking back on it – Glen saw an advert which this guy who used to tour-manage for Badfinger had put in the paper for a rehearsal space to rent at 6–7 Denmark Street. It was right in the heart of the old Tin Pan Alley, where all the guitar shops were. Malcolm promised him a load of money, which he may or may not have finally given him. I hope he did, because he was a really nice old guy.

His name was Bill Collins, and I only recently found out he was the dad of Lewis Collins from *The Professionals* – which was a funny coincidence, cos that's what me and Cookie would end up calling our next band a few years later.

Things had gone to shit for Badfinger due to a load of record company bollocks. One of them committed suicide a few months before we moved in and his best mate in the band – who found his body – would follow suit a few years later. I used to wonder if the first guy had done the deed in Denmark Street and that was why we'd got the place cheap, but apparently he hanged himself in his garage in Surrey. Either way, it was an ill wind that blew the Sex Pistols a load of good. Not only did we now have somewhere right in the middle of town where we could leave our gear set up the whole time, I actually had somewhere to fucking live.

Of course, no one was meant to live there, but there was never any doubt that I was going to. I'd been kipping on people's couches for long enough and I was hardly going to pass up the chance for a place I could call my own. There was a bookshop round the front and you'd come through there and up some steps, out into the open yard and then into this funny little square building out the back which had a downstairs – where all our gear went – and an upstairs which wasn't a liveable space when we got there but I made it one soon enough. There was already an Ascot water heater and I put a bed and a little black-and-white TV in and generally ponced the whole thing up. Eh voila – chez Steve.

I fucking loved being in Denmark Street. It's probably my favourite place I've ever lived. It was right up the West End, in the middle of all the action. You only had to walk out the front door and all the brasses would be there – I was living the dream!

It was dead quiet in there at night, too, so you could even sleep really well. I think John resented me having my own place in the middle of

Soho, but it was all right for him – he was still living at home with his mum and dad. He used to crash upstairs sometimes anyway – Cookie had a fight with him up there once, as did Glen, whose folks had moved out to the distant suburbs so it was harder for him to get home than it used to be, especially once he started at St Martin's art college just over the road. Chrissie used to come and stay over too sometimes but obviously that wasn't so much about sleeping.

There was also a period when I was knocking about in Ladbroke Grove with this bird with big tits – not the one who used to get onstage with Hawkwind, a different biker groupie chick I had a little thing with. She was a proper greaser and we'd buy speed off Lemmy and lurk in those boozers down Portobello Road where the Pink Fairies and Hawkwind and the people that became Motörhead used to hang out.

That's a part of West London a lot of people associate with good times, but I've never really liked it. Although while we're in Notting Hill I should probably mention my uncredited cameo appearance in a film which was shot there around that time. It's a British gangster flick called *The Squeeze* which has Stacy Keach and the comedian Freddie Starr in it, and at one point early on you can see me walking through Portobello Market wearing a Hawaiian shirt (the West-Coast-A&R-man look's only appearance on celluloid). Cookie saw it by chance on late-night TV once and nearly fell off his fucking sofa. Anyway, I digress.

This bird I was shagging lived in a squat in Ladbroke Grove with all these biker dudes. When I'd go round there I remember thinking 'Fuck this shit. This is not my cup of tea at all.' Obviously the whole squatting lifestyle would become very associated with punk later on, but it wasn't my scene in any way. It was dirty, the houses were always shitholes, and I found the squalor of it really depressing.

I need my surroundings to be a certain way – I like to be tidy and I like nice things. I don't want to be sleeping in a place where you don't know what's going to happen from one day to the next. Even the fact that it was illegal wasn't for me – I suppose if you're as prolific a law-breaker as I am, you don't want your home to be another possible entry on your ever extending rap sheet. I know that technically what I was doing in Denmark Street was squatting, but you wouldn't have known that to look at the place. I'm very organised and clean by nature – I guess it's the mod in me.

As well as my first proper home as an adult, Denmark Street gave me something else I really needed, which was somewhere to practise the guitar. When you've got nowhere to kip apart from your mates' sofas, opportunities to bone up on your bar chords are few and far between. Plugging in your Gibson Les Paul and playing along to The Stooges' *Fun House* doesn't tend to go down too well with the mums and dads. Now I finally had a place of my own, I could hammer along to 'TV Eye' and 'Dirt' to my heart's content and at any volume I wanted. The New York Dolls' first album was my other favourite for playing along to – cos it was simple and I could grasp it, it was the perfect thing to learn from.

I would play the guitar by myself for literally hours upstairs at Denmark Street – just figuring out how it worked. If you're wondering how someone with full-on ADHD and the attention span of a fucking mosquito managed to concentrate for long enough to become *Rolling Stone's* 97th greatest rock guitarist of all time, well, the answer is very simple: speed. Not sulphate, but the diet pills you get on prescription from doctors. Some people call them black bombers, others call them black beauties, but either way, you'd better get plenty of Mandrax to take afterwards if you ever want to get to fucking sleep.

Malcolm was very big on wanting everyone to be skinny so the band would look the part, and I think that's how I persuaded him to hook me up. He'd send me down to a quack doctor on Harley Street to get them:

sixty pills and sixty Mandrax each time. All the models and the people out of *Who's Who* went to this guy for their diet pills – he'd be in there writing prescriptions all day long. Once I turned up and the guy was so tired from all the bullshit scripts he was writing that he was actually nodding out on the counter. I think he got struck off in the end, but not before he'd given my guitar-playing the chemical leg-up it had been crying out for.

Those black beauties weren't a drug you'd take just for a laugh – the level of focus they gave you was beyond anything normal. You'd hear stories of housewives that had done one too many being up all night washing dishes or cleaning their floors with a toothbrush, just completely obsessing over the tiniest little detail. I could relate, as I approached learning the guitar in pretty much the same spirit.

Don't get me wrong, I loved music and I had an ear for it; it wasn't just a mechanical thing. But I honestly don't think I could have become a professional musician if I hadn't had the pills to help me along. A lot of people who get sober will tell you that drink or drugs did nothing but fuck up their lives – and they may well be right – but in my case I don't think I'd have got anywhere without them. Some of the best things that have happened to me have been largely if not entirely down to drink and/or drugs. That's why this shit's so hard to give up.

I didn't generally like speed, but I loved the feeling those pills gave me. The excitement of knowing I could actually focus on something for once would be hard to get across to anyone who hadn't struggled in school like I did. It ain't easy to learn an instrument properly and left to my own devices I'd probably have got bored and lost interest. I just wouldn't have had the patience to stick with it – whereas all I had to do was pop a couple of those pills and boom! One hundred per cent attention. And the quicker the progress I made, the more I got into it. It was pretty much like Chuck

Berry said in his classic hit 'Jonesy Be Good' – I may not have learnt to read or write so well, but I could play that guitar just like ringing a bell.

I knew I was getting better, but my band-mates took a bit of convincing, especially Cookie. He was still doing his apprenticeship and I think it was pulling him away from us. He said he wouldn't go forward with the band unless we got someone in who could actually play the guitar properly – which I couldn't quite yet, even though I was getting there. Obviously I took that a bit personally at the time, but I'm over it now.

Cookie's very much a playing-it-safe kind of guy – he's the opposite to me in that regard. I'll dive in headfirst, but he always wants to know all the ifs and buts of what's going to happen. I think Rotten hates that about him, but you've got to have a balance for the chemistry to be right, haven't you? A band with four hotheads in it isn't going to get very far.

We put an advert in the *Melody Maker* looking for a 'whizz kid guitar player' who was twenty years old or under and 'not worse looking than Johnny Thunders'. We put that in to keep the Yes types away – though, with hindsight, jamming with Steve Howe might've given me something to bounce off – and it seemed to work because very few real musos showed up.

Basically there were a few urchins and some total fucking clowns. We auditioned all sorts – about thirty or forty people altogether. My favourite of the real idiots was a guy called Fabian Quest – I know, it's a great name, isn't it? He showed up with all these fancy pedals and whatnot but the shame of it was this silly cunt couldn't play a note. There was also a kind of hippie-rock guy right near the end who could play his arse off. The only downside with him was he was obviously high on smack while he was doing it. I wish I could find out who he was and whether he went on to do anything else afterwards, because he was an excellent guitarist.

Even though it felt like a massive waste of time while it was going on,

In the early Nineties, I went back to Benbow Road for the first time since I'd gone to America. The place had come up a little, but once a shithole, always a shithole

Riverside Gardens from the other side of the flyover, right by the nonce underpass

Teddy Boys – my real dad, Don Jarvis, is on the far left. That's where my fashion sense comes from

My mum having a laugh – it did happen

Showing off the silky football skills that would later see me turning out for Hollywood United alongside Vinnie Jones, the actor Anthony LaPaglia and Chelsea's Frank Leboeuf

Before I discovered food

A narrow escape at Selfridges – at the time I didn't realise how young I was

This monkey you could get your picture taken with at a show at Olympia was having a good feed off the lice on my head

The uniform looks good, but I
didn't learn a thing

Me and Jimmy Macken out
on the town

Pinball Wizards

Recording at Wessex studios with my Flying V – don't think much of this guitar actually made it onto the album

The Pistols on the 'Anarchy' tour

Filming the video for 'God Save The Queen'. I like the way we look like waxworks at Madame Tussauds

John 'Boogie' Tiberi took this one – it must have been abroad because they didn't have bidets in England

Getting on a plane to go to Sweden – you can see it's Viking Airlines

Here comes trouble

Gaye Advert menaces me with her snake, but sometimes it's the snakes you can't see that are the most dangerous

Me 'n' Cookie – passport booths were the only place you could do punk rock selfies

At the place in Bell Street that Paul and I shared. Cookie is rolling a spliff

That's McLaren in drag, filming *The Swindle* in Chesham – Malcolm makes a lovely woman

Only the two original Pistols still standing by this stage. This was shot right by Shepherd's Bush roundabout – note the corrugated iron in the bottom right hand corner

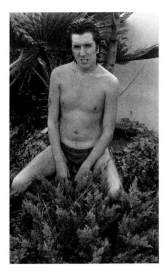

Hi, my name's Steve. I'm new in town. I'm looking for a hot meal, a shower and a bed for the night

Jimmy Page gets to meet one of his heroes at the ARMS benefit at the Forum, 12 December 1983

Me and Chrissie tearing it up in LA, March 1984

Chequered Past rehearsal – this is not a face you'll see me pull often

As on point as our Eighties fashion was, Chequered Past was also about the music

Backstage with Chequered Past – who says real men don't use guyliner?

Double dating with Nina Huang, Iggy and Iggy's bird of the moment

Sadly no photographic evidence remains of my 'Manager of Poco' fashion phase, but here is my 'Poldark' look as some small compensation

Onstage with Iggy – starting to get the Fabio vibe going here

Alone in the desert with
my black Gibson

My dogs – first there were Buster and Winston, then just Winston II
(the boxer – the sweetest dog)

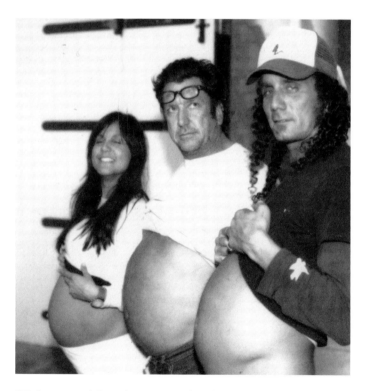

With my good friends Laurie and Richard and the twins (in the
foetal stage) – sorry you didn't make the picture, Jesse Jo

With Paul Simonon on our bikes in the Mojave Desert

Nina looking cute

The Neurotic Outsiders, 1996. This was a great band, but I guess it wasn't meant to be

Why am I so good looking?

1996 Reunion Tour in LA at the once-known-as Universal Amphitheatre

With Vivienne, whose fashion sense has also developed since the punk era

I'm wearing a chastity belt under this

Crystal Palace, 2002. After the show, I went to Chelsea Bridge Hot Dog Stand to stuff my face. I'm standing where many a ted and greaser stood. I wouldn't dare to walk past this gaff in 1977

Here I am in all my glory, a true perfumed ponce

A rare photo of me taking a bath with some friends.
A far cry from the tin bath

The Big 5–0 with Laurie and Jesse Jo

Anita, me manager, or me uva
muva

Me at the station on *Jonesy's Jukebox* with some of my guests – (clockwise from top left) Dave Grohl, John Taylor, Henry Rollins, Jack Black, Linda Perry, Gary Oldman, Gene Simmons and Iggy Pop with Josh Homme

this audition process worked out really well, because it finally convinced Cookie that I was the only game in town, at least for the kind of band we were going to be. My style of guitar-playing was shaped by lack of knowledge and lack of experience, which was why it complemented John's vocals so well, because he had exactly the same raw, natural quality. Cookie could just about hold a beat by then and Matlock played a bit of bass, but as far as me and John were concerned we were learning as we went along. That was what made the whole thing such a blast.

People often comment on the fact that a lot of the covers we played when we were working out the kind of band we were going to be – 'No Fun', 'Don't Give Me No Lip, Child', '(I'm Not) Your Stepping Stone' – had the word 'No' in the title. That was nothing to do with McLaren, who as I've said didn't have much input into the musical side of things. It was partly coincidental and partly down to Rotten's attitude. Anything that was remotely positive or involved any kind of happiness or love or appreciation made him want to vomit; that cunt never knew the meaning of the word *obrigado*. But the way he'd sneer his way through the lyrics really gave those old songs, especially cheesy ones like Dave Berry's 'Don't Gimme No Lip, Child' (the original of which I fucking hated) a bit of extra bite.

One more positive record which was a really big deal to us but never got as much credit as it should've was the first Jonathan Richman and the Modern Lovers album. Judy Nylon had an early copy that she used to play me, and it felt like a much bigger deal than any of the other East Coast 'punk' records, all of which seemed to be made by guys (or women, in Patti Smith's case) with long hair who'd been around a while and were much older than us. I didn't like the Patti Smith album at all when it came out – I wasn't drawn to her in the slightest. Richman's 'Roadrunner' was better than anything that lot could do, which is why the Sex Pistols ended up covering that song, not some Television tune with a twenty-minute guitar solo.

When it came to writing original songs, Rotten's anger was an energy there too. The two main tunes of our own we had before he came along were 'Did You No Wrong' and 'Seventeen'/'Lazy Sod'. The second of those was the first proper song I'd ever come up with, and I remember Johnny moaning he couldn't read the lyrics in my handwriting (which was no wonder, as I still couldn't write properly), so he changed them to suit himself. Funnily enough, that was one of the first times I remember listening to the lyrics of a song with real attention, and that was because they were partly mine and I was straining to hear what Rotten had done to them. I never thought, 'What's he doing fucking my song up?' though. I could hear straight away that his version was better.

I think this is the only Sex Pistols song that wasn't a cover where the lyrics are kind of half and half; normally it's him doing all of them. It goes back and forth. 'We like noise it's our choice' – that is me. Not caring about long hair is him. 'I don't work, I just speed' is me, as is 'gotta lot to learn', but 'You're only twenty-nine' is 100 per cent Rotten. It's not quite Lennon and McCartney, but it's getting there. And once we had a couple of our own songs up and running, Glen and Johnny got down to work together (which I was fine with, as I'm a lazy sod, like the song said).

It didn't go smoothly. John always moaned about having to go round Glen's house. I don't think John liked where Matlock came from. Even though John was like an art student, where he lived with his family he was always around real 'erberts – the Arsenal mob. Not that he was directly involved with that stuff, but Glen just had this very different background of nice home, nice parents and nice school which really got on John's wick. That tension ended up going into the songs in a way that really worked out for us, but you couldn't necessarily have predicted that from the beginning.

I would love to have footage of us rehearsing right at the beginning. You'd see Cookie not feeling confident and worrying that he might be better sticking with his apprenticeship, I'd be lazing about in my Denmark Street kingdom, coming up with the odd riff, and John would be sitting in the corner writing lyrics – on those rare occasions when he and Matlock weren't at each other's throats. You couldn't fault Rotten for some of the words he came up with – for a nineteen-year-old to write 'Pretty Vacant' and 'Anarchy in the UK' was pretty fucking impressive. I might not have been too bothered about lyrics before, but I knew a fucking classic when I heard one.

The only problem was that as well as songs that would stand the test of time, you could see a few long-lasting grudges building up as well. The fact that Cookie and I were best friends outside the band was definitely an issue. Glen used to say we were like Fred Flintstone and Barney Rubble, but it was John who was really bothered by it. Because he is very insecure, he didn't like how close we were. He still doesn't like it forty years later. I can see now how the fact that when rehearsals finished me and Cookie would generally fuck off together must have left him feeling a bit isolated. You'd have thought maybe the two of them would hang out a bit more to balance the whole thing out, but it never worked that way, because they didn't really get on.

The one area where there was never any conflict, funnily enough, was over the money from songwriting. We agreed to split it equally from the off. John was different then – it was more 'one for all and all for one' in the early days, even if we were at each other's throats most of the time.

17. THE SPUNK TAPES

As far as making ends meet went in the early days at Denmark Street – from moving in there in September 1975, till our first proper gig a couple of months later – it was the same old story as far as I was concerned: i.e. I was still nicking stuff. Food, guitars . . . anything I could get my hands on, basically. I've seen things written about us being on the dole. Maybe some of the others were, but I certainly wasn't. The idea of signing on to get it just seemed too complicated and official. It was like the driving test, except you got money at the end. And anyway, I was doing all right under my own steam.

Later on, signing on would be seen as an integral part of the punk thing. But for me the dole was like squatting – shit I never wanted anything to do with. In an ideal world, I would've preferred a luxury pad where I could live in comfort with my leopardskin rug and my nice stereo. Denmark Street was still some way short of that – I do remember rats and mice being around. Malcolm even went down to Club Row pet market in the East End and got us a cat to help keep them under control.

We had to put net curtains up to get a bit of privacy because the

Hipgnosis people had their art studio just across the courtyard from us. They were the ones who did all the hippie album covers for Pink Floyd. One of the guys there, Peter Cristopherson, who'd end up being in Throbbing Gristle (when he called himself Sleazy), persuaded us to let him take weird photos of the band. He had a different theme for each of us. Mine was being an escaped convict in pyjamas with handcuffs on, Paul was covered in bullet wounds and John was in a straitjacket. The only one of us who wasn't happy was Glen, because he had to dress as a rent boy. I would say 'if the cap fits', but that cap actually wouldn't fit – Glen was way too strait-laced to do anything that interesting.

As well as wearing my fingers to the bone playing along with The Stooges, I'd been focusing my criminal activities on accumulating the stuff we'd need if we were going to finally play gigs. The twin reverb amp I had from the beginning – that's the same kind of key detail as the skinhead not wearing Brutus shirts. I went by what the Faces used, as only the best equipment was good enough for them. I always thought the reverb came from a band supporting Bob Marley and the Wailers at Hammersmith Odeon, but they didn't actually play there till 1976 so I must've got that timing a bit muddled. Maybe my trusty Cloak had developed a time machine function because I can remember clear as anything lurking backstage like it was where I was meant to be, then wandering on before Marley hit the stage and just wheeling it out the back door.

It's amazing I never got caught and given a good kicking but when people see you pushing an amp off the stage they just think you're a roadie. Another night at the Hammersmith Palais they used to have a revolving stage with two bands on it, basically session musicians playing covers. I'd go in there wearing a big coat and then when the stage turned round I'd go round the back and snaffle whatever I could get away with. That's where Cookie's cymbals came from – I just took them off the drum kit, put them under my coat and walked out across the dance floor. No one thought twice about it.

The star of our first proper gig – in terms of our equipment, at least – was my huge 100W Marshall amp. We were playing at St Martin's art college, which was conveniently just the other side of Tottenham Court Road from Denmark Street. The other band on were a pub-rock act called Bazooka Joe that had Adam Ant in (he wasn't dressing as a pirate at that stage), and when we had a go on their stuff at the soundcheck it didn't sound loud enough, so we crossed the road and wheeled in this giant fucking amp.

The gig was only in a small room and once that amp was cranked up it was so fucking loud it was like having a jumbo jet landing in your living room. I was so nervous that I had a couple of pints and a Mandrax before-hand to calm me down. The Mandy came on during 'Did You No Wrong' and I remember looking at John and leaning on him for a second as we were playing. He kind of pushed me away a little bit and at that moment I was thinking, 'This, right now, is the best thing in the world.' He was the singer and I loved playing in the band with him and the whole thing felt fucking great. Sadly, that feeling wouldn't return too many times, but at least I'd always have the memory.

It's possible that the volume was a bit much for people who weren't on Mandrax. Bazooka Joe hated us so much that they turned us off after a few numbers and there was a fight, but it didn't matter. Pandora's box was open for fucking business. We did another show the next night and soon Malcolm was sneaking us onto bills left, right and centre. Because he didn't want anyone to make the mistake of thinking we were just another new band on the pub-rock circuit, McLaren put a lot of energy into mak-ing sure we played different venues to the run-of-the-mill places other bands would play.

Whether this meant milking Glen's contacts to get us onto the art school circuit or booking us to play strip clubs or cinemas or fashion parties or lesbian bars, we'd always turn up and do the job the same way, whatever the surroundings. Once I'd got over the fear of that first gig, I found I didn't need the Mandrax any more. I was still so nervous I would usually throw up before each show, and I'd always have a few beers to get loosened up, but I was never drunk. In terms of playing, we were quite professional – we always did our best to make it sound as good as it could. We just wanted to do the songs – we didn't want any fucking nonsense.

Obviously we didn't get so much as a sniff of a roadie, so we had to hump all the stuff around ourselves. We had our own PA system that I'd nicked – I can't remember where I got it, but it was definitely out of someone's van. It was more or less just two big speaker cabinets plugged into an H and H head guitar amp. The amp was quite a modern piece of kit at the time; kind of transistorised, not valves or tubes or whatever they used to have before. We never had monitors – just these two speakers, the amp and a couple of mics going into it. I don't even think we miked Cookie's drum kit up, because if you're playing in these small gaffs you don't really need to.

You could see how much we were breaking new ground from all the weird fucking places we played. And the people we played with: because there weren't any other bands around like us, we'd find ourselves playing ridiculous gigs like supporting Screaming Lord Sutch in High Wycombe. I remember standing watching him, and the whole show was just a joke. There was a bit of a row because Johnny smashed up their microphones and then denied point-blank that he'd done it, even though loads of people – including the Lord himself – had seen him with their own eyes.

Doctors of Madness, up North somewhere, that was another busy one. They wouldn't let us use their monitors and that really gave me the hump. So when they were onstage I went into their dressing room and nicked all their wallets. And there might have been an incident under the stage while they were playing, with me shagging this big American college bird who was one of their penpals. What with all that and playing a set of our own, I was exhausted by the end of the night.

Because there was no scene for us to fit into, we had to make our own. If that meant playing a party at Andrew Logan's fancy warehouse near Tower Bridge one night – it was all arty toffs in that crowd, no 'erberts allowed (except us of course) – and then supporting Eddie & the Hot Rods at the Marquee two days later, that was exactly what we were gonna do. The Marquee show was a funny one because quite a few people saw us for the first time that night. A guy from the *NME* was there and everyone got quite excited about Rotten and Jordan throwing some chairs around. What they didn't realise was the reason he was doing it. Because we'd never played with monitors before, this was the first time he'd been able to hear himself properly. He was so shocked by how bad he thought he sounded that he totally freaked out. After that, he got more into the singing lessons Malcolm had booked him in for. I don't think they made any difference really, and thank fuck for that, because the way Johnny sang was a big part of our sound.

There's a little bit of Super-8 film footage Derek Jarman shot of us at the Logan thing – only about thirty seconds, but enough to get the idea. I think it's the first proper film of us playing live, and you can tell it's early because we all look about ten years old. I loved doing gigs like that, where there was something different. It was a lot more fun than Northern working men's clubs where everyone except maybe two or three people at each gig took an instant fucking dislike to us. Some of these weird gaffs full of Northerners with moustaches wearing flares were terrifying, to be honest. You know those cunts ain't gonna like you but when they start throwing things at the stage, it's not a good feeling.

On the upside, we had started to pick up a few fans along the way. There were the Bromley people for a start, who we didn't even think of as fans because they were totally cool and seemed on the same level as us. They weren't Johnny-come-latelys, they were Siouxsie-come-earlies. As well as Siouxsie there was Steve Chaos (who became Steve Severin once the Banshees got going), Billy Idol, a few others. All these people were around from the beginning and it was good to have them along. They started turning up to as many gigs as they could and it really made us feel like we were getting somewhere. The funny thing was, they all seemed to come from places I'd never been to round the outskirts of London – that was what John wrote the song 'Satellite' about. He wasn't talking down to them; well, he was, but they didn't mind, cos they hated the suburban shitholes they came from even more than he did.

The most exciting time is always just before everyone knows what something is. Ask any band when they were happiest and they'll probably tell you the greatest moments were just before they were known – when the *NME* do their first little interview with you and you're driving up and down the M1 in a Transit van. That's always going to be the purest, most genuine time, because you feel like you're all in it together. No one knows who you are, so you don't have that other element that creeps in later on: when you get famous, people change. We hadn't even done a record then, but I'd love to go back in time and see the four of us, driving up to those fucking working men's clubs with everyone spitting and throwing bottles at us.

If I'd been a kid at that time, Johnny Rotten would've probably been my idol the way Rod Stewart was to me five years before. He didn't just have a fantastic look, he also had a sharp wit and a real intellect, and no one else could get close to the lyrics he was writing. Even if some of the songs took a while to find their right titles – 'Anarchy in the UK' started off as 'Nookie', and 'No Future' eventually turned into 'God Save the Queen'.

I'm not trying to take the credit away from Glen for the original song-writing, but the reason he and I worked so well together was that he'd come up with something quite fiddly – the 'fucking Beatle chords' that drove John up the wall – and then I'd drive a bulldozer through it. You hear some complex chord progressions played exactly right and they go in one ear and out the other. Give 'em to someone who's not too bothered about sevenths and elevenths, and all of a sudden they work on a whole other level. Glen was so polite that if he'd played guitar on our records I don't think anyone would've noticed them. Once I took over the chords he'd originally written, we ended up with something that was brutally direct but not simple-minded; an iron fist in a velvet glove.

There was definitely a feeling that we were leading the pack, but a few upstarts were already snapping at our heels. Mick Jones came down to Denmark Street around the time of the auditions for a second guitar-ist. At the time he was dressing like Johnny Thunders or some other glam guy with the long hair and the platforms. He played along with us and it was exciting because he actually knew what he was doing, to a certain extent. The next time we saw him he'd got his hair cut and he was wear-ing shirts with writing all over them.

It was the same with Joe Strummer. He was in a band called The 101ers that we opened up for the first time we played at the Nashville. They were like a pub-rock thing but with more of a Fifties style to them – they reminded me of the early days of Let It Rock. I think we made him feel a bit out of date, though, cos he was converted straight away, and the next thing we knew, him and Jones were in The Clash together with Bernie Rhodes managing them.

I liked The Clash once they got going. And The Damned, Buzzcocks – even The Stranglers, though they never really got accepted because they were older. It was great to have some decent new bands around for a change. We were the tip of the spearhead, but they weren't far behind, and I never looked down on them for starting after us. After all, there was fuck all else going on, so I never blamed anyone for gravitating towards their version of what we were doing.

It's easy now to look back and think it wasn't that big a deal, but at the time everyone was like, 'Fuck yeah, I'll have some of this.' The feeling that everyone was falling into line behind us was really exciting, and we were totally aware of what was going on. It was like a virus that had been incubating for a long while and then all of a sudden everyone was catching it.

We couldn't afford to let the grass grow under our brothel creepers, though, or someone else would come along and nick all the glory. The first proper studio we went in was Majestic in Clapham. Mickie Most – who was like the Simon Cowell of the Sixties and Seventies, except he actually made some good records – used that place a lot and I think maybe for five minutes Malcolm thought about us signing to his label. Or more likely McLaren just told him that so we'd get the place cheap. Either way, we were in there for a day in May 1976 and recorded three tracks. There was no time to get the full Sex Pistols wall of sound together, but it was a cool experience.

Even going there in the van was exciting, and I liked being in a proper studio from the first minute I walked into the place. I loved recording as much as – if not more than – I hated rehearsing. Putting songs together in the studio became my favourite part of the whole process, but only when there was time to do more than one overdub. For the moment, the three tracks we did – 'Pretty Vacant', 'Problems' and 'No Feelings' (which would become 'God Save the Queen') – came out very bland and drab. If

you listen back to that demo it actually sounds like a Mickie Most pro-
duction, because it's very dry.

The guy who produced it was Chris Spedding, and I used to watch
him practising with his band The Sharks in between moving sand around
in a barrow and nicking Ariel Bender's guitar at that studio off the King's
Road. He'd had a hit single since then with the song 'Motor Bikin'',
which I'd seen him do on *Top of the Pops*, but he was basically a session
guitarist who'd worked with Roxy Music and Nilsson, not to mention the
Wombles. He was a pretty good guy to have on hand the first time we
were in a studio, but we still had a way to go before we worked out how
to get what we were doing down on tape.

The way we did that was through making *The Spunk Tapes*, which
were demo versions of our best songs. We recorded them on a four-track
in Denmark Street over a couple of weeks at the end of July in the long
hot summer of '76. We'd done a load of gigs at the 100 Club and a couple
of mini-tours of Northern shitholes by then so we were getting pretty . . .
well, polished would be the wrong word, but shit hot would just about
cover it. The great thing about recording in Denmark Street was that the
equipment was set up all the time, so there were unlimited opportunities
to experiment and I could do loads of overdubs.

That was a really fun time. The only slight downside was that the
geezer we recorded them with – a complete fucking hippie called Dave
Goodman who'd rented us our touring PA – would later claim that
everything good about how we sounded was down to him, while making
a mint by selling off shit-quality live bootlegs – which showed how high
his standards were when he was left to his own devices.

Another consequence of the earlier Chris Spedding session had been
that this German bird called Nora came into the picture. She was Chris'
girlfriend at the time. Bernie Rhodes said he remembered her knocking

about with Jimi Hendrix a few years before, so you couldn't accuse her of having a type. Anyway, she came to see us play quite early on, we locked eyes, and the next thing I know I'm hanging out with her. She's got a really nice flat, and it's my first taste of the high life. She even bought me a Flying V guitar, which pissed Malcolm off – I think he saw her as an intruder. Like the girlfriend character in *Spinal Tap* a few years later who mispronounced 'Dolby'.

I couldn't see what his problem was at the time. She was a very sweet lady, plus this was at the up-and-down-the-motorway-in-a-Ford-Transit time when having a German sugar-mummy was just another little adventure. She had serious money, like real heiress dough – I think her dad owned a newspaper or something.

It wasn't just McLaren who disapproved. Rotten resented me seeing her as well. He used to coat me off for it: 'What are you hanging out with her for?' If someone had told us then that he'd end up getting married to her and they'd still be together more than thirty years later, I don't know which one of us would have been more surprised.

The order all this happened in has added to the many complexities of my relationship with John over the years, but I was no romantic threat to him in the long term. I can't be intimate with anyone, because I'm just off looking for more. I only get attracted to strangers, that's my thing. It's not about making love, it's about fucking someone in an alley, or paying a hooker – that's what turns me on, where there's no fucking feelings involved. Once feelings get involved, I'm done.

We did the second of the two Free Trade Hall shows around this time, which the geezers in Joy Division and loads of other Manchester musicians, including my good mate Billy Duffy of The Cult, would later say were the reason they all decided to form bands. Looking down from the stage, you wouldn't have known Morrissey and everyone were out there. Apart from anything else, it wasn't that big a crowd, and they just looked like a standard bunch of Northern cunts with moustaches and kipper ties from where I was standing.

Fair play to Tony Wilson, though. He was the one who had the balls to put the Sex Pistols on his Granada TV show, *So It Goes*, when hardly anyone else had heard of us. It was really exciting doing our first bit of telly. I remember being kind of nervous that we were going to fuck up, but luckily we didn't. That's the famous 'Anarchy' with Jordan in it, which is one of my favourite of all our TV appearances. Unlike the more notorious one a couple of months later, it didn't go out live. Tony Wilson was a real sweetheart; it was a great shame when he died young. I guess what he achieved by helping Joy Division turn into New Order after Ian Curtis killed himself shows what a difference it can make to have a manager who wants to resolve your issues rather than encouraging you to stick the knife in.

18. WHERE'S BILL GRUNDY NOW?

By September 1976, things were really cooking. Cookie even gave us the ultimate vote of confidence by quitting his job. We were playing a special gig in Chelmsford nick the night he finished his apprenticeship, and Paul got so pissed he fell off his drum stool. Roll over Keith Moon and tell John Bonham the news.

The night we played at the opening of some club in Paris on my 21st birthday was another big one. It was the first time I'd been on an aeroplane; my only trip abroad had been to Calais on the ferry with Jimmy Macken a couple of years before. Because I knew Jim could take care of himself, that gave me more licence to be a jack-the-lad than usual. I ended up offering out the whole nightclub and we got beaten up by about fifty geezers. We were lucky to get out alive, really, especially after I nicked some bloke's camera off the hotel balcony as a souvenir. It's funny, that British mentality of going abroad and starting fucking trouble, isn't it? I suppose it goes back to the Empire.

Anyway, I was moving in different circles now. My friendships with Macken and Hayesy had dropped off a bit – I think they felt left out with all the band stuff happening. And that weekend in Paris was amazing. The place was packed out with John Travolta kind of disco people, but we didn't care. Billy Idol drove the Bromley mob over and they all slept in his van. Malcolm got me the special birthday gift of a brass – obviously not my first, but still, it was the thought that counted – and there are some funny pictures in Ray Stevenson's Sex Pistols photo book of me looking totally shagged out after I've kept everyone waiting while I got the maximum return on McLaren's investment.

Ray was the photographer brother of Nils, who was kind of our tour manager and mediator whenever trouble broke out (which obviously it did a lot). Nils was basically Malcolm's guy, but I liked him too cos he was a deviant pussy-hound like me. Between the two of us, we were fucking everything that moved. Cookie wasn't doing badly either and Glen liked the odd one, though he never exactly steamed in, but Rotten . . . nothing.

Someone showed me that bit in Viv Albertine of The Slits' book where she's trying to suck Rotten off but he's not into it and he's blaming her, saying she doesn't know what she's doing. Typical Johnny: even when everything's going his way, he's still moaning (and I don't mean in ecstasy). I wouldn't have complained, that's for sure.

There was so much shagging going on at this time – at least, there was on my part. Any chance I could get I'd be trying to get my end away, usually in a cupboard or a toilet or an alley round the back of the venue. Those furtive encounters were a big turn-on for me. The funny thing was that, publicly, punk's attitude to sex was very disparaging. That was one reason punk birds in general weren't really my thing. From a standing start (which was usually the kind of start I was getting) it just wasn't a look I found particularly attractive. But there was a whole ridiculous ethos that you weren't supposed to date models or birds from the fashion or showbiz world. Fuck that! No one minded when Rod Stewart did it.

The longer punk went on, the thicker the clouds of bullshit surrounding it became. Fuck knows where all this hot air came from – 'Oh, we're down with the people, we're anti-establishment, we don't want any money, we could never leave our squat.' One thing's for sure, it didn't come from me. It was still a real nause, though. And as we started to really get somewhere, our success was a double-edged sword: the better we were doing, the less we were allowed to show it. I felt guilty just thinking about buying a motor. As I say, I have no idea where all this shit came from, but our lead singer's whole anti-rock-star thing definitely contributed, and especially when it came to sex. Rotten was always saying it was no big deal. Speak for yourself, Johnny!

In Viv Albertine's book she writes about how I try to get hold of her in the stairwell outside the Royal College of Art disco. I come off a bit menacing for a minute, but then Mick Jones – who she was going out with at the time – turns up to pluck her from my clutches like a knight in shining fucking armour. In my defence and for the record, I would like to state that when I ask her to suck me off and she says no, I do offer to go down on her instead, which by my calculations makes me the perfect gentlemen; a feminist, even.

Was I a cunt to birds at that time? I hope not. I like to think I was pretty upfront with women about what they could expect from me. I couldn't have the kind of relationship where actual feelings were involved because I was too fucking damaged, but I was definitely good for a shag round the back of the Nashville. To some extent I did have that chauvinistic thing going on where I would see women as sex objects first and anything else second, but I don't think I was the only man in the music industry in the 1970s who committed that misdemeanour. In fact, it would be harder to find one who didn't.

I was definitely guilty of not taking Chrissie Hynde seriously as a musician. She'd be going on about wanting to be in a band and I'd be like, 'Yeah, whatever – suck this.' She tried out for most of the new punk bands that were getting started at the time, but the harsh truth was that no one wanted her because she was a girl. Chrissie had the last laugh on that one by having a load of massive hits with the Pretenders. And in the end people like her and Siouxsie and The Slits and The Runaways and Gaye Advert, who was hot at the time, did do a lot to open things up, so people didn't think it was weird for chicks to be in bands any more.

Would I be lying if I said I did everything in my power to fight sexism in rock 'n' roll? Yes, I fucking would. But at that point I was just a bit of a lad trying to get laid as often as possible. Everything was still pretty new to me, and the crazy wolfman of my sex addiction was years in the future. I'd have to get sober for that shit to really kick in.

In the meantime, there was a lake of fucking booze to be drunk and a lot more adventures to be had. The place we played the most – and where we probably felt most at home – was the 100 Club on Oxford Street, just up the road from where I got skanked for a tenner by those fuckers with the dice as a kid. We'd done a gig there pretty much every week throughout the early summer. It started out with just the odd punter who'd seen us and liked us and maybe made the attempt to look a bit similar, but by the time we got to the 'punk festival' there at the end of September, it really felt like something was happening.

I know Matlock didn't like us being called 'punks', but it never bothered me. I think Caroline Coon had something to do with that word taking off – she mentioned it in an article and it sort of caught on. She was all right, Caroline: another of those posh ex-hippie birds who kind of latched onto the whole scene in the early days. She ended up going out with my mate Paul Simonon from The Clash for quite a while.

Anyway, back to the punk festival at the 100 Club. All the insiders who'd been hanging around for a while were starting to get their own bands together by then. As well as The Clash, there was the Subway Sect, who'd seen us at the Marquee the time Rotten heard himself for the first time, and an early version of Siouxsie and the Banshees where Siouxsie and Steve played with Sid (on the drums – best place for him) and Marco, who ended up in Adam and the Ants. Of course, they were no good, in fact they were awful – none of them could play a note – but that didn't seem to matter much back then.

Audiences were starting to get an idea of how punks were meant to behave. Aggression and even outright violence were definitely a part of that. Sid had taken his chain to Nick Kent by then, and a bottle he smashed at the 100 Club Punk Festival took a girl's eye out. Vivienne Westwood used to like starting the odd scrap as well – she was very punchy – but I spent more time trying to stop fights than I did starting them.

The tension onstage was definitely part of what drew people to us. Whether it's Mick and Keith or me and Rotten or Slash and Axl, when bands have that invisible pull that sucks you in, it's not usually because of how much they like each other. You don't have to actually see it: it's not like I was giving Johnny dirty looks all the time while he was winding the crowd up or blowing his nose or whatever he was doing – it's just that's what the source of the energy is.

Sometimes people – even people who knew us pretty well – would get the wrong end of the stick when it came to the flare-ups we'd have onstage. Often there was a simple practical cause behind what looked like an emotional outburst. I remember one earlier time at the 100 Club where Rotten flounced offstage and Glen nearly had a fight with him. Chrissie Hynde's book talks about me ripping all the strings off my guitar and having a bit of a tantrum, which she thought was because I was so upset with Rotten, but really I was just fucked off with the shit Rotosound strings I had on this Sunburst Les Paul I'd acquired. It had a Bigsby tremolo bar and the whole thing would go out of tune every time you fucking used it. So I smashed it up.

What we had to do was find a way of focusing our anger to make a definitive statement of what the Sex Pistols were about. Signing to EMI – the most old-fashioned and best established of all British record labels – and releasing 'Anarchy in the UK' as a single would be back of the fucking net as far as that was concerned. By the time we went into the studio in early October, we weren't just messing about any more – we really knew what we were doing.

Unfortunately Dave Goodman, fucking hippie that he was, hadn't got that memo. Or I should say fortunately, because if we'd carried on doing it with him, *Never Mind the Bollocks . . .* would've probably ended up like The Clash's first album did when they got their sound-guy to produce it – listen to that record and the drums sound like a fucking packet of crisps. Dave had smoked so much weed that when we were in the studios trying to cut 'Anarchy' he made us do it about a hundred times. His ears were so glazed over, it was never going to be good enough. Eventually we thought, 'Shit, this is not happening,' and got Chris Thomas in instead.

Once we were in Wessex Studios with Chris, he picked the second take we did. As soon as we had a proper producer it was like, 'Fuck me, at last – this is what it's all about.' I can't remember what the original connection was, other than the fact that Chris had done the Roxy Music albums which Cookie and I really loved, but he was the perfect man for the job. Not middle class exactly, but kind of hip. He just gave us that confidence that he knew what he was doing. Plus he wasn't a punk guy, which was good. The last thing we needed was some cunt with spiky hair coming in who had the look but didn't know one end of a studio from the other.

I've always preferred being around pros. That's why I like big record companies – I don't want to be around some Mickey Mouse indie label where everyone's having committee meetings about who's going to go out to buy the falafels. That was another real misconception about punk – 'Oh, write your own magazine, start your own label.' I couldn't give a shit about that stuff. If you're any good, you'll be able to get a proper paying gig at one of the places that's already there. It's not meant to be a fucking hobby.

Everything was set up perfectly. We mimed 'Anarchy in the UK' in front of a load of fans on the BBC TV show *Nationwide*, there was a punk documentary on ITV and the single was coming out in the last week of November with our biggest tour yet booked to follow it up. And then, on 1st December, Bill Grundy happened.

I think it was Queen who were meant to be on originally, but they couldn't do it, so EMI sent their up-and-coming label-mates the Sex Pistols instead. The *Today* programme was a lame London local news magazine show in the early evening. Matlock found out afterwards that the host Bill Grundy had been arguing with his producer because he didn't want to do the interview. So I don't know if he'd got drunk to show his producer he didn't give a shit, or maybe he did the show like that every night.

Either way, he was pissed, and so was I – I'd necked at least two bottles of Blue Nun in the green room, maybe three (and if there'd been some Green Nun in the blue room, I'd have had that too) – but it worked out better for me than it did for him. This would be another of those times they don't like to talk to you about in rehab, when drink or drugs really help you out. I'm not saying I'd have been too scared to take on

Grundy if I hadn't drunk that wine, but if you gave me a drink at that time I was bold as fuck, so in terms of making things happen, it was kind of a tool of my trade. I would respond instinctively to situations without caring about the consequences.

From the second we walked in there, Grundy didn't like us. The angle he was coming from was all about making us look stupid – he had no interest in talking to us on a normal level. That was kind of the MO in those days; it was the old British class system operating at full strength. People in those positions – journalists, TV and radio people – would always talk down to you and try and catch you out by asking how much money you were making. Like you were some shit-covered peasant who should be grateful you weren't polishing the master's boots with your fucking birth certificate.

If you look at early Beatles interviews at airports or wherever, the mentality of the journalists is exactly the same. The worst part of it was, it's not like they were a secret club of perfect gentlemen; those arseholes got up to all kinds of fucking bollocks behind the scenes and then covered up for each other. Look at all that shit about Jimmy Savile. Rotten tried to tell the truth about him in a radio interview in 1978 and the BBC fucking shut him down. Now, generally I would advocate taking what Johnny says with a pinch of salt, but imagine how many kids' lives wouldn't have got ruined if they'd listened on that occasion.

On the Grundy show, though, the boot was on the other foot. I've decided to include a transcript of the whole thing because sometimes you see versions which make out that what happened was all down to Rotten saying 'shit'. In fact I swore first, but I think Grundy was too half-cut to hear it (either that, or the word 'fucking' just seemed normal to him coming out of my mouth). Unusually, the whole band did work together on this one (well, all except Cookie – trust Mr Safe not to pipe up). Glen sort of wore Grundy down by being a bit cocky and annoying, then Rotten had a go and really riled him up, and finally I came in with the big guns after the sleazy old sod started cracking onto Siouxsie (who was sitting at the back with a few of the Bromley people).

The funny thing about seeing it all written down now is how not very outrageous it looks. You'd practically see this kind of thing on the news now, and no one really bats an eyelid. At teatime on ITV in the Britain of 1st December 1976, though, this was – at least as far as the next day's tabloid papers would be concerned – pretty much the most appalling thing that had ever happened. So dig it out on YouTube, settle back with your popcorn, and see if you agree . . .

Grundy: I'm told that that group have received £40,000 from a record company. Doesn't that seem slightly opposed to their anti-materialistic way of life?

Glen: No, the more the merrier.

Grundy: Really?

Glen: Oh yeah.

Grundy: Well, tell me more, then.

Me: We've fucking spent it, ain't we?

Grundy: I don't know. Have you?

Glen: Yeah, it's all gone.

Grundy: Really? Good Lord! Now, I want to know one thing . . .

Glen: What?

Grundy: Are you serious or are you just . . . trying to make me laugh?

Glen: No. It's gone. Gone.

Grundy: Really?

Glen: Yeah.

Grundy: No, but I mean about what you're doing . . .

Glen: Oh yeah.

Grundy: Are you serious?

Glen: Mmm.

Grundy: Beethoven, Mozart, Bach and Brahms have all died . . .

Johnny: They're heroes of ours, ain't they?

Grundy: Really? What? What are you saying, sir?

Johnny: They're wonderful people.

Grundy: Are they?

Johnny: Oh yes! They really turn us on.

Grundy: Suppose they turn other people on . . .

Johnny: Well, that's just their tough shit.

Grundy: It's what?

Johnny: Nothing. A rude word . . . Next question!

Grundy: No, no. What was the rude word?

Johnny: 'Shit'.

Grundy: Was it really? Good heavens, you frighten me to death.

Johnny: Oh alright . . .

Grundy: What about you girls behind?

Glen: He's like your dad, in'e, this geezer, or your grandad.

Grundy: Are you worried or just enjoying yourself?

Siouxsie: Enjoying myself.

Grundy: Are you?

Siouxsie: Yeah.

Grundy: Ah, that's what I thought you were doing.

Siouxsie: I've always wanted to meet you.

Grundy: Did you really?

Siouxsie: Yeah.

Grundy: We'll meet afterwards, shall we?

Siouxsie: [blows a kiss]

Me: You dirty sod. You dirty old man.

Grundy: Well, keep going, chief, keep going. Go on, you've got another five seconds. Say something outrageous.

Me: You dirty bastard.

Grundy: Go on, again.

Me: You dirty fucker.

Grundy: What a clever boy!

Me: What a fucking rotter!

Grundy: Well, that's it for tonight. The other rocker, Eamonn, I'm saying nothing else about him, will be back tomorrow. I'll be seeing you soon. I hope I'll not be seeing you [to us] again. From me, though, good night.

As the credits roll over the theme tune, you can see Rotten looking at his watch and me doing a bit of a hip-thrust in my leather trousers, like Elvis would have on *Ed Sullivan* if they'd not blocked him off at the waist. I'm not saying this was the British equivalent, but it certainly caused a stink. We knew we'd been a bit naughty, but we hadn't fully twigged that it had gone out live until we went out the back and all the phones started ringing in the green room. All these angry members of the public were calling in to say how outraged they were. Me and Siouxsie were answering the phones and telling them all to piss off, which didn't do anything to calm them down.

I was still pretty drunk and having a good old time. We all were, except Malcolm – the master media manipulator and creator of everything – who'd gone white as a sheet. Cookie used to say Malcolm was always going on about anarchy, but whenever we actually did anything a bit anarchic he'd shit himself, and that was true. He'd get a bit bold if he had a couple of drinks in him, but basically he was a pretty meek geezer. Fair enough, on this occasion he thought we'd ruined all his plans; and the EMI driver who came to whisk us off home seemed to be taking it pretty seriously as well.

McLaren cheered up quick enough the next morning when he found out we were front-page news – 'The Filth and the Fury', some nutter who was meant to have kicked in his TV, all that shit. When that happened, it didn't take Malcolm long to realise that the whole thing had been his idea in the first place. I didn't mind that. That was how the band was supposed to work: me and/or Johnny doing things spontaneously and Malcolm coming up with a manifesto to explain why it was cool afterwards. What was outrageous to me was that a couple of swear words you'd hear out in the street every five minutes could upset everyone so much. People nowadays find it hard to understand – I know I do – but I guess back then it was still a big deal.

Looking at us on the front page of the tabloids the next day, I had the same feeling of satisfaction I'd got hearing on the radio about Bowie's stuff getting nicked – 'I did that!' I was proud of it. I might not have been so pleased with myself if I'd known how much it was going to change things. Grundy was the big dividing line in the Sex Pistols' story. Before it, we were all about the music, but from then on it was all about the media. In some ways it was our finest moment, but in others it was the beginning of the end.

19. VICIOUS – YOU HIT ME WITH A FLOWER

Everything prior to Grundy was good, in my book. It was like the normal progression you'd expect of a band – we'd just made a great record, people were showing up to see us and getting converted, there was a real scene. Getting recognised for what we did by the music press was fun and it was something we could cope with. But then overnight we were on everyone's fucking breakfast table and the *Sun* and the *News of the World* were doorstepping us in Denmark Street.

Grundy didn't just catapult us to a new level of fame, it took the whole thing into another dimension in a way that was hard to grasp. Don't get me wrong, the notoriety was a good laugh, and it definitely brought us a lot of new fans very quickly. But the best way I can think of describing how it felt is like in *Star Trek* when they're just flying along normally in space, then Scotty presses the warp speed button and, whoosh, they're fucking gone.

In terms of the Sex Pistols having any kind of long-term future, this sudden acceleration was the worst thing that could possibly have happened. I still think we'd have got really big in the end without it, but the whole process would have been much slower and maybe less traumatic. I guess it was just never our destiny to be a normal band who make a few albums and then fade away. Grundy was definitely the point where everybody's egos started to spin out – McLaren's probably most of all.

He was as prone to believing his own publicity as any of us, maybe more so. I think he'd never really thought about what was good for the band; the idea of looking out for his boys wasn't in his genetic make-up like it would be for most normal managers. He wasn't one of those muso guys who plays a long game like Peter Grant or Andrew Loog Oldham. And from this time on, the music – which had always been the most important thing to us – took a total back seat as far as Malcolm was concerned. Everything started to be about him playing the system.

The first nightmarish situation McLaren had to try and make out was a deliberate strategy was the Anarchy Tour. By rights this should've been one of the highlights of the whole punk thing – us at the peak of our powers on a nationwide tour with The Clash, The Damned (who'd both played their first ever shows supporting us back in July, and were actually getting pretty good by this time) and Johnny Thunders & the Heartbreakers, who Malcolm had flown over from New York to give us an American angle. I think they arrived on the night after the Grundy thing, so they didn't know what kind of shit-storm they'd walked into.

The police were banning us, local councils were banning us – everyone was fucking banning us. It was exciting at first, showing up at all these places and finding out whether the specially convened meeting of all the most stuck-up people in the town thought we should be allowed to corrupt the young people of the area with our punk rock filth. But it got boring pretty quickly. We were driving round the country in this big flash tour bus, getting told everywhere we turned up that we couldn't play, sometimes right at the last minute. There was nothing else to do but get pissed and cause trouble.

Even that got old after a while. It didn't feel as spontaneous as it used to. It was like everyone had an idea of what to expect from us, and we were just giving it to them. Of course, Malcolm was relishing the whole thing, because us getting banned everywhere made for so much great press, but it would've been nice to play a few more gigs as well. Especially as at the small number of shows we did actually get to do – like in Caerphilly, the one there's some really funny footage of in *The Great Rock 'n' Roll Swindle* – all the Bible-thumpers came out and told us we were the Devil's children.

By the time we got back off that tour, Vivienne had changed the shop from Sex to Seditionaries, with all the bombing of Dresden pictures on the wall. Bomber Harris – that would've been a good punk name; almost as good as Fabian Quest. I would still go in there after that, but it wasn't as cosy as it used to be. They took out the couches and the jukebox, so it felt very clinical, and it wasn't really a hang place any more. Apart from anything else, there'd be all these punk kids knocking around wanting to talk to you, and they weren't as cool as the Bromley people – some of them were complete fucking idiots.

A bit of a siege mentality had been developing at the shop for a while. As if the angry Teds threatening to smash the place up weren't bad enough, Malcolm and Vivienne had been getting quite paranoid about people turning up at the shop and trying to steal their ideas. It was no wonder, really – when Don Letts came round from Acme Attractions he'd practically bring a notebook. A lot of fourth-division people were starting to capitalise on the whole punk thing. Boy was the worst – that place stank of tuppencery. It was the same with music; after Grundy, every Tom, Dick and Harry in London who owned a leather jacket seemed to be starting their own punk band.

The crowds were settling into a formula, too. Instead of thinking for themselves like they used to, the people who came to the occasional gig we did actually get to play seemed to have almost a code of conduct in their minds of how they should behave. They'd read that spitting and pogoing was the thing to do, so they fucking did it.

Sid was meant to have started the pogo by jumping up and down at the 100 Club because he couldn't see one of the bands. I think that one would probably come under the heading of 'good stories that might or might not be true' (especially given how tall he was). Rotten's claim to starting the spitting was probably a bit better, because he did have some problem with his sinus so he was always having a good clear-out, but whoever started it, it was horrible. Joe Strummer got a massive green one fully in his open mouth once and caught something. It really was fucking disgusting. I guess it was another thing that marked us out from the Led Zeppelins of this world, but not necessarily in a good way.

The thing that did really make us special, which was the music, seemed to be getting left by the wayside. The Grundy business had put the kibosh on the EMI deal, and they were looking for a way to get shot of us. The word was that the boss of the label used to go to dinner with the Queen and he didn't want to be associated with these foul-mouthed yobs any more. As far as the band was concerned, the one thing we all shared was that we wanted to make an album of the songs we'd written and performed live – I think that was everyone's main goal. But while Malcolm was in the process of negotiating a new deal with A&M, we kind of lost sight of that.

Tension had been mounting between Glen and John for a while, and when they had a really big row right around the time Glen started asking Malcolm awkward questions about where all the money was going, Matlock's days were probably numbered. Julien Temple says that getting rid of Glen and replacing him with Sid was the last project he saw Rotten and Malcolm really work together on. I'm not trying to get me and Cookie off the hook by saying this, as we did go along with it of our own free will, but it was one time when Malcolm's puppetmaster fantasy probably had a bit of truth to it. He certainly knew how to stir the shit-pot.

I can't really put my finger on the exact nature of those manipulations, but they were definitely going on. There was no denying there were some good reasons for getting rid of Glen. For all the big contributions he made to the songwriting and getting the band off the ground, he just didn't fit into the urchin vibe. Rotten calling him a 'mummy's boy' was unfair, but Matlock never quite looked the part. You could see he'd never gone without a meal, and he'd started to act up to being the toff of the group in a way that was quite embarrassing.

At first he'd been happy to wear clothes from Sex, but as time went on he seemed to be more and more into his Beatles thing, and it was all getting a bit painful. It wasn't just that he was more respectable and strait-laced than we were, it almost felt like he thought he was too good for us. The fact that he had a deal set up for his own band the minute he left – and with EMI, of all people – would kind of show where his loyalties lay.

On top of that, as we were building up the sound of the band, it was becoming very powerful; overwhelming, even. This meant there'd been less and less room in it for Matlock's dicking around with sevenths and elevenths. I don't think any of these factors loomed too large in Johnny's mind, though. He just wanted his mate along for the ride so he'd have a bit of back-up against me and Cookie. He'd always hated the fact that I had a mate in the band and he didn't. Malcolm's motivation was a bit harder to work out. To Cookie and me, it just didn't make any sense to have someone who couldn't play a note trying to fill Glen's shoes, but it was never about the music for McLaren. In fact, he didn't give a shit about it. He was always on a different trip, and getting Sid in the band was the ultimate expression of that.

I didn't mind having to play the bass on the album, in fact I was happy to do it. But teaching Vicious where to put his fingers on the fretboard so he could make some attempt at playing live was a total pain in the arse. Me and Cookie would just look at each other, like, 'Fuck me, what have we got into here?'

Obviously kids today don't give a shit that Sid couldn't play bass. They love him because he looked so fucking good. And not just for how he looked, but the attitude and the death and the whole mystique of him. Believe me, I get it. When I first saw Sid walk down King's Road on his way to Sex – this was before Rotten had joined the band – he was already a superstar in the making. He didn't have the spiky hair yet, but he was wearing it short (which was unusual at the time) and he was tall, with a great boat race and a generally stylish air about him.

Even then, he was bad news. He was taking a lot of speed and already knew Johnny (in fact, he got his name from Johnny's hamster). I had the same uneasy feeling about the two of them that I did about Jordan: you just didn't really feel safe hanging out with them outside the shop because they drew so much attention to themselves. When I'm not drunk and looking for kicks my instinct is always to stay out of trouble – I just prefer to slip off on my own and mind my own business (however nefarious that business might be). Put a couple of drinks inside me and that's all reversed, obviously, but I wasn't one of the low-class clientele who made a habit of getting pissed in the daylight hours.

It was never too early for Sid to get pissed or stoned, though. And his craziness was catching like the fucking clap. The day we signed to A&M, for example – 10th March 1977 – was a total nightmare. We started hitting the bottle at about eight in the morning, just drinking vodka in a room, then we got driven to Buckingham Palace to do the fake signing, then we went to hear the finished version of 'God Save the Queen' at Wessex Studios (this was the only good bit, as I couldn't believe how amazing it sounded: not just cos I was part of it, but generally, as a fan). Then we had a fight in the car, then we went to A&M and all kinds of fucking carnage ensued. It was a long fucking day of getting pushed from pillar to post and by the end of it we were all so pissed we didn't know what we were doing. In so far as Malcolm had arranged the whole thing, he was in control of it, but he had no way of knowing what was actually going to happen.

From the minute Sid joined the band, nothing was ever normal again. I get that it was great the way him and John looked together, and the media frenzy certainly sold a lot of newspapers, but as far as I was concerned, that wasn't what the Sex Pistols were meant to be. I hadn't minded being second fiddle to John, but now I was playing third fiddle to this fucking idiot; maybe even fourth if you went along with Malcolm's increasingly delusional certainty that we were all his puppets.

It wasn't so much that my pride was dented, though that was part of it, it was more just being around this fucking chaos. That night at the Marquee the year before when John heard himself for the first time, I'd told the guy from the *NME*, 'We're not into music, we're into chaos.' I was proud of that one at the time and it's still a blinding line, but I found out afterwards that it wasn't really true. Be careful what you fucking wish for! I *was* into music. We all were – not just Rotten playing his Van der Graaf Generator on Capital Radio – but now we'd got chaos instead, and it was shit.

People from more established bands had been a bit wary of us from the beginning – probably with good reason, to be honest. I remember me and Cookie being at the Roxy the night Jimmy Page and Robert Plant came down and noticing that they didn't really talk to us. Another time I was sitting in the Roebuck with Gary Holton, who was in a band called the Heavy Metal Kids. He came to see us early on and his advice was: 'You know, what you should do after a show is always bow and say thank you.' Obviously this is a lesson that has served me well. Gary was probably thinking, 'Fuck me, these rude cunts are gonna put me out of business.' He didn't get that it wasn't showbiz any more; well, it was, but in a different way.

Once things got going with the Pistols, a lot of my old fandom kind of went out of the window – I guess I was getting a bit older so I wasn't going to be idolising people so much any more. But one person I was still excited to meet was Pete Townshend. I was always a major fan of The Who and what with him coming from Shepherd's Bush way, I felt like we had a bit in common.

The funny thing was, on the night me and Cookie met him down the Speakeasy it wasn't us that were causing trouble, it was him. I think he'd been drinking all day at some business meeting in Tin Pan Alley, and by the time he got to us he was pretty lit. He kept saying 'Who the fuck are you?' to everyone and afterwards he credited that meeting with inspiring the song 'Who Are You?', which was their last big hit before Moonie died. If you listen to the lyrics you really get a sense of how belligerent he was. There's a photograph of us with him from that night. To be honest, I found it kind of inspiring that he was even talking to us because I dug him and his band so much.

There was no chance of that kind of thing happening once Sid was in the band, though – he'd probably have threatened to glass Pete Townshend like he did the DJ Bob Harris. That was at the Speakeasy as well. I think we showed up separately but the minute I saw him there I thought, 'Oh shit, this is a nightmare.' It was, as well. The guy's nickname was 'Whispering' Bob Harris, for fuck's sake – he wasn't an East End gangster. He didn't need a fucking glass pushing right up in his sound engineer's face or one of Rotten's mates threatening to kill him. Anywhere you went that Sid turned up, you knew there was going to be trouble. He kind of got off on that. Well, I assume he did as I don't know why he would've done it otherwise.

All this happened the day after the official signing to A&M, and once Harris' lawyers had been on the phone, we were off the label in less than a week and the release of 'God Save the Queen' was shelved. That was a disappointment, and we couldn't help wondering if we were ever going to get to finish our fucking album. At this point, Malcolm had the bright idea of getting us out of the country till the heat was off while he shopped around for a new deal.

First we went to Jersey, where we got thrown off the island within a day, and then to Berlin, which was horrible and bleak – the same kind of weather as London. Malcolm's paranoia had pushed Nils Stevenson out by this time so this guy Boogie was with us as McLaren's fixer. There's some 8mm film of this trip somewhere – we stayed in a dreary hotel, went sightseeing a few times and dropped in at a couple of weird tranny clubs. The only good thing that came out of it was 'Holidays in the Sun'. That was my music and Rotten's words. You can hear how pissed off we were at the time in that song. The funny thing is, an actual holiday in the sun might've cheered some of us up a bit.

After Matlock got the boot the pressure was on for me to pull my finger out and write a bit more. The song 'Bodies' was another example. It was my tune and Rotten wrote the words about this woman from

Birmingham called Pauline who was a bit of a nutcase and carried her abortion round in a bag. It was weird. She was a good-looking bird who didn't dress like a punk or anything – she looked like someone who would work in Safeways. I remember fucking her down an alley off Wardour Street. It might've been after the Marquee show. Either way, we used to draw these nut-jobs to us: it was part of what gave the band its special character. The only problem was, now we'd got one of them in to be our bass player.

20. NEVER MIND THE BOLLOCKS . . .

Even Fagin gave his pickpockets a roof over their heads and an apple. There was a woman called Sophie Richmond who was Malcolm's assistant and ran the office for him. We used to go to her for wages – we never questioned how much money was coming in, that was how stupid we were with the dough. You're in a band. It's exciting, things are good, you're getting drunk, you're getting laid. Why would you want to rock the boat by saying, 'Where's mine?' I didn't even have a fucking bank account.

Anyway, Sophie was a big part of the scene and she seemed like a sensible sort of character, even if she was going out with Malcolm's cover designer guy, Jamie Reid, and she helped us all get somewhere to live when the pressure on Denmark Street got too much. The first gaff me and Cookie shared was on Bell Street in King's Cross. When Sophie was organising the flats, the one they got for Sid was on an even shorter lease than ours. Apparently she raised the issue with Malcolm and he said, 'It's OK, he'll be dead by then,' so maybe he did know the future.

To be fair to Malcolm, that wasn't just him being cynical – Sid used to say that kind of thing all the time too. I don't know if he was glassing people before punk happened. I think he felt like he had to act a certain way once he was christened Sid Vicious. If only we'd called him 'Sid Kind', he'd have been out running soup kitchens and helping old ladies across the road . . . Well, maybe. Sometimes it's hard for people who didn't know him to accept this on the basis of how he acted in public, but there was a sweet side to Sid as well; a kind of childlike quality he had about him.

Although Vicious coming in was the start of the Pistols going skew-whiff and becoming a bit of a mess, it also kind of made sense in terms of the image of us that was being sold in the media. The hype that was drawing people to the band was all about how outrageous and out of control we were, and then Sid was brought in to make that come true. I don't think McLaren knew what was going to happen once we'd got Sid in the band – it was more a question of Sid taking on the role of being Sid, and then all the publicity happening and him just milking it more and more, rather than Malcolm specifically encouraging him to be an idiot.

Of all the people whose head the whole thing went to (and that was all of us – me included), it went to Sid's head the most. To be fair, he was the one who got thrown in the deep end the most, too. We hadn't been doing it for long, but at least we'd had a bit of time to adjust. He was this really gullible guy who came in when the madness was already at its height with the pressure of thinking that it was his job to keep it going. On the surface he was OK with that, but underneath I think he just didn't know what to do.

At first he did at least attempt to fit in on the musical side. He tried hard at the rehearsals and for his first few gigs he started out with his bass held up really high so he could actually play it, not down by his knees where it ended up in America. Unfortunately, that horrible bird came along with the heroin, and from then on all he was interested in was getting high. It wasn't totally her fault either – no one was twisting Sid's arm to make him put a spike in it, not even Nancy.

Nancy Spungen turned up at the very first gig Sid played with us, which was our second Notre Dame Hall show in March 1977 (the first had been with Matlock the year before). I think she had some connection – no prizes for guessing which kind – with the Heartbreakers, and the vibes around her were bad from the beginning. Suddenly this groupie junkie chick from America who was a complete fucking outsider was hanging around at soundchecks and none of us were in any hurry to accept her. That's not to say we were great judges of character – we probably wouldn't have been accepting of any bird at that point, as the atmosphere around the band had become a bit more of a boys' club than it had been at the beginning.

No one in the Sex Pistols had girlfriends around the band too much, maybe because they knew I'd end up shagging 'em. It had become what was expected of me at that point. So of course I took one for the team and fucked old Nancy. It was in the little room I stayed in sometimes at the back of Helen the midget's house, round the corner from Bell Street. She was fun, Helen – she had to be, because apart from her I was a bit prejudiced against midgets; the little fuckers gave me vertigo. I really liked hanging out with her, though. There was never anything sexual between us, but she was a sweet person. I'd go round there and we'd smoke weed and listen to old Fifties songs together; it was kind of a safe place for me. I wonder where she is now – I hope she's doing OK.

Anyway, back to La Spungen. I don't know why I had to do it, fucking other people's girlfriends was just a compulsion with me. It wasn't to put one over on Sid, and I don't think he ever found out, but I don't think he'd have been too bothered even if he had – there was quite a bisexual kind of energy about him. She was so whiney I was bewildered by what he could've found attractive about her – she just seemed to have so little to recommend her as a person. So a part of me (and again, no prizes for guessing which part) was curious to try and find out for myself. I will spare you the gory details, just to prove that chivalry's not dead.

One person even fewer people seem to have a good word for than Nancy was (and is) Richard Branson. But I had no problems with him. He was the only one out of all the label bosses we dealt with who you could actually talk to. All the others were just blokes in suits you never saw, who would probably cross the street to avoid you if your paths crossed outside the office. Even though Branson was a public school toff, he was definitely approachable. We went on his boat up by Maida Vale and he didn't seem to mind us taking the piss out of the way he looked by calling him Catweazle. Fair play to him on signing us as well, because a lot of the other fuddy-duddy labels wouldn't touch us with a shitty stick by then, and if it hadn't have been for Branson, *Never Mind the Bollocks . . .* might never have found a home.

I don't know if McLaren might have been thinking Branson was someone he could pull a fast one on, but Virgin was the only label that would have us by that stage. They were the smart ones – they'd seen the writing on the Berlin Wall. The good thing was they kind of needed us as much as we kind of needed them, because as a company they'd had their big moment a few years before with Mike Oldfield's *Tubular Bells* and then pissed all the money up the wall on jazzy prog shit like Henry Cow and Steve Hillage . . . Now, there was someone Sid should've glassed. Him or Rick Wakeman, who would've been a sitting duck in that cape of his.

Whatever Malcolm's devious plan was, Tricky Dicky Branson would have the last laugh by flooding the market with substandard Pistols product once the whole thing went to shit and McLaren was out of the picture.

But I didn't even hold that against him, because that's exactly what record companies are meant to do – capitalise on their assets – and Malcolm would have done worse if he'd had the chance. I guess he kind of did with *The Great Rock 'n' Roll Swindle* in a way.

The best thing about Virgin was that they rubber-stamped our choice of Chris Thomas to produce the album and then just let us get on with it, which was really good for me and Cookie as musicians. One of the factors in *Never Mind the Bollocks . . .* having such a distinctive sound is that bands normally start a recording with the rhythm section – bass and drums – and then add the guitar later, but because me and Cookie knew each other so well and we weren't fucking about, we'd start with the guitar and drums and then I'd put the bass in after. 'Anarchy in the UK' is the only song on that album where Matlock's on bass and it's the three of us playing together, but even then we were so locked in that you can't hear much difference.

Because a lot of later punk and post-punk bands would make a point of not being able to play, people don't necessarily understand how well drilled we were. We didn't go skipping into Wessex Studios saying, 'Yay, let's do it.' We weren't just having a laugh. We never wanted anything to be sloppy – the whole 'anyone can do it' element of punk had completely passed us by. In fact, me and Cookie were the opposite of that: we were really dedicated in the studio. Sometimes if he was dragging a bit on the beat, I'd say, 'Let's fucking do it again.' And I spent many happy hours doing guitar overdubs with Chris Thomas. He and the engineer Bill Price were always willing to experiment to get things right, up to and beyond the point of leaving a flight case by the amp to 'harden up' the guitar sound. Fuck you, Phil Spector, we're gonna drive a tank through your wall of sound and then build a better one on top.

The only reason all this was possible was because me and Cookie were left to our own devices. Not long after Sid joined the band, he was laid up in hospital with hepatitis for quite a long time and couldn't do anything, which was a godsend really, cos it meant I could get on with playing the bass. We needed him hospitalised on a permanent basis. Unfortunately, when he got better he kept wanting to play. You can hear him farting around a bit on 'Bodies' – there's two basses on that to make sure one of us gets it right – but I think that's the only song you can really pick him out on.

Rotten leaving us in peace was even more of a miracle: the more he stayed away from the musical side and just wrote lyrics, the better we sounded, and he certainly didn't need our help in the verbal department (once 'Lazy Sod' had pointed him in the right direction, of course). He'd never trust other people to do their jobs like that now – he's got way too controlling.

Chris Thomas was the best possible example to us of how you should set up a creative environment. He'd listen to my ideas – 'What about if I do this 'ere?' – and when it came to me playing the bass, he'd tell me what he thought and I'd do my best to execute it. I had so much fun doing guitar overdubs in the studio with him – that was a fucking great experience, probably the best part of being in the Pistols for me. There was no publicity, none of the madness, we were just in the studio, grafting to make a great record.

The one part of the process I didn't enjoy was tuning up the guitars. That was the only bit that felt like work, and Chris always made me do it myself, which I hated. Luckily I had a strobe tuner which I'd nicked, ironically off Mr Thomas' old friend and employer Bryan Ferry (though I never mentioned this to Chris at the time).

Island records had an office and a studio near the Chiswick flyover; I don't know if it's still there. One night when it was snowing – I think I'd been up till the early hours on speed – I saw a Ford Transit parked outside with just the windows at the end rather than the metal back door. That was always an incitement. I looked in and saw some tasty stuff so I put the window through and got in there. Inside was a strobe tuner and a Bryan Ferry gold disc, for the solo album where he's wearing a white tux by the pool on the cover like James Bond. Obviously the tuner would come in handy, and there was no way I was leaving that gold disc behind. After all, I was a big fan.

In early June 1977, we took a brief break from our labours to overturn a few tables and piss in the punchbowl at the Queen's silver jubilee party. Virgin did a good job getting the single of 'God Save the Queen' out in time for that. I never really paid much attention to all that jubilee bollocks, to be honest. That was more Rotten and McLaren's end of things – I was too busy in the studio to notice. The gig on the Thames riverboat was a good stunt, though – one of McLaren's best ideas. I don't think he even had anything personal against the Queen, really – he was just being Brian Epstein, looking for strokes he could pull to get attention.

The weekend that the single would've gone to number one, the record industry fixed the chart to stop us. As if radio stations refusing to play the song in case it started a revolution wasn't enough of an obstacle to get over, it came out in Branson's autobiography that the British Phonographic Institute sent a special directive obliging the people who compiled the chart to discount returns from all shops associated with record labels (the main one being Virgin, which would have provided a lot of our sales), then mysteriously reversed it the week after. Who was the beneficiary who got to be played at the end of *Top of the Pops* instead of us? Who else but Rod fucking Stewart! I swear that man was stalking me.

Even though I was pissed off about it at the time, I realised afterwards that lots of shit people have got to the top of the charts, but no one else has managed to mobilise the whole might of the British record business to stop people knowing a single had got to number one. It's a badge of honour I am proud to wear to this day.

In terms of how the public responded to us when we were out and about, 'God Save the Queen' was almost as big a gear-change as Grundy had been. But this time it definitely wasn't a lurch in the right direction. The jubilee might not have meant shit to me, but it was a big deal to Britain's racist Teddy boy community (which was quite substantial at the time), and egged on by the tabloid media, it was open fucking season on anyone who looked like a Sex Pistol. Cookie and Rotten and several other people around us got physically attacked in the street. I was lucky enough never to have any problems in that area – if I saw anyone dodgy coming towards me I'd just put my Cloak on. And the useless hairdresser's hair I couldn't sculpt into spikes like Vicious and Rotten's probably did me a favour too.

Getting jumped by Teds and skinheads all the time didn't do anything to bring the band closer together. It wasn't like we had bodyguards or anything, we were just getting on buses and tubes the same as everyone else, and Rotten and Vicious attracted so much attention because of the way they looked – and behaved – that if you hung out with them it felt like you were making yourself a target.

Even Cookie was spiking his hair up by that point. In fact, I was getting totally left behind on the image front. I had to up my game if I wasn't going to disappear off the radar altogether. So I started wearing the knotted white handkerchief on my head like a Gumby from Monty Python – to hide the shame of my giant unspiked bonce. I did it first around the time we were shooting the video for 'God Save the Queen'. The cartoon element would not have come to the fore so much if Glen had still been in the band, but I figured if the end of the pier was the direction we were heading in, I might as well get there first.

Although the next single, 'Pretty Vacant', actually got us on *Top of the Pops* when it came out a month later, it seemed like – between the media, the police, the fucking bastards at the GLC, every other local council in Britain and Malcolm getting bored – there was some kind of conspiracy keeping us from playing live in the UK. So we fucked off to Scandinavia and did a tour there instead. It was true what they said about Sweden. It wasn't just how good-looking the birds were, they were really into sex, as opposed to what we were used to, which was grudging Northern slags with big ankles and spotty backs. I'm sorry if the truth hurts.

Sweden and Norway were mental, and then just to show the grudging Northern slags we hadn't forgotten about them, we actually managed to do some proper shows in England. The S.P.O.T.S. tour (it stood for Sex Pistols On Tour Secretly) was as good as it was going to get for us playing live with Sid in the band. Our disguises – all the different names we used – were just good enough to fool the authorities but not so good as to leave us playing to empty venues. Tax Exiles, Special Guest, Acne Rabble, The Hamsters, A Mystery Band of International Repute – sounds like a festival worth going to. It was exciting – the clubs were all full of kids who really wanted to see us; just what a secret tour should be. I remember Malcolm not being around so much – probably busy doing our American deal with Warner's or fucking about with the film he was determined to make – but those were fun times. Sid was wrecked by the end of it, though.

By the time *Never Mind the Bollocks, Here's the Sex Pistols* finally came out – at the end of October 1977 – we were a very different band to the one we'd been when the earliest songs on it were written, two years before. But the great thing about the album was, not only did it still sound fresh, it felt like the defining work of a band putting all their ideas into practice at once. I'd supplied the title – half-inched from a cheeky-chappy hot dog guy at Piccadilly Circus who I'd heard say 'Never mind the bollocks . . .' a few times when I was off to Soho on my red-light missions.

There was definitely a connection between my raging fucking libido and how the album sounded. Being a bit of a drummer on the quiet gave me a very percussive way of playing – that rhythmic *djung-djung-djung-djung*. It seemed like the automatic thing to do. I didn't feel comfortable going *dah-dah-dah* and then leaving air. If you take a song like, let's say for instance 'All Right Now' by Free, there are gaps in it. Now I love that song, but I could never write or play anything like it, because I always wanted to keep driving, and the concept of not doing that just seemed really bizarre to me. Even with 'Submission', where it goes *djung-djung dah-dah*, I'm still kind of djunging in between. That's my thing – I just can't leave a hole unfilled.

With the album there was no record business conspiracy to keep us off the top of the charts (although a Virgin record shop did get sued for displaying the word 'Bollocks', like it was a retail version of flashing). They actually won the case. We got our number one at last, and it seemed appropriate that the Sex Pistols should have established a legal precedent for people showing their bollocks in public. We celebrated by doing a couple of special Christmas Day shows for striking firemen in Huddersfield, a matinee for the kids and then a proper show at night. There are some funny pictures from that afternoon of Sid with the kids, like both sides are trying to work out which is the biggest child.

It was getting pretty dark around him by that time, even if it didn't look that way when all those kids were throwing pies around. Trouble was also starting to boil up in terms of tensions between Rotten and Malcolm, between me and Cookie and the other two, and even between Sid and Rotten, who weren't getting on too well either. Once Malcolm's brilliant plan to kidnap Nancy and force her to go back to America had failed, Sid was pretty much lost to the heroin, and John had a big problem with that. It didn't feel like the writing was on the wall yet, though, and we had no idea when we were playing it that the gig for the firemen would be our last show in the UK and that by the end of the short American tour we were about to go on, the band would have broken up.

At first we were refused entry to the US for visa reasons – they were trying to save us from ourselves. Our stack of criminal convictions (we all had a few, but I had the most) meant that Warner Brothers had to pay a load of money to the American government as a bond to guarantee our good behaviour. Betting on the Sex Pistols to keep the peace at that time was like backing a three-legged chihuahua to win the Grand National – not the best investment they would ever make – and Warner's sent this record company enforcer guy called Noel Monk along to protect it.

That tour was a complete fucking circus from the very beginning – I think the couple of Vietnam vets Warner's assigned to do security for Sid wished they were back fighting in the jungles by the end of it. We were very big news in America then, and there were so many people following us around trying to get exclusives – which of course Sid was only too happy to provide – that the whole thing was crazy. Almost as soon as we arrived, the magazine *High Times* filmed him shooting up in a hotel room. That was enough to get us slung out of the country on its own, but somehow it got squashed by Warner Brothers. It's amazing what they can get you off when you're making them money.

Meanwhile Malcolm was still on his wanting-us-not-to-be-like-any-other-band trip, so instead of playing in New York or LA, where there would've been a real buzz, we had to play all these fucking cowboy places like Texas and Atlanta. Maybe this was a good idea in theory, but in practice it meant all the fucking Bible-thumping redneck crazies coming along to throw dead animals at us. Obviously shit like that didn't bother McLaren, because he never had to actually go onstage and deal with it, but it was the worst, man.

We might have got through it if the four of us could've put on a united front. But the band was splitting into two camps because me and Cookie couldn't stand being around Johnny and Sid any more. You couldn't turn round for a minute without Sid starting a fight with some cowboy at a bar or smashing his bass over some geezer's head. We were just trying to get by and he was busy being Sid Vicious and making life impossible for everyone.

Then on top of that you had Rotten, who was on his own trip and basically thought he was God by that stage. Even Sid had lost respect for him with his outfits and his silly hats. They'd been mates at the start, but from the moment Vicious joined the band they kind of pulled away from each other. I guess there was a bit of rivalry there, and they argued about Nancy and the heroin. Rotten is always moaning about junkies, but the effects of excess booze are just as terrible.

I hated flying, but anything was better than being stuck on the bus with those two. The whole thing was such a horrible nightmare that I've kind of blocked it out. Cookie says the plane we were on got struck by lightning going into Memphis and I don't even remember that. By the time we got to San Francisco at the end of the tour, I'd got the flu. The Winterland seemed like a great venue for a proper rock 'n' roll show, not like the shitty cow palaces we'd been booked into up till then. Unfortunately, we were awful. My guitars were all out of tune as I'd bought this fucking Firebird that was shit, and Sid was being a complete clown. Looking at it from the audience's point of view maybe they thought, 'Wow, this is wild, this is crazy,' but from my point of view, we were just utterly fucked.

A load of new West Coast punk bands like The Avengers and The Nuns played before us. It should've been exciting to think we were inspiring all these bands to form in America the same way we did with The Clash and The Damned back home, but I don't think I heard them play a note. I couldn't have cared less about the music by then. I was too busy concubining it up backstage.

I went to town at the Miyako hotel after the show that night. Even though I had flu, none of the conveyor belt of birds going through my room – in you come, suck that and thank you very much – seemed to be bothered about catching it (or anything else). I lost count of how many there were but let's say it was six because that's how many chambers there are in a magazine, and this Sex Pistol had just shot his last fucking bullet.

The pressure had got too much, so I did what I always did – I bolted. Rotten has tried to twist what happened next to look like he broke the band up, but he loved the Pistols and really wanted us to carry on. His plan was for us to get rid of Malcolm and continue. Looking back, he was right in a way, because McLaren's ego was destroying everything, but when it came to the crunch of choosing sides between our manager and our singer, there was only one place Cookie's and my loyalties could lie.

However much of a nightmare Malcolm had become, he was still a big part of the whole thing and we couldn't just ditch him. I'd been staying at his house for years before the Pistols even got off the ground, and I considered him an ally and a friend. Plus Malcolm was giving us the chance to do the Ronnie Biggs thing in Brazil and finish the film *The Great Rock 'n' Roll Swindle* – both of which we were quite excited about. They certainly seemed way more appealing as options than sacking Malcolm and trying to make the Pistols work with Rotten and Sid, who was overdosing every five minutes by then. At the end of the day, it came down to who we felt more comfortable spending time with, and that was a no-brainer. So me and Cookie fucked off to Rio to have fun with a Great Train Robber, Lydon went to Jamaica on Branson's dollar to discover reggae, and Sid and Nancy got a one-way ticket to their own public junkie hell.

PART III: AFTER

21. THE BOYS FROM BRAZIL

Me and Cookie had a great time down in Rio. Just being away somewhere new and not having to deal with Rotten and Sid and all the daily fucking fiascos any more was such a relief. It was sunny, it was tropical, it was great. Plus nobody in Brazil knew who the Sex Pistols were back then, so the pressure of everyone either loving us or hating us all the time was lifted from our shoulders from the minute we arrived.

It was a good laugh hanging out with Biggsy, too – he was just a normal guy trying to live up to the myth. I guess we had more in common with the notorious Great Train Robber than we realised at the time. Even though Ronnie was free, he was a prisoner in a way. The only reason he was allowed to stay in Brazil was because he had a kid there, and they had this bizarre rule that because he was a criminal he wasn't allowed to work. So the only way he could make money was from English tourists who wanted to go and visit him. It was like the Rock & Roll Hall of Fame, only for criminals.

We were round at Biggsy's gaff a couple of times when the tourists turned up. This little red bus would come trundling up to his gate, he would bullshit with them for a while – maybe give them a beer – they'd take a picture, someone would slip him a bit of money and then

they'd fuck off. I don't know how much he got out of it, not much probably, but I liked the way he handled the whole thing. He was fun.

In fact, I was enjoying myself so much that when we finished filming
and Cookie and everyone else went home, I stayed on for a couple more
weeks. It was relaxing to be by myself in the hotel for that fortnight. I
only know one word of Portuguese, *obrigado* – it's either 'please' or 'thank
you', one of the two – but that was more than enough to get by.

Returning to London at the fag-end of the winter of 1978, I hit the
ground with a fucking crash. I suppose we could have tried to sort things
out with Rotten, straighten Sid out and get back to writing some new
stuff. But Sid was too much of a mess by then to ever get clean, Malcolm
and Johnny hated each other so much they couldn't even be in a room
together, and the one attempt we'd made at writing a song over the last
few months of the Sex Pistols had been Sid bringing 'Belsen Was a Gas'
to the table.

That was a pretty stale leftover from his early band The Flowers of
Romance. There's a photo of us playing the riff together and when I look
at that picture I can actually remember thinking, 'Oh man, this is not
good, in fact it's crap.' It just kind of felt like, 'What's the fucking point?'
Too much had happened for anyone to be saying, 'Oh, let's write some
songs and do another album.' Those days were fucking gone and they
were not coming back.

The best time to be in the Sex Pistols was before Grundy, when we
were writing the songs that ended up on *Never Mind the Bollocks*. At that
point we weren't famous and we were all equal. There weren't so many
egos around . . . well, there were, but the tensions between Glen and John
or me and Paul and John were bringing energy into the songs. Whether
it was me crunching through Glen's Beatle chords, or John battling to
make himself heard over me and Paul, or all four of us kind of kicking

back against Malcolm, the struggles within the band were taking on a creative form. That's why there was no fixing the problems that ultimately destroyed us, because they were the same things that made the band work in the first place.

That's also why, when you look at the big fucking picture, the whole thing was perfect the way it was – beginning, middle and end. There's no point trying to dissect everything, saying, 'Oh, if Glen had stayed in the band instead of bringing Sid in, we could've done this or that.' Maybe the chemistry would've sustained us to do another album if Matlock had hung around, but it wasn't our destiny to have a progressive phase where we made a folk record and went on tour with Barclay James Harvest. The Sex Pistols were born to crash and burn, and that's exactly what we did.

I guess the one lesson you could learn from it all would be about trusting who you're with and not trying to be too controlling, because the magic was always the bit that *none* of us could control. We just didn't know how to handle how big we became after Grundy, really. We were like those fucking idiots who win the football pools, then blow all the money and end up committing suicide.

Instant gratification – always a weakness of mine – was a big part of the problem. Not so much in the traditional areas of sex and drugs (though obviously we weren't holding back there either), as in terms of the kind of things we'd do to get attention. Once something which happened spontaneously on TV caused that much outrage it became a bit of a game. It was like we'd got the keys to the machinery – 'If we do this, we'll get on the front page' – and the whole thing lost its innocence.

The sense of us being an actual band got swept away in a flood of tabloid bullshit. Malcolm got more and more obsessed with the circus element to the detriment of the music – that was how Sid ended up in the band – but we were all guilty of it. I remember one time somewhere in

Europe – could have been Amsterdam or Luxembourg, I don't fucking know, I didn't keep a diary – where I fucked this old fat bird from one of the big Fleet Street rags because I knew she'd give me a good spread in the paper if I did it. There I was on the page a few days later, the young stud running through the forest with these boots and a T-shirt on, and I felt kind of ashamed afterwards.

It was embarrassing, man, and that side of things got worse as time went on. I remember going to the Palm Restaurant in Los Angeles with Malcolm after the Pistols had split up. His ego had exploded by that time so all he would do was think of supposedly outrageous stunts to get more publicity, and on this occasion, he instigated me messing about with these lobsters in the restaurant in the hope that when we went outside there would be some big paparazzi thing. And there was – a bit, but not a lot.

Unfortunately, the impulse to prove what a master manipulator he was turned out to be what was driving McLaren when it came to *The Great Rock 'n' Roll Swindle* as well. Russ Meyer had been and gone as director before we'd even left for the American tour. I think it was his appointment that gave John a bad vibe that the whole thing was heading in more of a 'Carry On' direction from the beginning, and he was totally down on the project from then on. All I knew was that this geezer made movies about birds with big tits, and that sounded great to me.

As it turned out, once Julien Temple took over, I ended up having to kind of carry the whole film by playing the part of the detective who was trying to work out where the money had gone. Now you could say – and John probably would say – that I was helping Malcolm make us all look like idiots by doing this, but as far as I was concerned no one who knew anything about what had really happened was taking anything McLaren said seriously by that time. He certainly wasn't going to be winning any Oscars for his acting. He was so hopeless at learning his lines that they had to write them on scraps of paper and leave them stuck on things just out of camera range. That's why his eyes keep moving in weird directions in that noncey scene where he's in the bath and the naked girl is standing there.

I found learning lines much easier than Malcolm did, despite not being able to read or write properly, and I enjoyed the acting side of it. That didn't mean I was having a good time in general, though. We'd been the talk of the town for the last few years and there'd been a lot of excitement around us, then all of a sudden, it was over. Filming *The Great Rock 'n' Roll Swindle* felt like a bit of a lifeline, but looking back it probably made things worse. All the stuff in the film where we're auditioning Edward Tudor-Pole and a load of other singers to stand in for Rotten, for instance . . . I suppose that was Malcolm's way of showing Johnny that the band didn't need him, but what it actually showed was the opposite.

I remember getting up onstage with Tenpole Tudor a couple of times at the Hope & Anchor – drunk off my arse. Me and Cookie did a few songs together for the soundtrack, like 'Frigging in the Rigging' and 'Silly Thing', where there are two different versions with me singing on one and Cookie singing on the other. Of course my version is better, but his isn't bad either – it's got a funny vibe to it, and the song ended up being one of our biggest hits. Still, the more records came out with our names on and had success, the more obvious it was that the band was over.

I'd walked away from Johnny and Sid in San Francisco because it didn't seem worth being around their madness any more, but it only took me a few months after the end of the band till I was tumbling into some madness of my own. You'd think being around Sid at that time would've been enough to put someone off heroin for life, but it didn't turn out that way. I'd always had a feeling of emptiness inside me which I guess the band had helped me fill. But once all that was gone, the gaping hole opened up even wider and dope was a perfect fit for it.

I suppose if I hadn't had access to heroin, I would've probably just stepped up the drinking. I remember me and Cookie getting sloshed pretty regularly to keep the fear and loneliness at bay when we had to do all these Virgin record shop signings on our own up North around the release of 'Silly Thing', but why take an Uber of addiction when a chauffeur-driven limousine is available?

The strange thing was, I'd done heroin a couple of times while I was in the Pistols and not liked it either time: once on my birthday in Paris, and another with Johnny Thunders at Leee Childers' flat on Wardour Street in Soho. I certainly wasn't one of those heroin addicts who has it for the first time and thinks, 'Oh, this is it for me.' In fact, both times I remember snorting it, throwing up afterwards, and not really liking the feeling.

I should say at this point that heroin wasn't nearly such a known thing then as it is now. I hadn't really encountered it, growing up, when it was mainly toffs who were doing dope and blow, and the street drugs were speed, hash, booze and downers. I suppose Nick Kent was one of the first people I came across who I knew was doing it, but it felt like that was more of a pose, where he was pretending to nod out to make himself look (even) more like Keith Richards. The perception at the time was that in terms of punk it was really the New York people – specifically Johnny Thunders & the Heartbreakers – who brought it over. That was certainly true (via Nancy) of Sid, and there was an element of truth in it as far as I was concerned too.

Did that New York junkie cool thing draw me in? Johnny was very influential in terms of my guitar-playing, and when you met him he was very slick and had a lot of charisma. But did I start taking heroin cos I wanted to be like him? I don't think so. I liked the Heartbreakers, they were a great live rock 'n' roll band, but I don't think I realised at the time the extent to which they were junkies and their whole life was just about trying to get dope all the time. That one wouldn't click until it was too late and I was dangerously close to being in the same position myself. For the moment, heroin was just another medicine – like stealing and sex had been – which could stop me having to deal with reality.

The moment I realised I was in trouble was actually on the set of *The Great Rock 'n' Roll Swindle* – filming with the porn star Mary Millington up at the Rainbow in Finsbury Park. Mary seemed a sweet girl but she was very fucked up – she'd be dead before the film came out, just as Sid would. By then I'd been snorting heroin every day for about six months, but for some reason that morning I left home without it. When I got there I thought, 'I don't feel good – what's wrong with me? . . . Oh fuck!' I split straight away, went back to my flat, had a bit of dope there and felt better immediately.

It was a horrible feeling, being dependent like that, but it just felt too powerful to fight against. All I remember thinking was: 'Even though I don't want to, I'm going to go down this road and there's nothing I can really do about it.'

I did make a couple of half-assed attempts to put the brakes on. I'd heard Pete Townshend had done this black box treatment where you put pads behind your ears and pressed them every time you wanted drugs. It was an acupuncture kind of thing, but when I went to this woman's office in Bayswater and had a go, I was just pressing them every fucking second. It was a joke, really. I also tried buying methadone off the street, but it was watered-down shit that didn't work. Cookie saw what was happening and tried to help, but you're powerless over other people in that situation. You can't stop anybody who's not ready to do it for themselves, and I had a good few years of addiction ahead of me before I'd get to that point.

The big step up, out of the second tier of junkie fuckwits and into the top flight, is obviously when you start injecting. I guess you could say the Heartbreakers played an inspirational role in this for me, but only because one of the two guys who started me off (actually the same guy who brought Nancy to see us at the Notre Dame Hall that time – yeah, cheers, mate) thought he was a Johnny Thunders lookalike. His parents owned a hotel off Kensington High Street and he and his mate, a black guy called Barry, lived in this flat round the corner. At that time, I'd been snorting dope – but only snorting it, because I didn't know what it was like to shoot yet – for what felt like about a year. I was hanging out with them one night when they copped some and shot up. They looked like they were having a better time than me, so I said, 'Fucking do it!' I hated needles then, but it was all over from the moment that thing was in me. When you snort heroin, it takes a little while to get to you, but the instant rush of this was like a whole other fix in itself. It's in your bloodstream straight away and it's like, wallop! Two minutes later, you're in a coma.

It wasn't first time lucky in every respect, though. This was the only time I ever shared a needle and I'm pretty sure I managed to contract hepatitis C, but that wouldn't show up for a few years, and since I wasn't going to doctors for general health check-ups, it took a long while for the bad news to come through. Don't share needles, kids! Now who says this book doesn't have a responsible public health message?

In the meantime, I was hooked. The most demoralising thing about it was that the way you copped dope in the UK at that time was by going round to the dealer's house. So I'd have to sit around in this miserable hippie geezer's front room listening to Yes and Genesis for six hours just to get a sliver or sometimes even a few crumbs of dope. The indignity of it! The Sex Pistols were meant to have got rid of all that shit, and now there I was, a captive audience for Rick fucking Wakeman . . .

22. SIOUXSIE INCIDENTALLY

My promotion into the junkie premier league came in the latter stages of filming *The Great Rock 'n' Roll Swindle*. If babysitting Sid through the recording of 'My Way' in Paris wasn't going to put me off the dope, I guess nothing was. That trip was beyond a fucking nightmare.

So Sid's off to Paris with Nancy, and he's got six big bottles of methadone he's taking over with him. I guess he's getting it legally now because he's trying to kick – that old routine. Anyway, they're filming over there and I've somehow got pulled into the mix to go over and be the musical director in this little studio with these French session guys. At that point, being around him and that bird ranked a little below hell on earth as a place you'd want to be. To be fair to Sid, he was totally out of it, and methadone is a nasty fucking drug. I heard the Nazis came up with it, although I don't know if that's true. Either way, because you drink it in liquid form, it doesn't have such an immediate impact, but it lasts way longer. As a result, it's actually harder to kick than heroin is.

Anyway, while Sid was busy climbing the walls, I got these guys to cut the track. I think the original plan was for him to do it slow all the way through, but once we realised that probably wasn't going to happen, speeding it up was the only way to go. The way the twiddly bit goes into time with the bass player came out all right in the end, and to his credit, Sid did kind of turn up for the vocal. When I took the masters back to England, I was actually quite proud of what turned out to be my first credit as a producer. These days I always get a chuckle out of the end of the movie *Goodfellas*, where my name is the last word you see on the screen.

I still don't think I've ever been fucking paid for producing 'My Way', to be honest, but it felt good to be doing something new. Once Malcolm had got some guy to write out string charts and they'd put the orchestra on, it sounded pretty good. Unfortunately, I'd started to go downhill with the smack myself by then, so I wasn't as interested as I should've been. I kind of came off it for a while when I got the call to go over to San Francisco and work with The Avengers and Joan Jett, but I was smoking a lot of weed and drinking too much to fill the hole when I was out there, to the extent that I might as well have been on fucking heroin half the time.

I was actually working with The Avengers when I got the call to say that Sid had died. Obviously Nancy had gone ahead of him to see if she could find a connection in the afterlife. I know that will sound dark, but it was a dark time. I've got no inside knowledge of what happened to either of them, but it was fucking grim. When I was told that Sid had died, I didn't have a lot of feelings about it. I didn't have a lot of feelings about anything at that stage, to be honest, so when some guy from *Rolling Stone* called me up, I just said the first thing that came into my head, which was: 'Well, at least we'll sell some records now.'

In hindsight it was probably a stupid response, and I could tell that the guy was shocked. But it was also a very Sex Pistols thing to say, which in a strange way – as the idea of the band meant as much to him as it did to any of us – was maybe what Sid would've wanted. Later on, I did feel sad about what happened, especially through talking to his mum, who I got on with pretty well. Sid was not an idiot, he was quite an intelligent bloke, but once he was in the band the logic of his situation pushed him down a very dark track. As I've said, if we'd called him Sid Kind or Sid Gentle, he might've tried to live up to that instead, but I don't suppose he'd still be on so many T-shirts.

I think John carries a lot of guilt to this day over Sid's death, even though it's buried so deep in his head he doesn't always recognise that's what it is. But I don't think Lydon deserves any more of the blame for what happened to Sid than anyone else does. It was his own responsibility how he chose to fuck up his life. Sometimes destiny is a motherfucker and that's all there is to it.

With Sid's death, it was finally clear to everyone – even Malcolm – that the band was over. Did it feel weird not to be a Sex Pistol any more? Well, you're always associated with it, and I guess my image of myself at that point was that I still had to act a certain way, even if I didn't really want to. My time in the band felt so close that I didn't know yet who I was going to be if I wasn't going to be that. It wouldn't be till the mid/late Eighties, when I'd gone to LA and got sober and let my hair grow long and started riding motorbikes and writing mellow songs, that I'd begin finding another way to be.

Rotten was smart enough to begin that process straight away, by ditching his punk name and going back to being plain old John Lydon the minute he started doing Public Image Ltd. The other thing he was smart enough to do was take Malcolm to court. This was difficult for me at first, because I was still pals with McLaren and I didn't want to have to take John's side against him. When the receivers got put in and found out what a mess all the finances were it was really fucking depressing, but the more time went on, the clearer it became that it had to be done, and hats off to Rotten for doing it. I give him a lot of credit for having the balls to take that initiative.

Obviously he was doing it for his own good rather than mine and Cookie's, but it benefited us, too, in the long run. It took the courts six or seven years to sort the whole thing out, but the basic problem was that Malcolm had spent money on the film that should've been ours. Whether you view that as straight robbery – as John did, and still does – or take the more sympathetic view that if McLaren was just a thief, he would have nicked the money for himself rather than to make *The Swindle*, the fact remains that this wasn't his call to make. And if he hadn't stitched us up by getting his own lawyer to do all our contracts, he wouldn't have been in a position to get away with it for as long as he did.

When it came to the legal crunch, the clincher was that we were all under twenty-one when we signed our original contract. It was dodgy all down the line. We didn't fucking know what we were agreeing to – or how wrong it was for us not to have our own lawyers. How were we supposed to know that wasn't normal? We were too busy having fun. It was a shame for Malcolm that it all ended the way it did and he came away from the Sex Pistols with no financial reward, but he had no one to blame but himself. If he'd have just taken the credit for the things he did do instead of spending all our money on a film which made us out to be a bunch of muppets who couldn't play our instruments, it would've been fine.

In the gap between *The Great Rock 'n' Roll Swindle* being finished and it finally coming out, me and Cookie were still working as a team – proving the film wrong by getting as much work as we could, and playing on some pretty good records in the process. Us sharing that place at Bell Street hadn't really worked out – amazing, really, given what a pleasure I must have been to live with – so while there was still a bit of cash in the Pistols' kitty, I'd ended up with my own place on Canfield Gardens, between West Hampstead and Swiss Cottage. You could see how dodgy the finances were by the way the money for that just magically appeared, almost like it was out of a petty cash box.

It was a short lease – maybe forty-five years – which was why it only cost fourteen grand. You might get the door for that now. There wasn't a long thought, process involved in the purchase on my part – I just looked at the place and thought, 'Yeah, this is great' – but I did put a lot of effort into doing it up. It was kind of ridiculous because I didn't really know what I was doing, but I made a shower and even put a little stage in there – showbiz or what? No one else in my family had owned their own place before, so I guess from the outside it must have seemed like I was a high achiever, but it didn't feel like that at all . . . I mean, I shagged a lot of birds in that flat, no problem. I had a little drawer in the coffee table with the blow, the heroin, the downers, the uppers, whatever, in it, and the birds kind of flocked around that: threesomes, foursomes . . . In retrospect it all looked great, and in a way it was.

I had a couple of nice second-hand cars around that time, even though I still had no licence or insurance. The first one was a black BMW 2002 which I bought off an Asian kid I went to school with and souped up into a really fucking tasty motor. Me and Jimmy Macken – who was back on the scene a bit, although he and Cookie weren't getting on too well – would drive it around London really fast late at night after going to gigs at the Music Machine. We'd be fucking drunk and flying around like lunatics, to the extent that I can't believe we never had a crash.

Later I bought a big copper-coloured Jaguar Vanden Plas. It was a cool car but it fucking guzzled petrol, which was a major nause because by the time I had that one, the 1979 fuel crisis was in full swing, so I'd have to queue for hours to get petrol then the tank would be empty again a couple of hours later. I know what you're thinking: 'Serves you right, you flash bastard, why weren't you driving a shit-heap like the rest of us?'

Me and Cookie were kind of guns for hire at that time, and our credit was still good in the industry, so we were getting to work with a lot of people who had been our heroes. When Johnny Thunders got a solo deal after the Heartbreakers ended, I played on some of the tracks on his first record *So Alone*. Looking back on it, one of the sad things about that album was that he did a version of 'Daddy Rollin' Stone' – Otis Blackwell, I think it's by – with Cookie on drums, me on guitar, and a different singer on each of the three verses. Phil Lynott did a verse, Steve Marriott did a verse and Johnny Thunders did a verse. I'm glad I didn't do one, as they were all dead by 1992.

We also teamed up with Lynott a few times as a kind of punk/hard-rock supergroup called The Greedy Bastards. We did a few gigs mixing up Pistols songs and Thin Lizzy songs, and we even had a Christmas hit together in 1979. We had a laugh, and I really liked Phil, but things turned a bit ugly between us towards the end once we were both on heroin. There's a white Falcon guitar of mine in his museum in Ireland which he conned out of me for a bag of dope, but you win some, you lose some. People who've nicked coats off The Rolling Stones shouldn't live in glass houses, as I think the old saying goes.

I liked playing with other people, and probably my favourite band to play with was The Clash. I got up onstage with them a few times to do 'Janie Jones' or 'White Riot' or '. . . USA' – those were the three main ones – and always really enjoyed it. Once (I think it was after doing *Top of the Pops* with Thin Lizzy on the Thursday night) I drove all the way up to Birmingham on my own to do a song with them.

To be honest, although I never mentioned this to anyone at the time, I'd have quite liked to be in The Clash then – it seemed more fun than what I was doing. It was before The Professionals were happening and I think I just felt a bit lost. I guess it was like me imagining the perfect family as a kid. I never got a feeling of rivalry from that band; they were always warm to me and I was always a fan of theirs.

I know the grass is always greener on the other side of the tour bus, and I'm sure The Clash had their own internal turmoil to deal with, but I related to those guys in a way I never could to Lydon. You could have a laugh with Joe or Mick Jones backstage and it was like, 'Oh, OK, so not everyone is a complete cunt like Rotten.' The problem with Johnny is that he's always 'on'. And if you can't even shut the dressing room door and be real with someone you're in a band with because he's always got to be that guy, then what the fuck is the point?

The Clash weren't the only band of people from around the scene making it pretty big by that time. I can't deny that seeing everyone jumping on the punk bandwagon bugged me a bit. Even though the ethos was meant to be 'Anyone can do this', when they all did you just thought, 'Oh, fuck off!' Or at least I did. I didn't feel that way about the Bromley people, though, because they'd been there from the beginning.

I hadn't paid too much attention when Siouxsie played her first gig at the 100 Club with Vicious drumming, because they were shit. But I appreciated the way she looked – she really went for it – and she obviously had some talent because the Banshees turned into a decent band in the end. Not so much after they went Goth in the Eighties (that applied to The Damned as well: their first LP, before the line-up changed, when Sensible was still on bass instead of guitar – that was always the one for me), but certainly before that. 'Hong Kong Garden' is still a pretty cool tune – they probably have a blue plaque outside the Chinese takeaway that was about – and I played on a few tracks on *Kaleidoscope*, their album where the writing goes round in a circle on the back sleeve.

Siouxsie gets a page pretty much to herself in the Steve Jones sexual scrapbook as one of the very few who got away. I definitely had an opportunity one night – unless I'm daydreaming – when the two of us drove out to the airport together. We'd both been up the West End doing speed and I had the bright idea of driving to Heathrow to watch the planes take off and land (I don't think she'd have believed me if I'd offered her a look at my etchings). That's how smooth I was in those days; it was years before they did it in *Wayne's World* as well.

Now that I remember, this was in another, different car – a Lancia I'd bought off a guy called Fachtna O'Kelly who managed The Professionals for a while – so it must've happened a year or so later. Either way, the two of us drove out to the airport and parked up. Unfortunately, by the time we got there I'd had so much speed I couldn't even think about making a move. It was fun watching the sun come up, but missing the chance to get hold of Siouxsie is one of my biggest regrets. Now who says true romance is dead?

Joan Jett stayed over in Canfield Gardens for a couple of nights when we did the demo for 'I Love Rock 'n' Roll', too. That song would end up being her biggest hit; well, I say 'her' biggest hit, but it was written by The Arrows. It was all covers with Joan.

Those were the good times, but there was also some horrible dark shit going on in that period when I was living on Canfield Road and lapsing into heroin. I guess the band which had been the closest thing I'd had to a home didn't exist any more and I'd lost my bearings. I'm not making excuses for going down to that shop in Islington (run by an old Sixties rocker but I won't mention his name as he's still alive and he might sue me) which sold Nazi regalia and buying a couple of old swastika flags to put up on the walls in the living room; I'm just trying to explain where my head was at, and why this dark shit was so in sync with how I felt.

I hadn't really got my head around the concept of the concentration camps by the time the Sex Pistols were happening – history being one of the many subjects at school I didn't pay attention to – so to me Vivienne's 'Destroy' T-shirts with swastikas on were just about being shocking. In the late Seventies those Nazi images broke out from there and took on a life of their own. There's one picture which crops up every now and again of me hanging out with Jimmy Pursey of Sham 69, when we were thinking of doing something together after the Pistols. I've got this Harrington on and under it there's a T-shirt which is just this big blatant fucking swastika. That and nothing else – no writing or anything.

Every time I see that, it makes me cringe. It was weird, really, because I'm not a racist and never have been. I suppose it was just a way of summing up the darkness I felt. I'd done the progressive phase and the manager-of-Poco phase, so the Nazi phase was the logical next step.

One thing that didn't turn out to be the logical step was working with Jimmy Pursey. When me and Cookie gave Jimmy a try, it was never going to be the Sex Pistols in our minds, we always thought of it as a new group. The odd thing about it was that we liked him, but when we got together to try and write some songs in a studio out in the country, he couldn't fucking come up with anything. His cover was blown – he didn't have the talents or intelligence that Rotten did; nowhere near. It was like the world was conspiring to make us miss Johnny.

I remember hanging out with Pursey one time in the dark phase. I went down with him and some of his mates to see The Undertones – the Irish guys who did 'Teenage Kicks' – at a gig on Jimmy's home turf in the outskirts of London, the Guildford Civic Hall, I think it was. This was in May '79. We didn't have anything against The Undertones, the plan was just to get up and jam with 'em, but it went cockeyed for no good reason that I could understand and all of a sudden these skinheads who were Jimmy's entourage kicked the band off the stage and started smashing their stuff up. I should've tried to stop it but I didn't. It was very bizarre but kind of fun in a dark sort of way. I don't think it was fun for The Undertones, though, because they had to run and hide in the dressing room.

I had a little thing going with Sporty Spice years later – not sexually, just playing on her solo record. She told me her auntie was The Undertones' tour manager at the time and had told her they'd all been scared shitless by how heavy and violent and horrible it was. And these were people who grew up in Northern Ireland in the Seventies! There was certainly a weird vibe around Pursey. I wasn't surprised to hear he'd ended up doing interpretative dance on TV a while later. I remember everyone going back to his house to party and me thinking, 'Where's Jimmy?' and he was taking a bath . . . I thought that was weird. In fact, even thinking about this time is giving me anxiety because of how depressing it was. I'd like to be able to say that I'd reached my lowest ebb, but it wouldn't be true. Far from it.

23. 'I PISSED ON ELVIS' GRAVE'

It wasn't long after *The Great Rock 'n' Roll Swindle* was finally finished that another movie project came up. I went straight from a twisted cartoon version of the story of the band I had actually been in, to a movie about an imaginary band which turned into a real one. This would have been enough of a head-fuck even if I wasn't going cold turkey in Canada at the time.

The second film was called *Ladies and Gentlemen, the Fabulous Stains,* and although there were loads of people involved in it who had been – or would become – really big, it was a weird low-budget thing. It felt like it was going to be shit at the time. It never really got a proper release, and for years no one had heard of it, but gradually a bit of a cult built up around it and if you watch it now you can see why, because it's actually pretty funny.

The director, Lou Adler, was a famous old hippie who'd produced the band Spirit, and one of the producers, Joe Roth, would end up as head of Disney – though I don't think he'd have talked about this film too much at that job interview, as it wasn't the sort of thing Uncle Walt would've approved of. The reason me and Cookie got involved was that Caroline

Coon was the music consultant. Her job was to give the film a punk feel. She was certainly an expert in that field.

The main story was about this teenage girl band – led by Diane Lane but with Laura Dern in it as well – who become really big by basically being a bit like Lady Gaga. They wanted two other bands as a contrast – one was a kind of worn-out hippie rock band led by Fee Waybill from The Tubes, and the other was an English punk band called The Looters, which was me, Cookie, Paul Simonon from The Clash and, on vocals, the actor Ray Winstone (who'd just done *Scum* and *Quadrophenia*). Ray didn't have a clue what he was doing at first, but he did all right in the end. We showed him some moves and I think he got away with it.

We were filming in Vancouver, because they wanted a lot of rain. The plan was to make out it was set in Pennsylvania or some kind of industrial American place, and we had to get there about three or four weeks before the filming to record some of the music. I was so strung out when I arrived, I thought, 'Oh, Canada, it's just like America – I'll be able to score, no problem.' But I couldn't get so much as a sniff. I'd been on heroin and methadone, so I was just out of my fucking tree with no sleep for about a month.

They had a couple of local punk bands in Vancouver – obviously it was a small-time scene but one of them, D.O.A., were actually pretty good. Once, when I was kicking, me and Cookie went to a club where some band or other was playing and there were all these long-haired cunts wearing flares and satin jackets. Talk about America being a year behind. In Canada it was more like a decade. I remember sitting in there shaking from the withdrawal, looking at these wankers with their beards and moustaches and just wanting to fucking die.

I didn't really take to the Canadians as a people. They seemed a bit slow to me. If you asked them for something it would take them about a minute to catch on, but I suppose it was probably because I kept begging them for some heroin and none of them had any. I can't have been very easy to be around then, and Cookie probably got the worst of it. But that trip wasn't a total bust. The songs we wrote and recorded with Paul and Ray as The Looters would end up being the foundation of our next band, The Professionals, and once I'd come through the worst of the kick – they don't call it Jonesing for nothing – I even started to have a pretty good time.

There were a lot of cool people in that cast and crew, and a fair amount of swapping of hotel rooms went on. Plus the place we were all staying in was the Denman, which was as close as Vancouver got to a rock 'n' roll hotel, so all the other bands passing through on tour would stay there too. I got in the habit of going up Grouse Mountain, the big local ski resort, to have hot toddies at ten in the morning, and ended up becoming a kind of tour guide for visiting members of the rock and pop aristocracy. Once I took Gary Numan up Grouse Mountain (now there's an enduring image) and I've got funny pictures somewhere of us messing about in the snow.

It was fun, and I suppose it paved the way for what I do on *Jonesy's Jukebox* now – I've always had that kind of sociable vibe when it comes to other people in bands. There was a fair bit of free time, and playing the guitarist in an English punk band wasn't too much of a stretch for me in acting terms; I'd been doing it ever since the Grundy show anyway. The only real nause was Diane Lane's mum, who I remember being a classic nightmare stage mother. She may have been *Playboy*'s Playmate of the Month in October 1957, but that didn't stop her being a major pain in the arse.

Me and Cookie had written some decent songs – 'Kick Down the Doors' was a good one – and we were still in demand at that time, so

Virgin were happy to sign The Professionals, but by then I was in no shape to make the most of the opportunity. To say the heroin was clouding my judgement would be putting it mildly, and you can tell how not on the ball I was by the fact that we ended up having three different managers.

First there was Fachtna O'Kelly, this Irish bloke who used to manage The Boomtown Rats, then there was Dave Hill, who managed the Pretenders. They were both good guys who did their best for us, but I was becoming a bit of a lost cause by then. Finally came a big, menacing old-school promoter called John Curd who used to have a boat by the Albert Bridge. He was a mistake that wouldn't have happened if I hadn't been on the dope, but when you're as loaded as I was you kind of lose track of what your own best interests are.

Even Curdy – who wasn't renowned as a philanthropist – had a go at straightening me out. He sent me to the Canary Islands with this other bloke as my minder to get me away from the dealers, and I did stop doing dope for a bit while I was there, but we were still doing blow and getting pissed, which kind of defeated the object. It was the same when The Professionals went out on the road. That was the only time I would stop doing heroin, but then I was just constantly, belligerently drunk, which wasn't much of an improvement. That was my concept of being fucking sober at that point: getting off the dope. Heroin was the problem area. Doing blow, getting drunk, shagging everything that moved and stealing everything that didn't was all fine. This was level 1 Steve Jones sobriety – I hadn't yet grasped the concept that to be sober, you actually had to stop it all.

I had a lot more damage to get through before I'd be ready to do that: my work was not yet done. The short run of two and a bit years from John joining to the Pistols imploding was such a whirlwind that when it ended we were left reeling. Much as I'd been ready to say, 'Fuck it, I'm out of here,' in San Francisco in January '78, it was like breaking up with a girl-friend. Even though it might be your choice not to be with someone, you're still devastated they're not there any more. I didn't process that feeling in the best way – I dealt with it how I always dealt with things: by finding a way to blot them out.

You could say The Professionals were unlucky, but I guess we – or at least I – made our own luck. Alongside the contract troubles and the album that wasn't as good as the demos, the worst thing that happened to us didn't affect me directly. Somehow, and I can't remember precisely how, but it probably had more to do with sex or drugs than with rock 'n' roll, I managed not to be in the van when the rest of the band were in a really serious car accident in Minnesota on our first American tour in 1981. It took some of them months to get over that, but I was too wasted to notice.

Something else that happened in the USA that I wouldn't technically be fully present for – and I will deny all knowledge if questioned about this under oath – was the lagging-on-Elvis'-grave incident a few months later. I did mention this on my radio show once, but kind of skipped around the topic, hoping no one was really listening. Even then I could hear them panicking in the control room, as it isn't something I've talked about in public too much. So let us say hypothetically that such an incident might have taken place, while not making an absolute commitment to the fact that it did.

If it had happened, it would probably have been in the daytime, and the perpetrator would've definitely have had a drink. The time frame we'd be looking at would be the Tennessee leg of The Professionals' US tour in 1982, and it would be important to emphasise that the Graceland of that time was very different to how it is now. It hadn't been tarted up as a big tourist attraction, which is what happened when Elvis' wife or the daughter took the place over and turned it into a money machine. You couldn't go in the house – all you could do was go and look at the grave. In fact, the place was such a mess back then that you could think of the piss that might or might not have taken place as a protest about the facilities – maybe it was even the piss that changed everything.

Another factor to bear in mind in defence of the sexy pisser (assuming that he – or she – was sexy, which of course they were . . . probably) is that it's good to urinate near a grave because it keeps the coyotes away. So maybe this frontier character only did it – if they did do it – to protect Elvis from coyotes. The reason I am being so discreet about all this is, first, because I do actually love Elvis and, second, because there is a bit of form when it comes to these liquid offerings of affection and respect from visiting British rock royalty to their American hosts being misunderstood. Remember Ozzy at the Alamo? If those angry Texans had only realised he was trying to protect that historic monument from chihuahuas by pissing on it, they'd have probably gone a lot easier on him.

The Professionals' relationship with the guy who produced our album was up there with Ozzy and the people of the Lone Star state when it came to getting off on the wrong foot (although I think Ozzy actually missed his foot). His name was Nigel Gray, and he had a lot of hits with other people – The Police, the Pretenders, Siouxsie and the Banshees even – but not with us. Maybe the heroin gave him a good reason, and there was also an incident with me nicking some of 10cc's guitars from his studio out in the country which probably didn't help, but I just didn't feel as if he liked us.

One night, Nigel drove me and Cookie home from his studio. He was going to drop us off at Paul's house, but just as we were getting near Hammersmith, a cop car pulled us over and searched us. They found a bit of dope in the car that was obviously mine but at first I didn't want to own up to it. When the police made it clear they were gonna do someone for it, and Nigel was pretty upfront about not wanting that someone to be him, I put my hand up and got nicked. Between that time and the case coming to court, I fucked off to America and didn't come back, so I was never found guilty. But the charge really naused up my visa, so it was touch and go for a while whether I was going to be allowed back to the US.

Fuck knows what would've happened if I'd had to stay in the UK. The way I was heading at that time, I don't think I'd be alive now, let alone writing my autobiography as LA's best-loved rock 'n' roll punk radio personality. The funny part of it was that I always resented Nigel for what happened. For a long time I even harboured a crazy suspicion that he'd maybe had something to do with us getting pulled over that night, which would have been a real shit-cunt thing for him to do. I just had a feeling that he had some connection to the law – like he'd been a copper, or his dad had, or something. It was only when I was thinking about this book that I realised what this law enforcement connection was. Nigel hadn't been an informer for The Police, but he had produced them.

Some people might say that's reason enough to be suspicious of him, but Sting and the boys did have some good tunes. Of course there were no mobile phones then, so how could he have set us up from the motor he was giving us a ride home in? I suppose this just shows how far someone who is taking heroin will go not to face up to their own part in anything bad that happens to them.

By the time we left England for what turned out to be The Professionals' last US tour, I had bigger problems than a bullshit possession charge hanging over me. The only question in my head at that time was, 'Where can I get some dope from?' In pursuit of – always temporary – answers to that question, I had sold just about everything I owned. Canfield

Gardens had been stripped pretty much bare by my relentless quest for drug money, and I even had to give up my guitar and amp to John Curd to pay a debt he'd come up with. It's never a good sign for a musician when your manager is taking your instruments off you. One of the last things I did before leaving for the US in 1982 was playing on 'Dancing With Myself' at Air Studios in Oxford Street with my old Bromley Contingent mate Billy Idol. He was heading to America too, but he was going to be a lot bigger there in the Eighties than I was.

If I was to try and add up my reasons for staying in England, it wouldn't take me very many fingers. In musical terms, me and Cookie were totally surplus to requirements by then. I went down to the Blitz club a couple of times – where all the New Romantic kids who were into dressing up used to go – and it just felt like punk was old news. No one gave a shit whether we were there or not. The charts were full of Kajagoogoo music. If not quite them yet, it was all Adam Ant and Big Country and The Human League.

I get that the world changes and people move on; I think I got that even then. But now even my old friends were turning against me. The bad feeling Jimmy Macken had (understandably) felt about not being a part of the Pistols had started to come out in ways that turned things ugly between us. Sometimes it feels like the flipside of that working-class attitude to success is always resentment. Cookie had been doing his best to hold the whole Professionals thing together against the odds, but even he was getting fed up with me. And if there's a clearer way of showing that your rock 'n' roll race is kind of run for the moment than (possibly) pissing on the King's lasting resting place, then I for one don't know what it is. The way I was going, things could have been a lot worse – at least I didn't shit on it.

24. HOME IS WHERE THE 8X10 PHOTO OF HEART IS

You know what they say, when the going gets tough, the tough fuck off to live with a lady of the night. Faced with the many different kinds of carnage involved in The Professionals' second and last US tour, I did what I always did when a situation had got so bad that the reality of it needed to be faced up to – I bolted.

There wasn't one specific thing compelling me to stay in America, but there were a fuck of a lot of good reasons for not wanting to go back to England. I didn't want to go back to the darkness, the junkies, the dealers, the possession charge and the empty flat in Canfield Gardens with no furniture in it cos I'd sold it all to buy dope. Even the Nazi flags had gone; that place just didn't feel like home without them.

Sometimes there are things that you just can't do, and the prospect of knocking the band on the head only to get on the plane with the others and fly home with our tails tucked neatly between our legs seemed like such a grim fucking outlook. So I said, 'Sorry, see you later, guys – I can't go back to London,' swanned off with a woman of ill repute, and didn't go back to England for fourteen years. That part wasn't premeditated, but the fact that one of my first acts after staying on was to sell my passport for some dough – I can't remember who to, but I didn't get much, maybe $80 – shows how ready I was to leave everything behind. I was set in a pattern of scaling back from the dope to the healthy option of heavy drinking and cocaine when I was on tour, then going straight back on heroin the minute the gigs were over. If I'd been organised enough to have any priorities, there'd only really have been one at that point, and it would've been 'Get more drugs'.

When it came to heroin, I'd always thought of myself as a cut above the scratchers you used to see around King's Cross who were basically zombies with no fucking life. They'd always whine about how they wanted to get clean, but you couldn't help thinking that wasn't really true. Even when I compared myself to, say, Johnny Thunders & the Heartbreakers – who would go from city to city and the first thing they'd do when they arrived would be to find out where they could cop – I thought of them as real junkies and me as somehow not a real one. But the clear blue water I thought I saw between us was filling up with old syringes.

Maybe this was just the denial which was part of the addiction, but I still don't feel like I was a junkie deep down inside, the way I was a thief. It's the same with alcoholics – there are some who life has pushed to drink too much for one reason or another, and others you feel were born to do it. I definitely fell into the second category as far as booze was concerned, but still think of myself in the first, heroin-wise. To me, dope was more a hole I fell down when I was trying to escape, but how much difference that made, if any, was another matter. The fact was that I was doing more and more of the kind of shit junkies did, and if it waddles like a duck and shoots up like a duck, then it is a fucking duck.

The brass I did a runner with had one quality which qualified her for the job – she knew how to get dope. As solid a foundation as that was for an enduring romance (well, it worked for Sid and Nancy), it didn't last long. Then I found another bird willing to put up with me who wasn't a lady of the night but more a social butterfly – hip to all the clubs. We ended up staying together for a while. She was a bit naive as far as drugs went, but after a few months of me staying with her she found a needle in my pocket and realised what was going on. I thought, 'Oh that's it, the game's up now,' but it turned out she wanted to try it too.

I've never seen myself as a role model, and the influence I had on this woman is not something I'm proud of. We carried on that way for maybe six or nine months. She had a decent little loft in New York, sort of East Village/Houston way. It was kind of sleazy, not all cleaned up there like it is now. You didn't get many tourists and it was dangerous walking around at night, but I was too much of a mess to care.

At first, all the money was coming from her, but I soon worked my way through that reserve, and once she was skint we were back to me going to clubs and nicking handbags or doing whatever other demoralising things I could to keep a habit going. Thievery had become more of an occasional pleasure when the Sex Pistols were happening, if only because there was so much else going on. But they do say it's good to have a trade to fall back on, and the fact that I never got caught once I hit the Big Apple shows you I hadn't got too rusty. It was always in a small-time way – I was no Great Train Robber. Mind you, Ronnie Biggs wasn't exactly a criminal mastermind either.

London street-smarts were very different to the New York variety back then. I'd see all the other junkies shuffling around with their eyes glued to the sidewalk without realising that they were probably doing it for a reason. Striding round Alphabet City (which was where I used to go to cop dope) like it was Canfield Gardens may not have been the smartest move at the time. It's yuppie central now, but back then it was the opposite: a run-down bunch of blocks controlled by Puerto Rican gangs, where I must have stood out like a sore thumb. It was a scary urban jungle vibe – completely different to what I was used to. And not only was I very much out of my element, but most of the time I was out of my head as well, so I was lucky not to get mugged.

I came close a couple of times. Fuck knows what would have happened to me if I'd woken up in a hospital with concussion. I didn't have a passport, I didn't technically have anywhere to live – I was ahead of my time as far as being off the grid was concerned. As shit as all this sounds, I'd be lying if I didn't admit there was an element of excitement to it, too. Alphabet City was definitely a whole different ballgame to sitting in some gringe's front room while he made me listen to *Tales From Topographic* fucking *Oceans*.

There were times when walking down there to cop was the last thing I wanted to do. But when you're sick for the dope, you've got no choice. It was scary, but I knew I had to do it. The thought of getting high was all that was keeping me going. There was no joy coming from anywhere, but at least I knew what the point of me was. This is going to sound pretty fucking weird, but being a junkie felt like a necessity after the Pistols ended. It would be crazy to say it saved my life, but that kind of is how I feel about it. It's never the down-and-outs that kill themselves, it's always the ones who've had something and lost it. I'm lucky that I've never had coherent suicidal feelings in my life, and you can't imagine what that feels like if you've never been to that place, but the hole inside me was yawning so wide that fuck knows what else I'd have filled it with if I hadn't had heroin.

It wasn't that I liked being a junkie. I never wanted to make being a mess a part of my schtick like Sid did. I knew how pathetic I looked. Standards were slipping in fashion terms with my baggy trousers and big hairy sweaters; the peacock of my Sex Pistols days had slowly lost its feathers and became a fucking pigeon. Filthy fucking vermin I was, and some of the shit I'd do to get a few bucks was so petty it was embarrassing. Nicking birds' handbags at clubs was bad enough, but the girlfriend I'd corrupted had lived with a rock photographer before we got together, and I think the low point of my New York junkie phase was when we nicked loads of 8×10 photos of bands he'd taken pictures of – nothing fancy, just standard press shots – and tried to sell them to passers-by on the street.

You know what a joke you've become when your chances of survival depend on flogging someone a stolen 8×10 press shot of the band Heart. I just used to grit my teeth and hope no one recognised me.

The funny thing was that even though I was not in a good place in personal terms, I was still happy to be in America rather than London. I'd felt used up and unwanted there, and at least New York was exciting. Big streets, places that were open 24 hours . . . it wasn't like that in England. There were still only three channels on TV and the grim London vibe hadn't woken up and smelt the Eighties yet. Now everything's more or less the same all over the world, people might not remember how different America was then.

Obviously New York was edgier than the rest of the country, and I know this might seem a weird thing for someone who was a junkie at the time to say, but I loved the fact that Americans still prided themselves on service. When you'd go into a restaurant – even if it was just a cheap cafe – people would bend over backwards to make you happy. Ask for a sandwich in England at that time and the geezer's crying because he can't get the piece of ham small enough.

After I'd been in America a year or so, another band came about. It was me, Tony Sales from Iggy Pop's band, Michael Des Barres, who'd been the lead singer of Silverhead in the early Seventies – they were kind of in Led Zeppelin's shadow but with a glammy edge to them, and I'd liked their second album, *16 and Savaged* – and Nigel Harrison and Clem Burke from Blondie. This was in the days when the music industry had a bit of money to spend, and people would give you a big wad of cash just to do a show. Obviously mine went straight in my arm, but we did the gig, which was at the Peppermint Lounge, and the whole thing came together pretty well.

We started out doing covers – I think 'Vacation' by the Go-Go's was the song we began our first set with, so that gives you some idea of the kind of sound we were aiming at. It was just a rock 'n' roll band with a bit of punk underneath, but I didn't have any better options at the time, so when someone said, 'This is pretty good – we should do more,' I wasn't going to disagree.

The name of the band – Chequered Past – turned out to be appropriate, given that the album we made a couple of years later is probably not the one I'll be most remembered for. But to be honest I didn't really give a shit about the music then – being in a band with Sid Vicious had beaten that out of me. All I wanted to do was get high, and this was a way to do it. But I certainly didn't feel I was betraying the spirit of punk by making a more traditional-sounding rock album. Even when I was in the Pistols I used to go back to the flat and play Boston and Journey. There's a certain clean-cut, very crisp, clear, melodic rock sound that I've always been really into, and when I hear a good song, I can't help liking it: whether the singer has a mohawk or is a man wearing a dress doesn't matter to me.

Of course Malcolm wouldn't have been happy if I'd gone around admitting how much I liked 'More Than a Feeling' in interviews in 1976. That would've been a no-no for a band who were meant to be the start of something new. But it wasn't us who came up with the stance that the Sex Pistols were against all old music, for the simple reason that we weren't against all old music. I agreed with drawing a line under bands like Emerson Lake and Palmer – cunts you could never get close to who had disappeared up their own arses with their grandiose wealth. I got that – I never liked them, even in my progressive phase. But by the time Chequered Past formed in 1982, the rituals of punk had become as set in stone as prog rock ever was.

I'm not bothered about all those Exploited types. I could never give a shit about them, or GBH, or any of the bands with big mohicans. They all looked like scratchers to me, and even if they weren't, they'd completely lost the plot of what punk was all about. The early stages was the cream. Everyone was dressing differently – it wasn't all about how high the spikes in your hair were and having a studded leather jacket. That's when it all became two-bob to me, when it changed from the excitement of what you could become to hanging on to a uniform, frozen in time. Once you're saying, 'Let's stay like this for ever,' you're not bringing anything new to it or responding to life as it's happening. At that point, you might as well be a Teddy boy.

Now I was definitely in need of a new beginning, so when the Chequered Past people said, 'Let's start a band, but we've got to be based in LA,' because that was where most of the guys lived, it took me about three seconds to say 'yes'. I'd first met Michael Des Barres at Dingwalls in Camden when the Sex Pistols were happening and we kind of hit it off. He was one of those people who actually came to our last gig in San Francisco rather than just saying he was there when he wasn't, like so many others. Cunts still do that to me now – say they were at our shows when they weren't. Why do they do it when they're only going to get caught out and look like a dick? I'll do that to them, too.

'Hey, I love your album . . .'

'Oh, do you? What's track three on the first side of *Never Mind the Bollocks*, then?'

I don't know why things like that bother me. I suppose I just don't like bullshit, which makes it funny that I should've moved to LA, pretty much the bullshit capital of the world. But when I first got to California, even the clichéd 'have a nice day' American attitude to life didn't bug me. In fact, I found how positive everyone was quite refreshing after the darkness of New York. I also liked being free of that narky fucking English vibe where everyone was niggling away trying to stab you in the back the whole time.

A lot of British people who move to LA talk about it being disorientating when you first arrive, but I found the place quite easy to get the hang of. It's all very open and spread out so you can usually see where you're going – one way's the beach, one way's the hills, one way's back to the airport and the other way's downtown. Downtown is more like the old garment district; that's where all the tramps congregate. Either there or Santa Monica, which makes sense for the old paraffin lamps when you think about it. If you've got to be homeless, do it somewhere the rents are high, so long as the police don't hassle you too much. Downtown LA is pretty much out of control these days – there's just tents, tents, tents everywhere and a lot of the people in them are crackheads, so it's a very weird scene, which I was lucky enough never to have to be a part of, although I came close once or twice.

25. DETOX IN TARZANA

The first time I'd gone to LA was after going back to San Francisco to produce The Avengers, that band who'd played with the Sex Pistols at the Winterland. I'd spent most of that time stoned out of my mind because the weed was so different to what I was used to in London, but by the time I moved on to LA to hang out there for a few days, my head was a bit clearer, and I managed to pull this bird who lived in a house with a pool in Beverly Glen. I thought it was a palace at the time, but in reality it was probably more of a shack.

The nights were very warm and she had a big old convertible – a 1960s Cadillac. One night we went to a drive-in movie and as we were driving down the San Bernardino freeway smoking a joint I was thinking, 'This is fucking heaven!' It stuck in my mind then that I was going to have to come and live there some day. And once I was back at home in my Nancy Spungen Love Palace in rainy, grey, miserable old London, I used to watch the TV show *CHiPs*, about a pair of motorbike cops in the California Highway Patrol (hence the title – clever, eh?), and think how much I'd prefer to be in LA – big fucking freeways, big billboards, big tits: I was sold.

By the time I finally made it there, which was probably some time in early 1983 (don't ask me to be any more specific – it's a miracle I can remember which decade it was), I didn't have a pot to piss in. I was sleeping on people's couches, but at least I was in a different place and it was sunny all the time. Then when some money came through after EMI signed Chequered Past (we wanted the cheque as well) things looked up a bit.

I decided around that time to try not to do dope any more. At the risk of sounding like an old hippie, I do feel like there was some kind of divine intervention involved in me making that choice. But there was a long way to go before I'd be able to fully put that good intention into practice. The coin hadn't dropped yet that I should really get sober – the machinery was moving, but the system wasn't fully operational.

The guy who got things rolling for me knew a fair bit about how that mechanism worked. It was Danny Sugerman, who'd managed what was left of The Doors after Jim Morrison died. (He later wrote the book that got turned into the Oliver Stone film, and another one about his life as a heroin addict.) One of the guys in Chequered Past knew Danny, who in turn knew a Dr Feelgood in this building in Century City who got me on a private methadone thing which took me off the hustle and saved me having to steal off people. While I was giving that a try, I ended up living out in the Valley for a few months with Nigel Harrison, who used to be in Blondie. Nigel's quite a reserved guy – very business-orientated, but with a funny sense of humour too.

That was a weird period – the mid-1980s – when no one seemed to give a fuck about punk. Now it's gone back to being a big deal again and it feels like it won't ever go away, but then it just seemed like something that had happened but was now over.

I never thought twice about it at the time: I'd been in a band, it had ended quickly, and soon it would all be forgotten. That seemed to make sense to me. Even by the time I was doing my first solo record with the longhair, which was 1986–87, still no one gave a shit. It was only from the late Eighties onwards, when Megadeth, Mötley Crüe and Guns N' Roses all did their versions of Pistols songs that the whole thing started to come back into focus. Looking back, I think that period of time out of the spotlight probably did me a favour, as it meant I had to reinvent myself a bit rather than living off past glories.

Once I'd had enough of living with Nigel in the Valley, I moved into a couple of different houses with Michael Des Barres, his wife Pamela and their son Nick. I lived with them for a couple of years in the end. I was paying 'em rent and not doing so much dope, but making up for it by doing a lot of drinking and blow and shagging a lot of birds. Who wouldn't want me as a lodger?

One of their places was right near a big punk hang-out on Santa Monica Boulevard. It was funny – I used to walk down there at night while they'd all be hanging about outside with their mohawks, and no one knew who I was. I'd slip away unnoticed. Which was what I had to do from the Des Barres house after I got back on the dope and nicked Pamela's Beatles albums and her leather jacket to pay for some. I still feel bad about that now. I made amends with her and Michael years later and I think they've forgiven me, but it took them a while; they wanted nothing to do with me for years, and I can't blame them.

It wasn't just other people I was fucking over at that time. I wasn't doing myself any favours either. Like the time I OD'ed in the sushi restaurant on the corner of La Cienega and Santa Monica boulevards. I was meeting the man in this sushi place and he was late – it's like Lou Reed says, they always are – so I was knocking back the sakes. By the time he finally turns up, I'm drunk. I go into the bathroom to shoot up, and straight away I'm out cold. Next thing I know, I'm being pumped up with some of that adrenalin shit and the paramedics are giving me electric shocks to bring me back.

I'd sat on the seat of the khazi to shoot up and when the heroin hit my bloodstream I slid down so my foot went under the door. Luckily for me, some geezer's come in to use the bathroom and seen it. If it hadn't have been for my big plates of meat, I wouldn't be here now. Imagine the 'Sex Pistol Dead On Sushi Toilet' headlines – I'd have been like a West Coast Elvis. That was the only time I remember fully OD'ing – and I do think it's something even I would remember – but there were a few scenarios that came close. Not a lot, but a few. The worst part of the sushi one was I couldn't wait to get loaded again the minute I got out of hospital.

'I'm Waiting for the Man' is one of the best songs ever written about what that feels like. I always loved The Velvet Underground, and there are a few of Lou's solo records I really like, too: *Berlin, Coney Island Baby, Rock n Roll Animal* – nothing wrong with any of those. He's a fantastic songwriter, but he was awful live, especially in the later years. It's bizarre how catchy those tunes are, because he could barely carry a note. I think maybe he's one of those guys who was as good as whoever he'd got around him. The reason *Transformer* turned out as well as it did was that Bowie and Mick Ronson were so involved. If Lou had done it all himself, it would've probably been a load of shit.

Anyway, Lou would've known even better than I do that you can't make someone sober till they are good and fucking ready. By the time I made my first vaguely serious attempt – in 1985 – I had a horrible drug problem. Someone was kind enough to get me into a rehab in Tarzana. Well, it wasn't a rehab so much as a detox place. It was fifty bucks for two weeks and what they were offering you for that money was a big room with a bunch of springy beds where they detox you with methadone.

It was me and a bunch of gang-bangers, basically. We were quite close to the bottom of the food chain in rehab terms, but I didn't want to just go cold turkey, and this was the best I could hook myself up with at that stage. It was actually OK in a no-frills kind of way. You're much better off in a place where everyone knows why they're there than in some fancy gaff where the whole thing's set up to fleece you for as much money as possible. I was on my uppers, so it was more a beggars-can't-be-choosers situation. I was more or less homeless at that point because I'd pissed off everyone I knew by stealing from them.

The Good Samaritan who didn't walk past on the other side was a woman called Linda I used to get high with. We'd do blow together and drive around LA doing wild shit, but at that stage she was newly sober, and I ran into her coming out of a 12-Step meeting at the place where the Guitar Centre used to be. I was in a pretty desperate state by that time – just walking around looking for something to steal. Linda saw I was in a bad way and said I could have a place to kip on her couch if I went to the 12-Step programme.

This was my first introduction to something it would take me five or six years to fully get my head around (and a further twenty-five years later, I've still got a way to go). I started to get into going to meetings and even put my hand up to speak at a couple. At one I ended up admitting that I needed somewhere to live and this geezer agreed to put me up at his place. Obviously he had his own motives – he was quite a nerdy kind of guy and maybe he thought having a Sex Pistol on his futon would make him look cool. Every home should have one; he should've let me stay there for free.

It worked out well for me, though, and I was grateful to him. I'd got a bit of humility by then and I was relieved not to have to be doing any of the shit I'd been doing to get dope. I didn't mind kipping on this geezer's couch. It was a safe place for me, and I ended up staying there for about a year.

His apartment was in Hollywood, around 3rd Street and Gardner, and there was a park there that I used to go running in. It was good for me to fly beneath the radar for a while, because my credit was not good in the music industry. It wasn't just that there wasn't much work about: people would actively cross the street to avoid me (I didn't blame them – I'd probably have done the same if I could've). I had to find some other way to bring in a bit of cash that wouldn't involve me getting in trouble with the law.

So I started giving plasma for fifty bucks a pop. I was going to a couple of meetings a day, shagging chicks that I met there, and getting on the bus to the Valley to give them my finest claret. There was probably all manner of shit going around in my bloodstream at the time, but I don't even know if they tested it for contamination. They certainly didn't use new needles – they just used to wash 'em, but I didn't give a fuck. It was fifty bucks (in the form of a cheque that I could give the guy with the couch for rent) and I wasn't nicking any more, which was all I cared about. OK, so I didn't stop completely – I still pilfered a bit in sobriety. It was such a natural way for me to get things that it took me a long time to stop altogether.

It took me even longer to start putting the two puzzles together so I could understand the way the different addictions overlapped. I'd have to do a bunch of years of therapy as part of that process, and there were plenty of times when I wanted to bolt, but eventually I learnt not to. When I was going to those early meetings, though, I was really damaged goods. I didn't have the first clue how to be a decent person. Everything was all about me, and I didn't care who else I hurt. So these were just the first steps on a long road – a road with no fucking end.

At that point I had no idea how to conduct myself like a normal person, or how to react to emotion – that was my main problem. It wasn't like I was a complete cunt to people, but if someone hurt my feelings, I wouldn't deal with it the way a normal person would. I'd have to act out or run off – just find any way of not dealing with it. I'd been wearing that Cloak of Invisibility for so long it was like a second skin.

Getting the dope out of my system was just the start. When you're in the very early stages of sobriety you tend to go a bit haywire emotionally, because you start experiencing a lot of feelings you've blocked out for a long time. Of course, all I wanted to do was fuck chicks, which was basically just another way of shutting out reality. But a big turning point for me came when someone played me at my own game, and for the first time in ages I was actually sober enough for something to matter to me.

The socialite girl I'd lived with for a while in New York (not the brass, the other one) came out to LA after the Chequered Past thing had happened. Her name was (and is) Nina Huang, and we're still good friends. She'd got sober too at that point, and for a while we were almost living together. Of course I was still fucking other chicks left, right and centre, but one day I spoke to her 12-Step sponsor who for some reason thought it was a good idea to tell me that Nina had fucked—Well, I'd better not print the name cos it'd cause too much trouble even now. Let's just say 'a major A-list Hollywood film star'. Much as I had no right to take offence, given the amount of shit I'd been up to, this fucking devastated me.

It was the first time someone had really turned things round on me so I wasn't the one doing the upsetting. This might be hard to believe, but I'd never given a thought to all the pain I was causing people before. Of course it wasn't the first time I'd been fucked over, but in the old days I would've just drowned whatever I felt in booze or drugs or thieving. This time, because I was newly sober, I had no choice but to actually experience it. I remember thinking, 'Oh, fuck me, this feels like *shit*.' It was a painful lesson, but it was also a great lesson, as it was the gateway to me starting to turn things round in the way I treated other people.

I had to find a way through it – but I also had to stay sober in the process. I kind of had to go cold turkey on not feeling emotions; I literally didn't eat or sleep for two weeks. That shit was a worse kick than methadone. But by the time I came out the other side, it had put me on the fast track to recovery. Well, when I say the fast track, me trying to find a way of treating other people a bit better was not going to be an overnight process. But at least my eyes were open now to the kind of shit I had to stop doing. The old ways had died hard, but my days of fucking my mates' chicks and not caring were on their way to being behind me.

Almost like a reward for making my first tentative steps in a better direction, things started to look up on the work front as well. Even in my darkest days I never lost my confidence as a musician – people always seemed impressed by what I did and that was enough for me. As a person, it was a different matter. I definitely didn't feel adequate, but then again, I never had done.

One of the first paying gigs that came through was to work with Andy Taylor of Duran Duran on his solo record. There was a lot of money in the record industry in the mid-Eighties, and Andy was hot then, so he got paid millions to do that record. Maybe not as many of those millions came to his co-writer as I would've liked, but I appreciated him giving me a chance when no one else would, so I was hardly going to kick the deal out of bed.

A few months earlier, I was a junkie who couldn't get my shit together. Now I was slowly building myself a new life – being sober in the sun, shagging some beautiful women. I even got to move off that geezer's couch. Andy Taylor had a few houses around LA, and one of them was just off Sunset Boulevard near the Hyatt Hotel – on King's Road, funnily enough. He was living out in Malibu and only came into town once in a blue moon, so he was fine with me moving in.

Word seemed to get around town pretty quickly that I was doing an OK job for him, and it wasn't long before I got offered a solo deal of my own. It was with a guy called Danny Goldberg who'd worked with Led Zep in the Seventies and would later be manager of Nirvana. He signed me to MCA to do *Mercy* – an album of mellow rock songs that sounded nothing like anything I'd done before. I guess it was my opportunity to do a soundtrack for the Poco manager look I used to wear up and down the other King's Road, and even though it's not the thing I've done that people ask me about the most, I was still proud to make a record while sober, and doing it was very meaningful to me.

I bought myself a GMC pickup truck with the first little bit of dough that came through. It was the first motor I'd bought properly since I'd been in America, and I've got a similar one now. Things were looking up.

26. IGGY, DYLAN & THE BIG O

The thought of being onstage completely sober was terrifying at first – I remember thinking, 'I'm never going to be able to do a gig without at least a pint inside me.' So I started various two-bob bands with other people who were sober, just to give it a try. The first one was called Dano and Jones: as the name suggests, it was just me and this guy Rick Dano. When I was maybe sixty days sober, we put this little band together to play at a venue which was called Central at the time but then turned into the Viper Room.

It was just traditional rock 'n' roll, but people loved it, and the adulation of everyone kissing my arse when it was over – and getting laid afterwards – was very helpful. From then on, it just got easier and easier. The idea that you play better when you're high was always a load of bollocks – maybe you sound better to yourself, but that's because you're high and your judgement is not to be trusted. If you really want to know what you sound like, try listening to yourself when you're sober.

Now that I think of it, the first person to give me a leg-up back into writing and recording again in sobriety wasn't Andy Taylor. Iggy

Pop was a much more appropriate mentor. When it came to getting your shit together and getting back on your feet, he'd been there and done that.

The Stooges had been a huge deal to me when I was doing my diet-pill guitar crash course back in Denmark Street in 1975, and I'd been really pissed off to miss the famous gig Iggy did at the Scala in King's Cross with the Flamin' Groovies a few years before, so I certainly wasn't going to miss the chance to play with him ten years later.

I'd first met Iggy when I was still with The Professionals. I can't remember how it came about, but we hung out in New York a couple of times. Then later on he came out to LA for a while and we wrote together for about a month. From those demos I ended up with I think four co-writes on what became his *Blah Blah Blah* album. Iggy was great in just the way you'd imagine – came up with really good lyrics and was just fun to be around. I remember thinking, 'Why couldn't writing with Rotten have been like this?'

OK, so Matlock had beaten me to the punch by playing with Iggy Pop already (on *Soldier*) but there was no way he could compete with the Sammy Hagar look I was working by the time me and Iggy played 'Cold Metal' from his next album, *Instinct*, on *Letterman* in 1988. The funny thing about that is, lots of the people commenting on YouTube don't think it's me, cos they can't handle my big hair.

I shouldn't have made myself as conspicuous as I did in my Fabio phase, really, because as aliens go, I was totally illegal. I shouldn't have even been in America, and I didn't have a green card for about ten years. That's why I couldn't go to Switzerland to play on the actual recording of *Blah Blah Blah* – if I had done, I wouldn't have been able to come back. It wasn't just the old English convictions that were hindering me; me and Cookie had got drunk in the King's Head in LA one day and I got done for nicking a sweater. It was only a misdemeanour, but it didn't help when I was trying to get legal. I suppose I was lucky not to be deported. As well as ruining my life, to be chucked out of the country for crimes against knitwear would've been embarrassing.

The Cloak of Invisibility saw me through a few more illegal years in LA. I ended up having to go back to London in the early Nineties to get a working visa, and at that point I managed to get into that system where you have to go back to England every year to renew it. It was a fucking pain in the arse, especially as England was the last place I wanted to be at that time, but I kept at it and eventually the green card was mine. For me a big part of the process of getting sober was getting myself on the grid so I actually left a footprint on the world like a normal fucking human being, instead of just drifting from one disgraceful action to the next. The Cloak had to go – I guess that was what it came down to.

The first step was to get a regular address of my own. I'd been down in the flatlands for my first few years in LA, but as soon as I was earning enough to cover the rent, I moved up to the canyons. It was a big leap for me – going up into the hills. I found the atmosphere of the trees and the quiet a little weird at first. Apart from anything else, it was the furthest out into the country I'd lived since I was in Banstead Hall. And not only did the Manson murders happen just round the corner, there was always the danger of waking up to find Joni Mitchell playing her acoustic guitar at the end of your bed, which I would probably have found scarier than the Manson thing, to be honest.

I rented two different places for about four years each before I got the dough together to buy somewhere. In the meantime, it wasn't just a passport and a driving licence and a credit card I had to sort out, there was the little matter of learning to read and write properly. I was in my thirties now, and knowing I was still not properly literate was a source of constant insecurity and embarrassment to me. Before I was sober I'd had so many other things to be embarrassed about that this one had kind of gone on the back burner, but now was the time. So I hired this Asian bird to teach me. She helped me a lot – she came over for maybe an hour twice a week for about six months, and once I got into it I found the learning much easier than I'd expected. She was a good teacher, which helped, and a great girl too. I think she wanted a portion at the end but I didn't bother because she was too sweet.

It made me feel a lot better to be able to do some of the things that normal people do, but there are limits. To this day, everything that needs dealing with goes through my management office, and if something turns up at home that I have to sign I go into a panic. I still can't really deal with bills and shit like that. It just freaks me the fuck out. It's not just that I don't want to deal with it – I don't even want to see it. That's why I don't think I could ever have held down a normal job. It's not that I think I'm above such things, I just can't be bothered.

Even while I was trying to buckle down to the discipline of sobriety, the freedom of those first few years in LA was great. It was a world away from being in some dingy basement in London picking your blackheads; in LA you could get someone else to pick them for you. And I loved the fact that you could ride motorbikes without having to wear a helmet. That was how me and Mickey Rourke ended up reviving the whole Harley-Davidson thing. There's no ego involved in me saying that – it's just the truth. When we started riding them no one else was doing it except the real greasers.

From driving round London fetching the samples for Malcolm and Vivienne's rocker clothes in the Too Fast To Live, Too Young To Die days, to helping bring back the Harley in LA, where it all began – it's a nice kind of circle. Seeing Mickey Rourke for the first time was a funny one. I had a Harley and he had one too, but we hadn't met. I bumped into him at some cafe one night. He wasn't too popular at that time and neither was I. We looked at each other and kind of checked each other out, the same way two not-Brutus-shirt-wearing skinheads might've done on Shepherd's Bush Market twenty years before, and it wasn't long before we started hanging out as part of a little team.

Mickey Rourke might seem a funny person to start hanging out with when you're newly sober, as he's not really a 12-Step type of guy, but even though I knew he liked to party, I never saw him fucked up around the bikes. Mickey had built this coffee shop in the heart of Beverly Hills called Nicky and Joey's. A few of us used to hang out there and it became a big thing more or less overnight – all of a sudden, there were fifty of us. We weren't real bikers, just posers on the weekend.

The big thing to do was meet at the coffee shop on a Friday night to pose around a bit on all the bikes, then drive to this club called Vertigo, a hipster place downtown. We'd take Olympic Boulevard all the way, go in there and stroll around like we owned the place. If things went well and a bird or two was impressed maybe there'd be a bit of suction in the alley afterwards. Then at about one o'clock we'd all go our separate ways. The big bike ride was five miles and that was it. I don't think any of these cunts had more than 500 miles on their clocks, me included.

I always loved motorbikes. I had one in England when I was about sixteen – got it out of the shop on HP and don't think I ever made one payment. It wasn't just a moped, I think it was a Honda 650cc; 450cc at the least. I was nobody's idea of a good credit risk, but I suppose they didn't care so long as they got the sale and then it became someone else's problem. Either way, I rode this thing till it broke down and then just left it where it stopped. I had no idea what I was doing.

Switching to a Harley once I got to America wasn't a betrayal of my skinhead roots. It was just horses for courses. I see these kids in LA now trying to re-enact the mod thing on their scooters; there's a whole little scene, but it doesn't really work if you've got to wear a helmet. For me, mod wasn't about wearing helmets – the cool part was, everyone could see you. I still hate helmets but I've got quite a collection now and I don't mind wearing 'em because I've seen some of the scary shit that's happened to people who didn't have them on. I still don't wear the full face – I prefer the open face. A geezer is putting horns on one for me right now.

I had a couple of quite bad motorbike accidents. In 1986, when I was in the early stages of sobriety, Linda, who got me started on that course, co-signed for me to get a Harley-Davidson Sportster. That was when Nina was still around. She was on the back, I'd had a couple of pints (well, I did say it was the early stages of sobriety), and neither of us were wearing helmets. I was nowhere near drunk, but I didn't know the LA roads that well yet.

As we were getting ready to come off Sunset up at Crescent Heights, I turned round to say something to Nina. The next thing I knew there was a car in front of us stopping to turn illegally and we rear-ended it. Nina was all right on the back of the bike, but I went flying into the fucking bushes and broke my wrist. My arm was pushed right up under me and I had to have stitches; there were also a few concerns about the break. It was to my strumming hand. Guitarists don't want wrist injuries, but luckily the hospital straightened the arm out OK, so I made a 100 per cent recovery.

Cut to a year or so later, and I'm riding home from Justine Bateman's house up at the top of Laurel Canyon and Mulholland. She was a big soap actress at the time and there were eight of us on bikes – all these actor kids, being tough guys and giving it the big 'un. I think the former teen idol Leif Garrett was there, too, for some reason. We were coming down the Canyon when these birds came up the other side in a car only way over the centre line so they smacked right into me. My bike rolled over with me and Nina still on it – bosh! I broke the same wrist and had to have a load more stitches. Again, I was lucky there was no permanent damage, or at least nothing to rob my guitar-playing of the subtlety for which it is globally renowned.

As shit as they were at the time, I actually appreciate having had those crashes, because they made me so aware of the dangers. I feel bad for motorcyclists who don't know the ropes. When I see people now who've just got on their bikes for the first time and they can barely take their feet off the ground, I think, 'Oh, you poor fuckers – you're going to get a wallop, it's just a matter of time.' I'm so grateful – my wallops could've been so much worse. Over time you pick up experience so you see things before they happen, which you need to nowadays, with so many car and van drivers too busy checking their texts to pay attention to the road.

There was definitely a motorbike element to one of my favourite stories from this time. One day I got a phone call from Bob Dylan. 'Hey, Steve,' he said, however he talks. 'Can you put a band together?' It didn't come completely out of the blue. There'd been a kind of courtship phase when he saw me around town a couple of times and he'd come running over and hug me. 'Hey, Steve,' he'd say. It was funny because Dylan's usually notorious for coating everyone off, and people couldn't believe he was giving me all this attention. I'm not sure if it was because he was into bikes too or maybe he was a secret Professionals fan, but either way, we did a session one night in March 1987, at the famous Studio 3 in Sunset Sound on Sunset Boulevard (where Jim Morrison had all that fun in the booth), and it was the weirdest experience.

When Bob asked me, I thought, 'OK, let's see what we can rustle up.' Paul Simonon was hanging out in LA at the time. The Clash were done and he was out here riding motorbikes and messing about with a band called Havana 3a.m. (The singer was a geezer I knew, who's dead now.) Anyway, I'd loved Simonon from the beginning – we'd always got on, and there are some good pictures of us riding motorbikes together trying to look like James Dean. So he was in. Then there was Pat Benatar's drummer Myron Grombacher – which is a pretty cool name, I'm sure you'll agree – and maybe a keyboard guy I can't remember.

We got there in the morning and set up all the gear. Then Bob arrived and put his lyrics on the piano in a big pile. He's standing there with his acoustic, me and the band are sitting waiting, and he starts kind of mumbling his way through the chords – 'C, uh D, uh G.' He just wanted us to play and see if anything started cooking, basically like a jam band. Now, I know this works for some people, but I'd never made music that way before. I'd usually go into the studio knowing exactly what I was doing and then we'd build the track up piece by piece. So there was a bit of a clash of cultures. He must've started about twenty different songs then he'd cut them off just as we were getting going. They got one track out of it for the album *Down In The Groove* and that was a cover of 'Sally Sue Brown'. It was a good job I'd not spent my whole life waiting for a Bob Dylan co-write to come along, because that never materialised.

What did happen was that Mickey Rourke turned up at the studio with a big gang of our biker mates. I was facing the glass window of the control room and Dylan was facing me with his back to the entrance. While he's talking away to me, I notice Mickey and about thirty of these other biker geezers come swaggering in. Then Bob turns round to see them all and does a massive double-take. I wish someone had been filming it, cos his face was a picture. I wouldn't say he was intimidated, but it wasn't long before he made his excuses and left.

The way music seemed to be bringing me out of the darkness in those years was just like when I was a kid and hearing Jimi Hendrix or Roxy Music gave me a bit of hope. Working with Roy Orbison was one of the best ones. That happened around 1987–88 as well. I'd signed to Danny Goldberg's label by then, as well as to him as a manager, and he was also representing Roy, who was trying to do an album at the time. Danny thought it was a good idea to put the two of us together, so I rode my motorbike out to Malibu to meet the big O a couple of times, and we started writing this song on a cassette.

'The Chains of Love', I think it was called, but it wasn't a bondage thing as Roy was no more into that shit than I was. It was coming out pretty good, and it only needed a few more lyrics from him and it would've been done, but unfortunately he died before we could finish it. Of course his wife couldn't find the cassette, and then the house got burned down. So maybe there's a cassette somewhere with me and him singing on it, and maybe there isn't.

Roy was a sweetheart – very soft and kind in his manner, one of those blokes you feel would've never lost their temper – and we got along great. He had the demeanour of a real Southern gentleman, and he was definitely the nicest of all the original rock 'n' roll giants I've met. It was such a shame when he died. I remember we were working on the song downstairs in his house and he was sneaking fags, going, 'Don't tell my missus.' You just don't get that from Jerry Lee Lewis.

I'd been two and a half years clean the first time I went out of the programme (the respectable way of saying 'got back on the gear') for a month before coming straight back in. Then I managed another three years before the same thing happened again. In the periods when I relapsed, I didn't socialise with anyone. It wasn't like I was falling out of the Viper Room into the gutter; people probably thought, 'Oh fuck, he's relapsed,' because I would just disappear. No one ever saw me high, because by then I was embarrassed to be seen not sober. I just kind of slunk away and kept myself totally isolated till I could get myself together enough to climb back on the wagon. I guess that was a sign I'd taken some of it on board.

The reason I kept hitting that wall was that I never worked any of the 12 steps. If you don't do any steps, eventually you'll end up getting loaded again, and that's what I did. For that first five and a half years or so I was just dicking around, really. I was going to meetings, picking up useful bits and pieces in my thick head, but only really paying lip service because it was a safe place and I liked the attention I got from the birds.

27. THE WOLFMAN OF SUNSET

Between my first solo album coming out in 1987 and the second one, *Fire and Gasoline*, a couple of years later: that was when The Wolfman was really off and running. I was slim then, and in good shape, plus I had the long hair and looked like Fabio, so I could get laid at any time. Yes, I went to meetings and shagged chicks I met there, but you didn't have to be an addict for me to shag you – I was all about equal opportunities.

Part of it was that doing dope for six or seven years kind of damps that part of you down and you don't worry about sex so much. So, as the effects of the heroin wore off and the old safety valves of booze and drugs closed down, all the pressure started to push in one direction. I was so horny that I was just going to 12-Step meetings looking for pussy, which isn't really a good idea in recovery terms. Once at the big Friday meeting on Rodeo Drive, a porn star called Ginger, who was highly rated by *Adult Video News'* list of the top 50 porn stars of all time, sucked me off in the toilets. What can I say? It was a romantic time.

You can only do that for so long before the realisation hits you that it's all the same thing. The nature of the addiction might be different, but whether the only thing you're thinking about is where your next fix is coming from or fucking chicks at 12-Step meetings doesn't really make too much difference – you're still behaving in the same obsessive way. I guess the truth was that I hadn't really hit rock bottom. Well, I'd hit a few rock bottoms, but not the right one.

I'd tried the 12-Step programme specifically related to narcotics but I couldn't connect with it. They just seemed like a bunch of cunts, topping each other's stories to glorify their pasts. The full-on junkie mentality is a different thing to the regular alcoholic's, that's for sure. I realise this might seem like a bit of a stretch, given that I did have a massive problem with heroin, but even now after years of various kinds of therapy I still think of myself as an alcoholic who ended up taking heroin, rather than as a junkie. I don't think I was one of those people who, when they get sober for a bit, everyone knows will go back to dope again. It was more like a form of escapism for me, from the emptiness I felt after the band ended.

The thing I could never escape was the effect alcohol had on me when I put it in my system, and alcoholism was definitely the road I would've gone down if heroin hadn't offered me the kind of short cut that a fan of instant gratification like myself was never going to be able to pass up. You might wonder, what's the difference between flying first class or economy when the destination is the same? The funny thing is, it's only people who've always flown economy who ask that question.

Once both of the crutches I used to rely on were gone, I started to lean on the sex thing more and more. The mentality of LA is very much about looking good at the best of times, and the more I got into playing the part of being the rocker guy on his bike, the more my natural-born Englishman's resistance to gyms and the pursuit of the body beautiful (my own, that is – I'd always been happy to pursue other people's) started to get worn down. Ridiculous as this will seem, given how hard I was trying to stay sober, I even went through a phase where I was doing steroids to get buff.

I only did a couple of cycles – I didn't go crazy with them – and the results were amazing. They work really quickly, and I can see why people get hooked on that hit of how much better they make you look, but instant gratification has always been my downfall. I definitely wouldn't recommend steroids to anyone trying to get clean. You don't really get high from them, but they do alter your head a bit, if only by making you angry and full of testosterone, which I've never exactly lacked. I'm not saying steroids were 100 per cent the cause of my second relapse, but I guess the fact that I carried on doing something I knew wasn't appropriate to sobriety shows you where my head was at.

I did look good in the Fabio phase, though. It will be hard for anyone who knows me now to accept this, but I was quite vain in those days – the peacock had grown its feathers back, and he didn't care who he showed them to. I don't know how exactly you measure it, but in that phase of short-term sobriety between the two relapses, I would say, technically I was probably a sex addict. If I couldn't pull a rock chick in the clubs on the Strip, I would cruise around in my truck till I found a woman who was ready, willing and able. To show you how dependent I was on pussy, one time I was cruising over in the Valley early in the morning when I started seeing things – I'd see fucking mail boxes in the distance and fixate that they were chicks. The worst part of it was, I was sober as a judge at the time. An old-school non-drinking judge at that, not one of those pisshead ones.

Meeting Axl Rose was another unlikely landmark on my long road to sobriety. I was on my bike outside the Rainbow on a Friday night – trying to get laid as usual – and Axl just walked up to me. He had a big leather coat on and a military cap and he was fucking goo-goo-eyed about talking to me, which was a nice ego boost. It was all new to him then, and he just wanted to hang out. It must have been at the time when things were starting to take off for Guns N' Roses, because there weren't loads of people around him trying to get his autograph, but I knew who he was.

A lot of those dudes from the hair metal and thrash metal bands would say they were into punk when really they were into metal. But while Slash and the other Guns N' Roses guys came from more rock backgrounds, Duff and Axl were real punk fans. We talked for an hour or so that night, and a few times after. I really liked Guns N' Roses – they were a real band with a classic rock sound, not like the Poisons of this world. And Axl was cool. He ending up singing on the version of 'Did You No Wrong' that was on *Fire and Gasoline*. Axl does a verse, I do a verse, and Ian Astbury of The Cult does a verse – like bringing three generations together.

All of a sudden, after we'd been in the wilderness for almost a decade, there was a lot of love coming to the Sex Pistols from a bunch of new bands. Mötley Crüe and Megadeth did versions of 'Anarchy in the UK', and Anthrax did 'God Save the Queen'. It made sense because that was where their music was coming from. I didn't care too much for thrash metal, to be honest, but it was a nice feeling to get a bit of kudos, cos there hadn't been too much of that flying around for a while. I guess you can hear me getting my confidence back in how much more of a balls-out rock 'n' roll record my second solo album is than the one before it. I know *Fire and Gasoline* is not to everyone's taste but some of the cognoscenti revere it as the Rosetta Stone of biker metal. No really, they do.

There's no VIP room in the 12-Step programme, much as some people would like there to be. It doesn't matter if you're rich or poor, gay or straight, black or white – nobody's special. You've all got one thing in common, which is the gene that gives you a fucking issue with alcoholism – obsession of the mind, allergy of the body, whatever you want to call it. And it would take one more relapse for me finally to commit myself fully to doing something about it. As relapses go, it wasn't spectacular. I didn't finally touch the bottom of the pool and then swim towards the oxygen with all the strength I had left. It was more a kind of 'I'm done' feeling – 'I can't be doing this any more so what do I have to do to stop?'

I was lucky that by the time the coin finally dropped after five or six years of dicking around, I was much more established than I had been at the start of the process. I wasn't fucking homeless and kipping on a sofa any more, I had a decent apartment to live in and enough money from my two record deals to pay for some proper treatment. It was funny that the day in 1990 when I took the pledge and meant it for good – 28th October – was the same date *Never Mind the Bollocks . . .* had come out thirteen years before. But I didn't pick that day for its historical significance. The time had just finally come for me to really get stuck in.

If all the people who flirted with the 12-Step programme actually stuck with it, those meetings would be like sell-out shows at the Staples Center. With my tiny attention span and history of fucking off when the going got tough, no one would've picked me out as one of the happy few the programme would work for. I don't know why that happened for me and not for so many others. I can't answer that question. It wasn't just that I was fortunate. I was lucky to even be alive.

In LA – at least among the people I knocked about with, it was different in the gay community – AIDS only seemed to become a big issue around the late Eighties/early Nineties. That was when it really felt like a problem. Prior to that, catching herpes seemed to be the biggest worry. Condoms just weren't on the agenda, and obviously, with the number of people I'd rumped without them, I was terrified by the idea that you could get AIDS though fucking. To be honest, I think some of those risks have been blown out of proportion when it comes to straight people, so as not to seem discriminatory, but anything involving blood and/or putting cocks in arses is definitely not a good idea. So I've had more than my nine lives there, given the amount of deviant shit I've done over the years.

I dodged a few bullets in injecting heroin, too. The key thing there was, I never lowered myself to use those shooting galleries they had then, which basically meant a dirty old bucket with a bunch of used needles in it and people would just bang in there to get a fix straight away. Even if I was sick and desperate for dope, I never did that; it just never seemed right to me. I always had my own needle, even though it did sometimes feel like taking your own cue to the snooker hall. Thank God I kept on doing that, because a bunch of people I knew are brown bread from going the other way.

The only one I didn't get away with was that first fix back in London all those years before, which I'm sure is what gave me hepatitis C, even though they say you can get it from snorting through a straw – all you need is a little blood particle on the end of it from someone else's fucking nasal membranes. The other big way of getting infected was through blood transfusions at hospitals. A load of completely innocent people picked it up that way.

The strange thing about that disease is nothing really happens to tell you you've got it, other than finding yourself napping a lot. I don't know if I used to do that prior to getting hepatitis C, but it seems as though I've been napping all my life. You can live with it for years without even knowing, but it will be affecting your immune system and the level of symptoms depends on how healthy you are in general. It's all about cleaning your liver, so if you're still knocking back booze and smoking and shooting up all day, that's obviously not going to help. If you keep over-loading your liver you'll eventually get cirrhosis, at which point you will either need a transplant or get cancer.

Thank God I never reached that stage, but if I hadn't sobered up, it would've got a lot worse than it did. It all comes down to the numbers of something called your Viral Load, which wouldn't be a bad name for a metal band. Mine was something like ten million, whatever the fuck that means. It was high, but not critically high. I think what saved me from anything worse was the fact that the span of time I was on dope was rela-tively short – from '79 to '85, and then five years of on–off sobriety with two short relapses of a couple of weeks each, before I finally made it really official.

I've been sober twenty-five years now, but it's never over. It's not like you ever get to the end of the 12 steps and think, 'OK, let's party!' It's just a way of thinking you have to stay inside until the day you die.

28. GROUP THERAPY

The main difference between group therapy and being in a band is that in group therapy everyone's trying to help each other. There's the therapist – who I guess would be like the manager in band terms, though heaven help you if Malcolm McLaren is guiding your recovery – and three or four other bods. The therapist would home in on you one by one and say, 'It's your turn to talk,' the others would listen and then they'd chip in with their responses afterwards. That might sound stressful if you've not done it before, but in my experience there was never any aggro. At first it was a challenge to be in the hot seat, but it got easier the longer you were there, and it was good listening to other people talk about their issues as well. That definitely helped me to open up.

Once I'd got the idea of talking these things through, it didn't make too much difference to me whether I was in a small group, one on one with the same therapist in his or her office, or standing up to speak at a 12-Step meeting. Each of the larger gatherings has its own character, and I know the map of different groups in LA like the back of my hand. It's funny how some of their names seem to remind you of drinks – like Sundowners – and they have different atmospheres according to the people who run them. A few can get a bit competitive and starry, others are more nurturing.

Bread and Roses – the stag (which just means it's men only, they don't show blue movies) meeting on Brentwood – does 'involuntary sharing', which some people find a bit of an ordeal. They just point at you and you have to spill your guts, which is fine if you're up for it, but if you're not you can get so consumed with worry in your head about the moment your turn will come – 'Everyone's gonna be looking at me, and I'll have to speak in front of them' – that you don't hear anything else that's said. That is definitely an alcoholic trait, which obviously you will see a lot of in meetings.

It's in the nature of the 12-Step programme that people bring a lot of baggage to it. And just because someone is trying to get sober doesn't stop them being an arsehole; quite the reverse. Even setting aside all the acting out that goes on, if a person was an arsehole drinking, there's a good chance they'll be an arsehole sober as well. It takes years of peeling layers off the onion to get to the cleaner bulb, and while people are shedding the tears that are part of that process, you're not necessarily going to see the best of them. This is the final house on the fucking block, after all – if you don't get in, you've had it – so in terms of how people interact, you've got to expect the worst of the worst.

Don't get me wrong, I know that nice people who've had tough lives come into the programme as well. But they aren't the ones you tend to notice first. And the whole experience is far from the goody two-shoes scenario that words like 'fellowship' and 'higher power' might suggest to those on the outside. The 12-Step programme is not like the Scouts. You're not volunteering because you want to be a good kid: you end up there because there's nowhere else to go and you might, if you're lucky, have found a last-chance saloon that will serve you something other than alcohol.

In the meantime, you get a lot of cunts coming in who are selfish and have their own manipulative agendas (I know, because I was one of them). When they first get sober, many people kind of go nuts, because the central focus of their lives – whether that's booze or drugs doesn't make too much difference – has suddenly gone. It's almost like you've lost your job, and what the 12-Step programme gives you is something to fill the space that's left behind. That's what the steps and the rituals and the regularity are all about: finding a way to stop that inner void pulling you in. It's not complicated, but it's hard, and it's not for everyone.

The first thing you've got to do is get into the groove of it, but then the novelty wears off and the monotony sets in. When everything starts to feel smooth and straightforward it's probably the time you're most in danger, because if you get too cocky, you're fucked. The programme keeps you on your toes by pushing you in new directions. If you'd looked at who I was when I was living in New York (in the 8×10s of Heart era), the idea of me giving talks in hospitals and prisons would've seemed totally fucking ridiculous. I would never have had the balls – or the motivation – to do anything like that without the confidence I've got from standing up to speak in meetings.

I get asked to do this a lot to this day, and to my surprise I've turned into a pretty decent speaker. I was terrified at first, and sometimes even now I don't want to fucking do it, but I found it easier to get up and speak in a 12-Step context than anywhere outside it. You know that at some level everyone there can relate to what you're saying, so you don't really feel like anything you can say could be 'wrong'. I guess I've taken that no-holds-barred approach onto the radio with me in more recent times (it's funny that a radio show has sponsors too, but not the same way an alcoholic does). One thing's for sure, *Jonesy's Jukebox* is one of the many good things in my life that could never have happened without the changes the programme has made in me.

The only thing going to meetings guarantees is that if you stick with it, you will stop drinking (or whatever). Sorting everything else out is up to you, but it's amazing how many different aspects of your life it seems to help with. I'd got a bit of baggage with managers by that point, but when I was working with Andy Taylor and doing those two solo records with Danny Goldberg, a woman called Anita Camarata had come into the picture. She was helping Danny out, and it was good to start afresh with someone who'd only known me in sobriety. By the time I was emerging from that solo deal, she'd overcome some of my trust issues with management (you should never surrender all of them) and we're still working together today.

In the early Nineties I got a little band together called Fantasy 7. It was me, this guy called Mark McCoy on vocals, and a couple of other geezers who weren't quite Sly 'n' Robbie on bass and drums. I liked Mark – he was cool. He was kind of a wannabe Iggy Pop on one level, but also clean and a veggie (which sadly didn't stop him dying of cancer a while back). One of the main things was that we looked cool. I'd had enough of the Fabio look, so we all shaved our hair off to look like skin-heads. It was funny, really, cos everyone else was doing that long-haired grunge thing, so no one knew if we were ahead of the times or behind them. Our music was back-to-basics punky rock 'n' roll, and the whole thing was good fun. We'd play around town in LA and show up for gigs in a van. We also did a couple of nights in Buenos Aires, strangely enough, and there are some clips of us playing on an Argentinian TV show.

My next band, The Neurotic Outsiders, came a bit later – maybe 1994. We were another one of those strange hybrid punks and rockers super-groups, like Chequered Past, but with a lot more going for us, not least a lead guitarist who wasn't only in it for his next fix. It all started when Matt Sorum, the drummer of Guns N' Roses, wanted to do a benefit for some bloke who'd got sober but had cancer. We did the first show at the Viper Room and the line-up was me, Matt, Duff McKagan, and John Taylor from Duran Duran on bass (not to be confused with Andy who I'd worked with earlier. John is actually a really good rock bass player who plays with his fingers, which gives a much warmer sound than a pick).

We did a bunch of songs and my mate Ian Astbury got up and joined us. People really enjoyed the show, and it grew into a residency which went on for a while in 1994–95 and was kind of the place to be on a Monday night in LA (we'd chosen the day of the week well so there wasn't too much competition). Loads of people I knew got up and did numbers with us – Iggy, Chrissie Hynde, Idol. One of our regular punters was Guy Oseary, who luckily for us ran Madonna's label, Maverick. He loved the buzz of it all and to celebrate gave us a million dollars to make a record. It's bizarre how much money was flying around at that time; nowadays we wouldn't get a million pesetas. And Guy manages Madonna and U2 these days, so it's not worked out too badly for him either.

We had a fun time making that record, and I think it could've done well if we'd all been around to give it a proper push. But there was talk of Guns N' Roses getting back together, so Duff had to rehearse for that, and I had some reunion business of my own to attend to by then. I ended up squeezing a load of Neurotic Outsiders dates into a three-week break in the middle of the Sex Pistols' Filthy Lucre world tour in 1996. I was knackered after that year, but it was a very good one for me financially, and set me up to the point where I was able to buy the house in Benedict Canyon where I still live today. I was forty by then, so it was about time I saw some proper dosh. If I'd had any back in the day it would've probably gone straight in my arm anyway, so I was all the more appreciative when it finally turned up and I was sober enough not to waste it.

We'd tried to get back together and do some shows earlier, but Lydon put the mockers on it for some reason. I'm not sure why John changed his mind when he did – maybe he needed a dollar, or his manager convinced him. Either way, at that time he was being looked after by a guy called

Eric Gardner, who was somewhat sensible, so once things got moving all the arrangements came together pretty smoothly. John was quite controlling, but a lot more liberal than he is now.

When all the court cases were finally finished ten years before, the Sex Pistols as a business was split up into quarters, with the last one divided between Glen and Sid's next of kin (just don't mention who actually played bass on the album). At first that meant his mum, Anne Beverley, then when she died in 1996 it was left to her sister; then she died soon after and it was left to someone else. Then they died, and it went to one of the kids a long way down the family tree. Say what you like about that family, they don't live very long, and Sid's been much less of a problem in death than he was in life.

His mum was a complex character, but she was always cool with me and I got on well with her, as – usefully – did Anita. I even got Sid's bass off Anne for a thousand dollars. She said, 'Look, it's been under my bed for seventeen years, I think someone should have it.' I said I would and she asked what it was worth, so I told her a thousand bucks new – which was true. When she agreed to sell it to me I got a courier service over there to bring it back the next day, before she could change her mind. I think he only had two of the white ones. He left one in a cab and this is the other one – with the strap that says 'Sid'. I haven't flogged it yet, but I've been offered two hundred grand. Obviously that looks like a hefty profit on paper, but bear in mind I did play it a lot more than he did. When you look at it in that way, it was a fucking liberty I had to pay as much as a grand for it.

When it came to the reunion of the band's living members, it was actually fine. OK, we'd all coated each other off a fair amount over the years – John and Glen hadn't exactly held back in their books – and I think John still had a resentment about the way the band ended, but we decided to put all that aside and be polite. The only thing Glen had done that annoyed me was to claim he was the humble songwriter who wrote all the hits, but given the shoddy way he'd been treated after John and Malcolm edged him out of the band, I couldn't really blame him for that.

One thing I would like to clear up is that I'm as certain as a man with as bad a memory as me can be that the story Lydon put in his book about me spunking up into Glen's sandwich and tricking him into eating it is not true. I presume John just said that to cause shit between us, which was a shame, because the raw material of that story was actually a very sweet scene which was more like something from *The Waltons*. One time when Glen was staying over at Denmark Street, I was giving him advice on masturbational techniques before he went to sleep. It's a service I like to provide – check in Glen's book if you don't believe me.

I was telling him how if you cut the top off an unsliced loaf (Mother's Pride doesn't work as well), scoop out some of the bread, and fill it up with warm water – room temperature, not boiling – then shag that, it actually feels quite like a cunt. It's all part of the doing-something-to-your-cock-without-your-hand-actually-touching-it thing which has always been so important to me. You can get a similar effect with a pound of liver, but that way is more expensive and the meat goes off quick – it gets rigor mortis. I'm not saying that telling Glen this changed his life, any more than the sex tips I gave him in Brighton did, but if you wanted to know why John saw fit to twist the innocent memory of our friendly exchange of information into something dark and cruel, you'd probably have to ask him.

Anyway, back to the music. After all the shit that had gone on with Sid, it was weird to go back to Matlock on bass, but also a major relief. I think it laid a ghost to rest for Glen, too, and it was good to have the line-up that wrote the songs up onstage again. When the Sex Pistols played Finsbury Park in June 1996, many people there were too young to remember how few shows we did first time round – a load of those kids hadn't even been born when we were playing the 100 Club and the Screen on the Green.

The shows we did from 1975 to 1978 were very rarely to crowds that actually wanted to see us. The S.P.O.T.S. gigs and maybe Brunel University near the end were among the few times I remember us being in front of big crowds who were excited to be in a room with us. Then we went to the States and it was back to square one with the angry cowboys. So 1996 was our time to get some appreciation from the punters. Plus we could play way better with Matlock than we ever could with Sid, so people who'd got into us later got a bit of a bonus.

As on any tour, there were a few horrible moments – like when we played in front of 100,000 people at Roskilde Festival in Denmark and a small crowd of cunts kept throwing cider bottles at us. We told them to stop because it was really dangerous but they didn't, so we fucked off on the third song. There was another festival show where it was Cookie's birthday and Rotten started celebrating three hours before the gig and was so hammered by the time we got onstage that it was a total disaster. But to be fair to him, it only happened once. He was pretty good about not drinking before the gigs, which was a relief, as he forgets all the words when he does.

The American dates were a great way of sticking it to all the people who went to the Winterland gig (or said they did) and thought we couldn't pull off a big show. We started at Red Rocks in Colorado – that was a good one. Then there were three shows in LA – two at the Palladium and one at the Universal Amphitheatre. All the punk kids came out and did the mosh-pit thing and there were some good moments. The only real mistake we made was to let it go on too long. Japan and Australia were OK, but by the time we got to Brazil and Argentina, old tensions were starting to surface (and not in a creatively fulfilling way). Blow had entered the scene, and the whole mood turned dark and ugly. At the final show in Chile, we were every bit as fucking sick of each other as we had been when the band first split up.

29. NO SLEEP TILL HAMMERSMITH

We wouldn't play live again till Crystal Palace, six years later. That's how keen the four of us were to spend more time together. In the meantime, I quit smoking.

Surprisingly, I managed it at the first time of asking. I'd never tried before because all I'd heard from people was what a nightmare it was to give up, but I went to a hypnotist and it wasn't too bad. Kerry Gaynor, the geezer's name was, and he had an office on Santa Monica. It's three visits altogether. The first one you don't actually quit for, you just go and sit in his Lay-Z-Boy recliner and he talks to you about all the reasons you want to give up and why it ain't a good thing to smoke. I was kind of talking myself out of quitting, but he's got an answer for everything.

Then he says, 'Now, you're going down,' and counts back, '10, 9, 8 . . .' to put you to sleep like they do in the movies. I thought I was just playing along with it, but maybe I was fucking hypnotised and didn't know it; all I do know is I quit and I've not been back on the fags since. I'm fucking grateful because I hate cigarettes and until I stopped I didn't realise how shit smoking was. It's technically illegal to light up anywhere in Beverly

275

Hills now – it's not like in Europe, you can't smoke in restaurants. Of course lots of people still do, but if a cop wanted to be an arsehole (which obviously a lot of them do) he could actually give you a ticket.

I'd given everything else up – except hookers and cream pies – but I never thought I'd be able to leave the fags behind. It was always implanted in the back of my head: even subconsciously there was still this voice saying, 'I'm eating all of this health food but I'm still smoking – it doesn't make sense.' I did want to stop, but I didn't believe it was possible. I didn't think I was good enough. I thought I'd carry on smoking till the day I died, so the fact that I've gone fifteen years without it is a miracle to me.

Of course, I still eat like an addict. That's the last fucking one, the food thing. The pussy thing's subsided a bit – though I still get bouts of it where I want to act out with birds who are strangers. It's weird how those two bounce around: if I'm not getting any pussy, I'll eat more, but if I am, I won't eat as much. On reflection, maybe it's the same for everyone.

The thieving seemed to drop off of its own accord once I didn't need money for dope any more. Obviously that hadn't been how it started, but it was how it ended up, and the humiliation of the Des Barres leather jacket episode was something I never wanted to feel again. On top of that, I saw a TV documentary about what goes on in American prisons that scared the living shit out of me. You might think I've got a bit of front with the tattoos and the bikes and everything, but when push comes to shove, I'm a total pussy.

I've given talks in LA County jail a couple of times, an experience that didn't make me any keener to go back to my old ways. I also spoke on a panel at Wandsworth nick when I was back in England for the Crystal Palace show, and again when we did five nights at Brixton Academy, five years later. You usually get a good turnout with a captive audience, though you never know if it's because people want to be sober, they like me cos I was in the Pistols, or most likely just because they want to get out of their cells for a bit. Either way, the punters seemed to appreciate it and I didn't get any weirdness, but boy I was glad when I could walk out of there.

The same was true of those extra batches of Pistols shows, although the weirdness count always went up a bit by the end. Luckily we had the good sense to schedule some shorter tours, so we had a busy couple of weeks in America in 2003, with a good show on my birthday at the Warfield in San Francisco when Rotten got the crowd to sing me 'Happy Birthday'. He'll do something nice like that every now and again, just to keep me guessing. The 2007 dates in Britain weren't too bad either, because we just did the shows at Brixton Academy, then one in Manchester and one in Scotland.

What we've learnt with Johnny is that he usually starts off a tour all right, because he's nervous, so he behaves himself – we have a laugh, sometimes. But then we get good, so he gets cocky, and everything goes to shit. Why we forgot that important lesson when we were scheduling the extended three-month summer 2008 tour that basically fucked us for ever, I will never know. But before we get to that horrible nightmare, there were some big things going on in my life outside music that I need to bring you up to speed with.

It all started with a Justin Sterling Men's Weekend. Oliver Leiber (the son of the Leiber half of the great songwriting team Leiber and Stoller), who was someone I knew, went through one and suggested it would be a good thing for me to do, so we went together. It was up in Oakland at this big Masonic temple. They're brilliant buildings – I love those places. Even though I don't have any links to the Sterling Institute any more, I'll be a bit vague about the details of what happened at the weekend, because I wouldn't want to spoil it for anyone who might be going.

Justin is quite a controversial character, but for me it was a fucking amazing experience. For a start, it was the first time I'd ever let myself cry in public. I'd never shed a tear in a meeting or in therapy before – if I felt myself welling up, I'd just damp it down and then bolt as soon as possible. But in that heightened atmosphere when one guy in the middle started bawling it just set everyone else off. We'd been learning all this good stuff about not letting women take our balls. Then suddenly we were all weeping about our own shit, and it felt good. That was one of the big benefits of the whole thing for me – to have a fucking breather from holding it all in.

It wasn't just about the one weekend, either. Sometimes you'd have to be a staff member, which meant watching the door at the weekends so no one could run out – it does get pretty uncomfortable in there at times. I was fucked after being on my feet for twelve hours doing that. Also when those first two days are done, they put you in a team according to where you're from. You have to come up with a name for the group, and then meet up every weekend and do something to better yourself. I lasted a full year, so you can tell I got a lot out of it.

What you learn in the group is mostly old-school proper geezer shit, like from the Forties and Fifties, which hopefully turns you from a bloke into a gentleman. One of my big weaknesses in life used to be that I always showed up late. I never thought it was a big deal until I arrived late once for the team and they made me accountable for it. As a kind of punishment, they made me sing in front of a crowded restaurant. I just had to stand there and belt a song out – it was worse than that Salter's Cafe gig in '75, cos I didn't even have a microphone.

I fucking hated it, but I did it. There were no Rod Stewart covers this time – I went for something a bit less predictable and sang 'Michael, Row the Boat Ashore', which was just about the only thing I remember from school. The rest of the team stood outside watching to make sure I did it, and I was never late again. Shit like that makes you a man.

A big part of what Justin Sterling teaches you about respecting yourself was 'forgive your fathers', so I tried to apply that to my stepfather, since he seemed to be the only game in town in that division.

Early on in sobriety, on a therapist's advice, I'd sent my mum a letter explaining about the fiddling. Finally telling someone what had happened to me in Benbow Road had taken some of the weight off, so I thought it might be worth taking the whole openness thing a bit further. Unfortunately, we hit a brick wall. I don't know if Ron intercepted the letter, or what happened, but I got a reply back from my mum basically saying, 'What are you talking about?' It was full of all the usual denials that seem to happen when people get called up on that shit. I guess she just didn't want to deal with it.

The next time I met up with my mum and Ron after this had happened, it had been quite a long while since I'd last seen them. He looked like such a feeble little dude and I seemed so much bigger than him that I could tell the power relation was reversed. Now I was the big guy and he was the one who was shitting himself. So because I'd done this Justin Sterling thing and I was trying to be the better man, I gave him a hug, and he kind of seized up like he thought I was gonna fucking stick a knife in him – that was the feeling I got.

It was the only hug I ever gave him, and I wasn't inclined to give him another one afterwards. To be honest, it wasn't my instinct to try to make it up with him, so I suppose I was just going through the motions of following other people's advice, but at least I tried. Unfortunately, I didn't really feel any benefit from it. I still hated the cunt and had a hard time forgiving him. I've always felt that what he did steered me in a direction which meant that to this day I'm no good at maintaining relationships with women. Obviously I've got to take responsibility for my own actions in adult life too; it's not all Ron's fault. But it's hard to forgive someone who won't even admit what they've done wrong. And he's brown bread now, so that's never going to happen; not that it was really on the cards anyway.

There was a more positive side to my 'forgiving the fathers' initiative, though – a few years later I managed to track down and meet my real dad. I should say at first that it wasn't my idea to do this, but in the end I was really glad I did it. One of the big benefits of sobriety is that I've got some friends who aren't fuck-ups, and two of the best of them are a couple called Laurie and Richard, who've got a lovely place out in Malibu where I go and stay sometimes. I knew them before their business took off and they're kind of a normal family with kids and everything – they've welcomed me into their home just like Cookie's mum and dad did. It's the same old 'Lonely Boy' thing – nothing changes, except something did, and it was all down to Laurie. She had told me about her dad's Dutch cousin whose job was tracking people down – sometimes from families that had been separated since World War II. I wasn't sure if this was a can of worms I really wanted to open, but Laurie kept pushing me, until eventually I gave him the name Don Jarvis, and all the information I had, which wasn't much.

He came back to me a couple of times over the course of about a year, and eventually he called and said, 'I've found him.' He'd tracked down a picture of my dad boxing and then phoned him – saying he was doing a documentary about amateur boxers, to check it was the right guy – but my dad twigged it straight away. I think maybe one of his son's kids had guessed because he was a metal fan who had seen the Sex Pistols documentary *The Filth and the Fury* where I actually mention his name. I was happy that when the Dutch geezer told him his son wanted to speak to him he just said, 'Yeah.' My biggest fear was that he was gonna say, 'No, fuck off, I don't want anything to do with him' . . . *again*. Once in a lifetime is enough for that shit.

Anyway, I called him and we spoke on the phone. It was a very odd feeling, to speak to him for the first time that way. Since the band was gearing up for the big tour at that point, it was simple enough to arrange to meet him once we were all settled in London. I got a train up to Nottingham (where he lived) and met him at the station, then we went to some cafe round the corner and bullshitted for probably two hours, before I got the train back down south again.

When I was looking into the crowd to find my dad at the station, I knew who he was straight away. He was quite dressed up, with a cardigan on and a shirt and tie beneath it. I sensed that he had made an effort with what he was wearing, which I thought was cute. Talking to him was a bit nerve-racking at first, but once we sat down and started chatting properly, it just felt normal. Thinking back, it was funny that it didn't feel more strange, as shit like that doesn't happen to you every day.

If you saw the two of us standing next to each other, I think you would probably guess that Don was my dad. He did remind me of myself a bit – he has the same handsome features, his voice is exactly the same and a lot of his mannerisms were quite familiar. Obviously that was a new experience for me, having always felt like I was on my own in the world, with no brothers and sisters or anything. I wouldn't say it was confusing; the surreal thing was that because I'd never been with him since I was a baby, I kind of felt like that baby inside again, even though I was fifty-two at the time.

He started apologising for not having been around but I said, 'I'm not here for apologies – I was just curious to find out what you looked like, if you were healthy and whether you still had your hair.' He still had it, so that's a good omen, and he seemed a happy enough dude – I got a good vibe from him. It turned out he'd been sent to Nottingham to do National Service soon after I was born, and not long after that he met the woman he married and they've been together ever since. So it's not like he was some cunt who was just going around shagging everything, like I did. He's got two boys and a girl – all grown up now, with kids of their own – who I suppose are my half-brothers and half-sister, although I don't feel that much connection to them.

I spoke to him on the phone a couple of times after our first meeting, and then that was kind of it. I guess it would be nice to meet up with him again some time, now that the dust has settled. Maybe then I could really see him, because it was a very intense thing – to be meeting your dad, who made you happen – and I felt like it all unfolded in a fog. But I think it's too late in the game, now, for us to have any kind of real relationship. A lone wolf can't change his spots.

I'm glad I finally got to speak to him, though, as it was a very positive experience. In fact, there were no negatives about it. It was one of those great things – like getting a bank account and a driving licence, and learning to read and write properly – that would never have happened if I wasn't sober, because I wouldn't have followed through with it. Did it change me a lot? I don't think so. There wasn't some great flash of enlightenment where suddenly I had a new picture of myself in my mind.

I suppose I've never found it too hard to put myself in my dad's shoes.

Did he fuck off?

Yes.

Was that a horrible thing to do?

Not really.

If you're not in love with someone and you've had sex on a whim and she gets pregnant, what are you gonna do? I don't think I should be mad at that. Despite all my mum's moaning over the years – which I can understand too, from her point of view – he did settle down afterwards, which proves he was a good guy. Overall I've got no grudges against Don Jarvis whatsoever.

One thing I do have now is a picture of him in the ring. It's a bit frayed around the edges, but that doesn't matter. I think his boxing record was that he lost more times than he won, so it's not a 'coulda been a contender' situation. There's also a clearer photo, of him and his mates when he was young where they're all dressed as Teddy boys outside a boozer. Malcolm would have liked that one.

And talking of Malcolm, meeting my dad brought back to my mind an incident from the time when I was first hanging around in his shop. There was a girl who came round to the flats in Battersea once when I wasn't there and told my mum I'd got her pregnant. I did remember shagging her in Battersea Park one night when we were walking home from the King's Road after being in the Bird's Nest pub. It was near the hotdog stand by Chelsea Bridge, where the Teddy boys used to hang out. We went back to the flats, I guess I shagged her again, then she just split in the morning, and that was the end of the story, for all I knew.

Between then and the time she came round, I'd had that fight with my stepdad and fucked off, so I didn't hear about this till later. And my mum gave me mixed messages as to whether the girl ended up having the baby or getting the money for an abortion. Then the trail went cold. So, for all I know, there could be at least one grown-up person out there whose existence is down to me the same way mine was down to my dad's. It would be a miracle if there wasn't, really, under the circumstances.

I was based in London for the duration of that big tour in the summer of 2008, so I went to see my mum a few times. I don't enjoy going back to England. Even when I'm working – which is the only reason I'd be there – that lonely kid still kind of comes to the fore again. There's a lot of deep-rooted stuff inside me that doesn't seem to be going anywhere. On this occasion I was trying to face it down and it didn't go too well, so it ended up being quite a dark time for me.

I had a lot of heavy-duty shit to be dealing with, and the one thing a doctor probably wouldn't prescribe for a person in that situation would be three months of Johnny Rotten. I'd agreed to do the tour on the basis that we wouldn't be travelling together and I wouldn't have to see him between shows. Of course that was never gonna be the way of it. We were based in London, then flying off to do festivals at the weekend in the worst fucking shithole places in the former Eastern bloc – Russia, Slovakia, Estonia, Poland. Dealing with John in those situations was a nightmare.

The worst thing you could ever hear when you're waiting in the airport to go somewhere with him is 'Flight so-and-so has been delayed', because then you know he's going to start drinking and the darkness is going to descend. A lot of the time you're on chartered flights – not private jets, two-bob fucking mini-planes with the whole crew of maybe twenty people on board and one prop held together with a rubber band. Early on we were on one of these flights and for some reason – maybe he was a fan – the pilot let Rotten smoke upfront in the cabin.

Cut to two months later. We're on the same kind of plane, so Johnny has got it in his mind that it's OK for him to smoke, but it's a different pilot who – quite rightly – isn't having it. Rotten goes absolutely ballistic. He's like a fucking baby having a tantrum – banging on the pilot's door, trying to open the windows and doors in the fuselage, basically risking all our lives cos someone's told him he's got to wait a couple of hours to have a fag. It's two in the morning, we're all knackered and everyone's trying to make out they're kipping, but no one is, cos a man in his fifties has gone into a full-on meltdown about not getting his own way.

I know where we were going – from Norway to Ireland – and because it was such a small plane it had to stop on the way to refuel. When we landed I thought, 'Well, that's it, he's nicked.' But nothing happened: no policemen came to take him away, he just stands smoking by the side of the plane while they refuel and off we go again. I think what I hate the most about these situations is that I can't be myself around him. With anyone else, you could just tell them to fucking pull their head in, but because in recent years he's surrounded himself with people who don't just tolerate his childishness and aggression, they actively encourage it, anyone who dares to prick that bubble will just be making life unbearable for everyone else. So you have to kind of go along with it – Yes, John, no, John, three bags full, John.

The funny thing was that, quite early on in the tour, we'd done a warm-up show in Austria before playing the Isle of Wight Festival the next day. Rotten decided out of the blue that he was going to change the set-list, he and Cookie got into it, and things turned really nasty straight away. This was the second show of the tour and we had thirty-two more to do. At that point, I was seriously tempted to fuck off. I was wondering if I could get out of the tour by pretending to break my back onstage at the Isle of Wight. I actually spoke to a couple of people about how to feign a spinal injury in a way that would seem legit. I guess there were a few Premiership footballers who could've helped me out with that.

I know it would've been letting down the fans who wanted to see us, but all I could see was the next few months stretching in front of me with Johnny's need to control everything festering throughout them. I was in hell. Of course when it came to the – fake – crunch, I couldn't go through with it. And I'm glad I didn't, because even though my prediction of how the tour was going to turn out proved roughly accurate, the Hammersmith Apollo show right at the end was worth . . . well, maybe not all the pain, but certainly most of it.

I fucking loved playing that gig, because I had so much history tied up in the venue. It was bizarre, when you think about all the times I'd been there to watch Bowie and Mott the Hoople (and to steal Bowie's amps). But I wasn't the kid lurking in the rafters like the phantom of the Odeon any more – now I was actually on the stage, standing in the same spot where Ariel Bender had stood. It was strange walking through all the corridors and dressing rooms. They hadn't really changed in the intervening thirty years since I used to break in round the back; they're quite clinical little rooms, there's not really any magic to them. But all in all it was a pretty good moment, to have come full circle and be back there sober, playing our songs to a crowd who really wanted to hear them.

It's always hard to absorb the significance of these things when they're happening, though, and I was kind of spaced out by it. It was the night before my birthday and Rotten did the 'Happy Birthday' routine with the crowd again, which I was touched by. That really added to how special it was. I remember playing 'No Feelings' and Cookie coming in wrong and it all being a mess – maybe because there actually were some fucking feelings involved. And after the gig, I felt satisfied. Me and Cookie even went and hung out for a while at this pub down the street from him which was his dad's local.

It would've been the perfect way to finish the tour. The show was a blinder – it meant something to me, and I'd have loved to have knocked it on the head there and then and relaxed. Unfortunately, we had one more poxy gig to do a few days later in that bit of Spain where they don't want to be called Spanish. My fairy-tale ending had been fucked by the Basques . . . and after all I'd done for them!

30. BOYS KEEP SPINNING

A lot of people in bands find it difficult to adjust when they get back from a long tour like the one we did in the summer of 2008. And on top of the usual dislocation, there was a nasty financial surprise waiting for us. We were supposedly going to earn a lot of money from that three-month stint – I'd been renting a place by Hyde Park in Knightsbridge and living high on the hog all summer in that expectation. Unfortunately, it turned out the pot of gold at the end of the rainbow was actually full of shit.

Between the first of those shows and the last, the world's leading economies went tits up, so what we thought we were going to come away with was very different to what we actually did. The bankers had fucked it all up for us; it turned out the only notes that mattered really *were* the ones that came in wads. Talk about the suits' revenge! Luckily for me, I had a job to come home to.

OK, playing records on the radio for a couple of hours each day might not be everyone's idea of hard graft, but it's the closest I've ever come to a regular nine-to-five. At that point, anything I'd have been doing that didn't involve Rotten would have been a joy. Faced with the choice of heading back out on the road with the Pistols or going to be hanged at

Tyburn with a crowd throwing cabbages at me, I'd have gone for the cabbages every time. So the fact that I was able to do something I really enjoyed and somehow make a success of it was just a bonus.

It was one of those weird flukes, how *Jonesy's Jukebox* came together. Because the station it started on – Indie 103.1FM – had only just gone on the air and they were trying to get something a bit different going, we were given an unusual amount of freedom. They'd started broadcasting at Christmas 2003, and I'd tuned in as a punter in the car and loved the fact that they played things like Buzzcocks and even the Sex Pistols, who you'd never hear on the radio at that time (or now, really, outside of my show), because for some reason we don't qualify as classic rock. After that it was only a couple of weeks later that I got a call asking if I fancied doing a show for them. There'd not been any contact between us in the meantime, so I guess the whole thing was just meant to be.

At first, it was a total joke. I had no idea what to say and no clue what I was meant to be doing. I guess there was a certain charm in a man trying to keep afloat in a leaky bucket on the super-slick LA airwaves. I think part of the attraction to people was hearing this buffoon on the radio who was farting and burping and leaving long interludes of silence while playing whatever music he wanted. It took me a little while to get into my stride and work out how I wanted to present the whole thing, but right from the off there was a lot of goodwill coming my way.

I met David Bowie for the first time at an LA gig he did the night before my first show and told him I was going to be playing a lot of his records on the radio. He replied, 'Good, cos nobody else fucking does,' or words to that effect. So it obviously wasn't just me who felt the parameters of Southern California radio were way too narrow. Even though the station had a small signal, people who cared about music really loved it, and it didn't take me long to adapt to talking live on the air. I guess getting up to speak at 12-Step meetings had given me some good training in making full confessions in public, and in how to create the kind of atmosphere that brings out the best in people.

I never wanted to be one of those DJs who deliberately set out to make their guests uncomfortable. I might say shocking things sometimes, but I'm the opposite of a shock-jock. You get much more out of people if they're relaxed. Because they know you're not just out to make them look stupid, they're much more likely to let their guard down and say something interesting instead of just going into their usual promotional routine. Also, from a personal point of view, it's nice for me to be able to give something back – to the bands I've stolen stuff off, as well as the listeners.

No one else is playing 'Virginia Plain' on daytime radio in LA these days, that's for sure. Maybe I've almost played it enough to pay Roxy Music back for that guitar tuner I nicked off them. There've been so many times when music has randomly reached out to me and made my life better – from hearing the Jimi Hendrix out of that Shepherd's Bush window onwards – that I love the idea of doing that for other people. And the fact that I get to meet and jam with a lot of my heroes is just the frosting on the cake.

Once I started to build a reputation for doing something a bit special, I got all sorts of top people coming in. Burt Bacharach was really good, and Sly Stone totally out of his mind – which certainly added an extra dimension to us jamming together. Robert Plant was great as well. I got to jam with him, too, and he turned me on to someone I was never hip to before who he said was one of his favourites. It was a Fifties guy called Ral Donner who sounded a bit like Elvis, and I really like his stuff now. If you listen again to a few of the old Zeppelin tunes straight after Ral, you can hear that Planty's nicked some of his licks.

Inevitably, there was the odd bad apple in the barrel. Brian Wilson was a complete cunt. Just because he's supposedly a bit nuts, that's no fucking excuse not to be a nice person. Jerry Lee Lewis didn't go too well either. Obviously he's known as a tricky customer but I've got total respect for his music – I love all his early shit. Unfortunately I made the mistake of opening up a can of worms by asking what it was like when he came to England (with that thirteen-year-old cousin he was married to). He turned on me a bit, but luckily he wasn't armed.

Although one of the selling points of the show is that I'll always say what's on my mind, I'm not a total idiot when it comes to things I should and shouldn't be saying. One of the only times I ever got a smack on the wrist was for harping on about that Xenu mob – the Scientologists – and saying their God who lives on another planet was a big herpe. I got called into the office for that and told, 'Look, knock it on the head. There's a lot of people in Hollywood who are into that and we don't want to lose sponsors.' So that was a no-no. Still, I did feel quite vindicated recently when I watched that documentary about them, *Going Clear*. That was hilarious.

What I was most proud of with *Jonesy's Jukebox* was that it was my own thing – it stood or fell by my contribution, so I could really enjoy its success because I felt I'd earned it. That was very important for me and gave me a lot of self-esteem. Rotten even came on once and was positive and polite and respected the fact that it was my show, not his. That was a bit of a landmark for me, even though it was stressful having him in there.

The DJ-ing thing was another example of the 12-Step programme steering me down a good path. It made me more confident that if I just go with my instincts, creative shit happens, and I don't need to be second-guessing myself and putting myself down so much. That's the biggest thing I've learnt in sobriety: to let situations unfold. Worrying about every little detail always backfired on me, where being more relaxed helped me be more professional so I could really enjoy not letting people down. Five days a week for five years is the longest time I've ever done one thing, and I would probably have stuck at it for a lot longer if the station hadn't folded.

That was a sad day, early in 2009, about four months after we got back from the tour. I felt bad afterwards because I knew the game was up, but no one had told Lemmy, who was scheduled to be my guest that day, so he turned up at the studio with his Jack and Coke in hand to find there was no station for him to appear on. It would be even sadder seeing Lem for the last time at his 70th birthday party, just before he died in late 2015. We'd had some good chit-chats over the forty years I'd known him, but it was almost like he wasn't there any more by the end. All these people had turned up for the celebration, but he didn't really know who anyone was.

The Grim Reaper's been doing overtime over the past few years. When Malcolm McLaren died in 2010, that was a big one for me. They had a memorial service for him and I sent a letter to his son Joe who I used to share the bedroom with saying, 'Where's the money? I wanna look in the coffin cos that's where the dough probably is.' It got a big chuckle from all the punters when he read it out apparently, but I wasn't making light of anything. I think Malcolm would've liked it, cos he always preferred the myth to the reality anyway, and I went on to say what a great impact he'd had on my life.

The one thing all humans have in common is that no one really knows what happens when you die. Everyone has their theory, but whatever you might think, you don't fucking know – all that bullshit about being on the slab and walking towards the light, that's just a chemical thing going off in your head. As a result, the 'higher power' part of the 12-Step programme is something a lot of people have a problem with. I know I did, at least until I realised that it doesn't have to mean believing in a Father-Christmas-looking bloke up in a cloud, it's just about realising that whatever God is, it ain't you. If you don't get the message that your selfish will is not the centre of the universe, you're never gonna get anything sorted out.

That said, one of the lamest sayings they trot out at meetings is 'God didn't bring you this far to drop you down'. Tell that to the geezer who just got AIDS and died of cancer! When I ask myself why I'm still here when I probably shouldn't be while a lot of people who didn't deserve to die are long gone, the best answer I can come up with is to understand that the whole thing is beyond my comprehension. Or, to put it a bit more simply, 'Shit happens, people.' I'm sure those poor fuckers who were on the plane that got flown into the World Trade Center hadn't done anything wrong. I personally can't imagine some bearded geezer upstairs picking who goes and who doesn't – 'He's all right . . . No, fuck him, he's a cunt' – but if you can, then knock yourself out.

Now I'm back on the radio five days a week again, it seems to be RIP someone or other more or less every day. I don't mind all the fuss when it's Lemmy or David Bowie. What I don't like is when someone dies who's been on a long down-slope, and then everyone gets on the pity pot and sentimentalises their addiction. Like my old mate Scott Weiland from Stone Temple Pilots, who I used to play 'Bodies' with. I went to a couple of meetings with him but he just didn't grasp it and was never going to. That's the reality. The big thing for me was that no one gave a shit about him the day before, but then as soon as he died, every radio station in LA was milking the fuck out of him.

I guess in a way that's the beauty of life: you don't know what's coming, and just when you think you've got it sussed out, something happens to turn everything upside down. When I first moved to LA and no one gave a shit about punk, I didn't know that Axl and Kurt Cobain loving the Sex Pistols and us getting back together was going to make it all such a big deal again in ten years' time. I'd have been even more surprised to know it was going to be bigger still another twenty years on. These days every kid seems to have the T-shirt with the picture of Sid – it's not even a fad any more, it's become part of the culture. It feels like punk won't go away now, but there's no way of knowing.

At the time of writing, the whole Pistols thing is a bit of a mess. We should be running a tight machine and figuring out ways to make dough, but that's not really what's happening. We keep getting offered shows, but I'm not sure if the dosh is ever gonna be quite enough to get us back together. People say, 'Well, The Rolling Stones are still doing it . . .' but I don't think they would be, on our money. Also, their business doesn't have to be run in such a way as to keep two imaginary cunts in some East London council estate happy. I get that it's good to be the real deal when you're twenty, but when you get older, things change. The two imaginary cunts have probably sold their council flat and fucked off to Essex by now, anyway.

Don't get me wrong, I'm not saying we should be doing mortgage adverts. You've got to keep the dream alive to a certain extent. That was one of Johnny's better moments, when we got put in the Rock & Roll Hall of Fame in 2006 and he sent them a letter at the last minute refusing to appear and calling the whole ceremony 'urine in wine'. Left to our own devices, the rest of us would probably have done the show, but in the long run what he did was best for the Pistols as an idea. Even though Anita would've liked more than 24 hours' notice.

That's the tricky part with John. If he was a total dick all the time, you could write him off, but every now and again he does something you have to commend him for just to keep us on our toes. The shame of it is that he doesn't need to be so insecure. No one questions John's contribution to the band. Everyone knows he was one of the greatest lead singers of all time, who put what we were about into words, an attitude and a vocal style. But still, he's not the one who has to turn up at the opening of the new Hard Rock casino in Vegas to see one of his quotes put into someone else's mouth. (They'd written, 'The only notes that matter are the ones that come in wads,' on the wall, which everyone knows was one of mine, and ascribed it to 'Johnny Rotten'.)

It's all so irrelevant anyway when you think about the endless fucking size of the universe. Here we are, these tiny little ants, self-importantly talking about why Wally got the sack from Swankers, but when the ants come into my house I get the spray out and murder about 20,000 of them. I'm like the Himmler of ants. In their world they're probably arguing about who's not done their ant chores, then I come along and press a button and they're gone. This is just the kind of inspirational stuff you want to be reading in a last chapter, isn't it? I don't believe in sugar-coating things.

Even now I've been sober twenty-five years, I still wake up kind of miserable a lot of the time, but I don't think you're ever going to think, 'Everything's gonna be great from now on, because I've discovered the true meaning of me.' I'm just happy not to be loaded. To that end, I do a lot of talks and sponsor a couple of other people as well, which I get a lot out of. Plus I still go to four or five meetings a week. I get there early and I thank the speaker afterwards. Gary Holton would be proud of me.

I've done a fair bit of making amends in recent years – you have to do the 12 steps in order and that's the ninth. The person you've done wrong might not accept your apology, but if they want to just tell you to fuck off, obviously that's their choice; it's all about cleaning your side of the road.

My big thing was: 'Oh fuck – am I gonna have to pay people back for all the stuff I nicked? Cos if so, I'm gonna be paying these cunts off for the rest of my life.' Luckily, no one's asked for the money yet. The guy from 10cc was a good example of how people normally respond. I got his number and rang him up to tell him, 'Look, I'm sorry, but I nicked one of your guitars – what can I do to make it right?' He just said, 'Do you know what? Don't worry about it. I appreciate the apology.' And when I went to kip that night, I put my head down feeling a little bit more like a decent fucking person who'd cleaned up a bit of the wreckage of my past. Obviously things might be a bit more acrimonious with Ariel Bender, but fingers crossed, eh? Maybe I should have him on the show . . .

I do a bit of meditation too, these days, to help me focus. Russell Brand got me into Transcendental Meditation when I was the one-man orchestra on his TV show for a while. You're meant to do it for twenty minutes on your own, morning and evening, but I can't always manage that. I go to group meditation on Wednesday and Sunday nights, which I find a lot better, cos when there are a bunch of people I seem to get more energy from the group so I can get a bit deeper into the whole thing.

I like TM cos it's one of the simplest forms of meditation. I'm not so good with counting beads and all that. With TM you just kind of sit there and let it happen; say your mantra every now and then; it's not hard. You do come out feeling a lot calmer. Of course I might go to the David Lynch Institute to meditate and then some cunt would cut me up on the road on the drive home and I'd just start screaming at him – the geezer in *Blue Velvet* with the mask on his face will still come out. I'm not walking around on a fucking cloud like people think, but I guess that's the same for everyone. Don't knock over the maharishi's pint or he'll have you.

The main benefit of TM for me is that it makes me bit more aware of shit that's going on; I can be a bit oblivious, left to my own devices. As I get older it's important for me to try to be nicer to other people. Not being a cunt – that's where my head's at. I still have selfish, consuming Steve within me, but as I've got older I seem to have become a bit more considerate of others – my fellow fucking humans, if you wanna dignify them with that title. I'm not sure if that counts as taking a more spiritual path, but it's as close as I'm gonna get to one.

My addictive impulses still show up out of the blue in unexpected ways, like the time a few years back when I had to have back surgery from doing too much spinning. It's a workout they do in LA. Not something you would necessarily want people to know you'd got hooked on, but I don't give a fuck. It's too late now to be hiding anything. Basically, spinning is aerobics on a bike. How it works is you have a bunch of people on stationary bikes, pedalling really fast (not the kind of pedalling I'm usually talking about) and looking at an instructor who tells them what to do. She says get out of the seat and you stand up on the pedals, get down and you go back down. There's usually loud music as well – not the kind I would normally listen to, either.

Anyway, I got so obsessive about this whole process that I did it six days a week for a fucking year. I even reached the point where I was the guy on the podium and everyone was looking to me for a lead. Look, Ma, top of the world.

I should say that I don't blame people for laughing when they hear about this. I do see that it's funny, and what made it even funnier was that obviously I never used to do stretches or warm-ups in any way at all. Until one day I suddenly realised, 'Oh shit, I've fucked my back up.' From then on, I went through hell for two years. I wanted to avoid surgery, so I went to every charlatan in town, which in LA is quite a lot of charlatans. Every cunt that was gonna fix it got my dollars, and it was just a waste of time. What I was suffering from was basically sciatica: every time you make the transition from sitting down to standing up, you reach a point you feel like you're getting stabbed.

The pain was so bad I ended up just staying at home. I wanted to avoid taking painkillers on sobriety grounds, so I tried everything else instead: steroids, acupuncture, chiropractors, osteopaths, that energy thing – I did it all. Unfortunately, the problem was too serious to be fixed by hocus-pocus, so I ended up having to get epidurals all the time. My face was horribly bloated from all the steroids they put in me and finally I had this thing called nucleoplasty: an incision with heat at the end which they use to burn off the edge of your vertebrae. Ideally there's no scar, but unfortunately my recovery from the operation went all wrong, so every time I walked anywhere it was like I was getting electric shocks in my nuts. This went on – up to a level where I was randomly keeling over in the street – for a couple more months before it finally cleared up. If I'd known what was going to happen I would never have got involved with the spinning in a million years, but you live and learn. Everyone has some kind of shit that happens to them.

My mum and I had never been close, but that last London trip was more or less the final straw as far as the pair of us were concerned. When she found out I was going to visit my real dad it was a bit of a thorn in her side, but we just about got over that. Then she came on one of the recordings of my radio show I was doing in London and it was funny as fuck – she was a bit like Alvin Stardust when he came on, in that she didn't quite get the concept that it was going out live in LA while we were doing it. It was such a success that we were going to do it again on my birthday, the day after the Hammersmith show, but she didn't show up. She just went missing – she wasn't answering any calls, it was like she'd disappeared.

When I finally got in touch a day later she said she'd forgotten, but that wouldn't really wash, because we'd sent a car and everything. After grilling her a bit it turned out that she'd got the hump because she hadn't been invited to the gig. I hadn't deliberately not invited her, it just never occurred to me that it was something she'd want to do. I thought it'd be way too crazy for someone of her age. Anyway, things got a bit heated on the phone, and we haven't really spoken since. I realise this is the kind of misunderstanding that could probably be cleared up pretty quickly in a normal mother/son relationship, but I guess you reap what you sow.

I've almost given up on the idea of ever being involved in a normal relationship with a woman. I'll get to a stage when I start really liking someone, and then I can't have sex with them any more. That's pretty much the size of it, and it's a hurdle I can't get over. I've been to Sex Anonymous and I've done a lot of therapy, but I've stopped now. I'm not putting those experiences down: they have helped, but once you realise that it's all the same drive – drugs, booze, fags, sex, pies; water will always find its own level – there's just nowhere else to go. I made a conscious decision to stop doing things that are gonna make me feel ashamed, and I feel a lot better for it.

Don't get me wrong, I'm not a monk. I still act out in various ways with birds who stroll into meetings. I'm sure they all gossip about me, 'Here he comes, who's he gonna latch onto now?' But I kind of own it, because that's who I am – a semi-retired sexual deviant who doesn't really act out so much any more, but still gets those urges from time to time. I've done more pervy things in sobriety than I ever did when I was drinking and using. You don't have the energy then.

In general I'm OK being single and getting a few birds over now and again, but there's a cold, lonely side to it, too. I can just about manage to look after a dog these days. I had a great boxer called Winston for about six years. It was funny how I got him. A bird I knew had him first. I used to go over and see her at weekends and I really bonded with Winston. Then she found some other guy who had a Rottweiler. The Rottweiler and the boxer didn't get along, so she gave me the dog. The idea of taking it on freaked me out at first: 'I'm gonna have this dog now, this is gonna be my dog all the time' felt like a lot of responsibility, but I actually handled it all right, and it went really well till he got a brain tumour and died when he was about ten. They seem pretty rife in that breed, the old tumours.

I was sad when Winston died, but the whole experience was definitely a step forward from the two bulldogs I got for a while when I was newly sober. I didn't know what I was doing at the time so I shouldn't really have got them, but I guess I was trying to give myself something else to focus on. They were brothers and my thinking was: 'I'll get two and they can keep each other company.' But it was a fucking nightmare – they drove me insane because they were untrainable. I stuck it out for nine months, maybe a year, till I took them over to this bird's house. She had a little poodle and they chewed it to bits. That was when I knew I couldn't handle them, so I just took 'em back to the breeders.

You never know till you try, though, do you? I've got to give new things a go every now and again, because the most important thing for me is not to get too comfortable and complacent. Left to my own devices I'd probably just stay at home by myself, watching TV, eating cream pies and jerking off – living the dream! I've got an app called WaterMinder on my phone which reminds me to get up and have a drink of water every now and again, so I'm not going to die of thirst. But being in that solitary place is not good for me, and if I do it for too long I'll most likely end up going the whole hog and relapsing.

That's how the Instagrams started, when I was doing nothing and realised I need an outlet for some kind of creativity. I'd done a bit of acting on the TV show *Californication* and really enjoyed it. That came from a phone call from the man who created it, Tom Kapinos, and I was on it for two seasons. Acting is fun, and I love the ins and outs of the whole business. I learnt a lot but of course knowing I ain't a pro they'd written a tour manager character who was basically me. They weren't going to have me playing a priest. I actually asked Tom, 'Have you ever had a scene where someone's getting his arsehole licked – the ol' tossing of the salad?' He said no, so I got them to write that into it, and it was pretty funny. In a way, I wish I did more of that kind of work, and I probably could if I wasn't so fucking lazy.

What I love about the Instagrams is I can do them all myself, so if anyone's going to mess up, it's going to be me. I've got all the stuff at home – I bought myself a light rig and I just set the iPhone camera rolling on a carbon fibre stand and then choose the best sixty seconds. Then I use an app for putting the music on, which is kind of like doing overdubs in the studio. I've got a pretty good collection of hats and wigs, and sometimes I'll put on one of the devil masks which this gay guy who works in a leather shop makes for me. But if I need a special costume – like the blue make-up for the Dave Bobbins video – I'll get someone in to help me. It's fun and it makes people laugh; and besides, this is the fucking information age, and if you ain't all over Twitter or Instagram you're going to get left in the dust.

It's hard to find the time to do Instagrams at the moment, because since I've been doing this book and then KLOS bought *Jonesy's Jukebox* back, I've actually been pretty busy, which I feel better for. When the show was first on Indie 103.1 I could literally play whatever I wanted – reggae, Norman Wisdom, anything. But now I'm on KLOS, a much bigger station with maybe two to three million listeners, we have to keep it in the vague ballpark of rock. I thought that was gonna be a real fucking challenge for five days a week, but it's working out OK for now. Luckily they give me plenty of leeway to sneak in a bit of Strawbs or Atomic Rooster here and there; I've got to change it a up a bit, otherwise what's the point of having me on there?

It's essentially the same show as it was when it started out: just my low, dulcet tones with some rock 'n' roll. So on an average day at the moment I'll maybe get up early to catch a Chelsea game on TV, or go for a hike in the canyons with Billy Duffy and Slim Jim Phantom, the drummer from the Stray Cats, and his dog the Great Bandini. Then I'll run downtown on my motorbike to pick up some *Jonesy's Jukebox* sample T-shirts, before doing the show at twelve bells. After that I might go and get some new headshots done. Oh yes, it's all go here. This is Hollywood, baby.

APPENDIX – THINGS THAT ARE NOT ROCK 'N' ROLL

I have decided to put this list of rock 'n' roll no-nos out there as a public service. I'm not a hypocrite. I know I've had the odd lapse in a couple of these areas myself, but rules are made to be broken. And how are we going to grow as people if we don't set ourselves impossibly high standards?

Things That Are Not Rock 'n' Roll:

Baldness

Double chins

Perspex round the drum kit

Electric drums

Ear monitors/earplugs/hair-plugs

Steinberger guitars (the little black ones that have no headstock)

Publicists

LinnDrums

Click tracks

Paul Shaffer

The Rock & Roll Hall of Fame

White people with dreads

Facelifts on old dudes

Old dudes trying to look young

White people trying to be cool

White people trying to dance

Benefit shows

Meet 'n' greets (but greeting the meat is OK)

Sandals

Selfies

Health food

Never having had VD

Being old

Dyeing your grey hair black

All Access laminates

Cunts hanging out on both sides of the stage

Cunts who say they saw you forty years ago, but secretly hated you back then

Cunts who get your signature on stuff then sell it on eBay

ACKNOWLEDGEMENTS

Steve Jones thanks:

I'm not going to thank everyone who knows me – this ain't the Oscars – but I would like to say something about Dawn Girocco. She's the general manager at the radio station, and *Jonesy's Jukebox* wouldn't be on KLOS without her. It's not just that, though. Dawn goes back right to the beginning of the show on Indie 103.1 and then forward through KROQ. Let's just say she's been a staunch advocate who's made all the difference.

Some other people I'm grateful to for helping make this book happen are Paul Cook for filling in the gaps where my memory ought to be, Chrissie Hynde for doing the foreword, the publishers Jason Arthur and Ben Schafer, the lawyers Peter Paterno and Jeff Silberman, the literary agent Anthony Mattero, the money men Paul Lima and Al Pivo, my manager Anita Camarata and her old man Michael Jewison who helped with the edit, my friends Lori and Richard, Nina Huang, and the photographers who let me use their pictures including Ray Stevenson, Dennis Morris, Boogie and Robert Matheu.

Ben Thompson thanks:

Jason Arthur for putting my name in the hat; Ray Winstone for vouching for me; Simon Petty for onsite LA limousine services; Paul Cook, Steve's auntie Frances via his cousin Wendy Brown, Chris Thomas and Julien Temple for additional interviews; Matt Thorne, Kelly-Lee Alexander, Wesley Stace, Richard King, Maya Biltoo, Jon Savage and Chrissie Hynde for helpful conversations; Johnny Marr and most of all Nicola Barker for editorial rigour.

PICTURE CREDITS

Section 3:

Page 1 © Robert Matheu

Page 2 Author's own/ Photo by Frenchie/ Photo by Laurie Stark

Page 3 © Robert Matheu/ Photo by Linda Nelson/ Courtesy of
Nina Huang

Page 4 © Chris Cuffaro

Page 5 © 1996 Jimmy Steinfeldt/ Photo by Laurie Stark/ © Robert
Matheu

Page 6 Photos by Laurie Stark

Page 7 Photo by Laurie Stark/ Photos by Jenni Cook

Page 8 Photos by Mark Sovel and Amanda Esep

The publisher and author have made every effort to credit the copyright owners of any material that appears within, and will correct any omissions in subsequent editions if notified.